T0248151

HADRIAN'S WALL PATH

NATIONAL TRAIL:
DESCRIBED WEST–EAST AND EAST–WEST

by Mark Richards

JUNIPER HOUSE, MURLEY MOSS,
OXENHOLME ROAD, KENDAL, CUMBRIA LA9 7RL
www.cicerone.co.uk

© Mark Richards 2023
Fourth edition 2023
ISBN: 978 178631 150 4
Third edition 2015
Second edition 2004
First edition (*The Wall Walk*) 1993

Printed in China on responsibly sourced paper on behalf of Latitude Press Ltd
A catalogue record for this book is available from the British Library.
All photographs are by the author unless otherwise stated.

1:100K route mapping by Lovell Johns www.lovelljohns.com
Contains Ordnance Survey data © Crown copyright 2015
OS PU100012932. NASA relief data courtesy of ESRI. The
1:25K map booklet contains Ordnance Survey data © Crown
copyright 2015 OS PU100012932.

Updates to this Guide

While every effort is made by our authors to ensure the accuracy of guidebooks as they go to print, changes can occur during the lifetime of an edition. Any updates that we know of for this guide will be on the Cicerone website (www.cicerone.co.uk/1150/updates), so please check before planning your trip. We also advise that you check information about such things as transport, accommodation and shops locally. Even rights of way can be altered over time. We are always grateful for information about any discrepancies between a guidebook and the facts on the ground, sent by email to updates@cicerone.co.uk or by post to Cicerone, Juniper House, Murley Moss, Oxenholme Road, Kendal LA9 7RL.

Register your book: To sign up to receive free updates, special offers and GPX files where available, create a Cicerone account and register your purchase via the 'My Account' tab at www.cicerone.co.uk.

Front cover: Milecastle 39 in Castle Nick

CONTENTS

Acknowledgements

First, David McGlade, who for almost 20 years was responsible for the day-to-day management of the emergent, and resultant, National Trail. Respected for his integrity and passionate commitment, David put in place high sustainability standards of custodial care. In 2017 David moved on to the 8th-century Anglo-Saxon frontier Offa's Dyke, and now steers its friends' charity, the Offa's Dyke Association.

With the same emphasis, I would like to draw walkers' attention to the original work of Amanda Earnshaw, who was responsible for the original routing and sensitive negotiations to create the National Trail at the Countryside Agency up to the formal opening in 2003. New rights of way were required within the World Heritage Site corridor, bringing into being a path that will long require careful management as the underlying archaeology will always be a cause for concern for the antiquarian community.

Two of their number have always been generous to me in imparting their wisdom, namely David Breeze and Tony Wilmott. They are not alone as I have had many conversations with others who have special insight into the Roman world and the physical frontier with all its yet to be fully understood secrets.

I have enjoyed the special pleasure of the company of fellow enthusiast Peter Savin on many a Wall ramble, too. Peter, I must say, coined the name Hadrian's Toon Trail! Having decided to follow the archaeological trace of the Wall through Tyneside, I consulted Graeme Stobbs and shared the research walk itself with Colin Earnshaw (yes, Amanda's husband) and Richard Young (appropriately of Wall village).

The daily care of the National Trail is accomplished with aplomb by Gary Pickles, with a string of volunteers who pick up litter and report issues back to Gary. If you find something you feel he should be aware of, send him a photo and note via Twitter @HWpath.

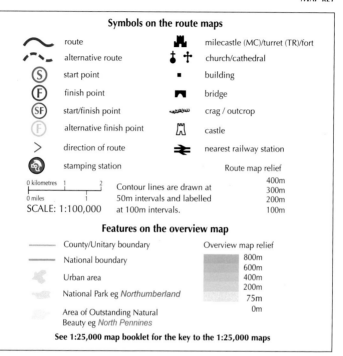

Symbols on the route maps

- route
- alternative route
- (S) start point
- (F) finish point
- (SF) start/finish point
- (F) alternative finish point
- > direction of route
- stamping station

0 kilometres 1 2
0 miles 1
SCALE: 1:100,000

- milecastle (MC)/turret (TR)/fort
- church/cathedral
- building
- bridge
- crag / outcrop
- castle
- nearest railway station

Route map relief
400m
300m
200m
100m

Contour lines are drawn at 50m intervals and labelled at 100m intervals.

Features on the overview map

- County/Unitary boundary
- National boundary
- Urban area
- National Park eg *Northumberland*
- Area of Outstanding Natural Beauty eg *North Pennines*

Overview map relief
800m
600m
400m
200m
75m
0m

See 1:25,000 map booklet for the key to the 1:25,000 maps

Dedication

To my darling wife Helen, whom I met at The Archaeology of Frontiers conference in Hereford in 1974, following which we walked Offa's Dyke Path for my third walking guide. My stalwart companion and support over the intervening years, she shares my passion for historic places, not least Hadrian's Wall.

Warning

The Military Road from Greenhead to Heddon-on-the-Wall (Stages 5–8) is a potential death trap for walkers as it is used and abused by drivers as a rat run to avoid the A69. Please avoid using it to create ad hoc circular walks.

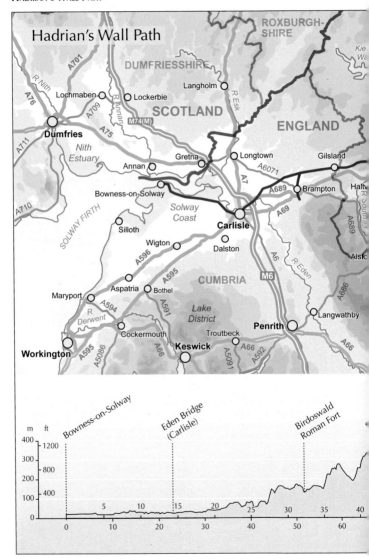

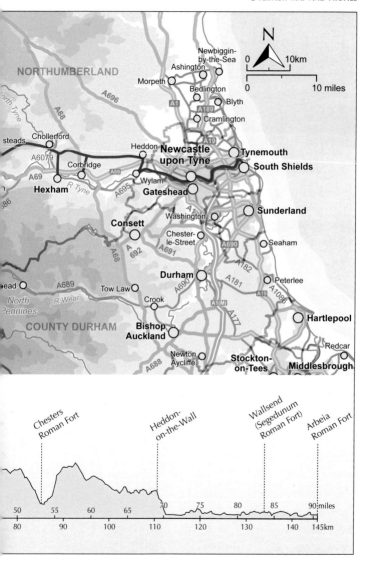

ROUTE SUMMARY TABLE

Places in bold are stage start and end points. Distances are rounded to the nearest ¼ mile (or ½ kilometre).

Location	Distance on miles (km)	Distance from western end miles (km)	Distance from eastern end miles (km)	Page
King's Arms, Bowness-on-Solway		0	91 (146.5)	36
Port Carlisle canal outflow	1¼ (2)	1¼ (2)	89¾ (144.5)	
Highland Laddie	1½ (2.5)	2¾ (4.5)	88¼ (142)	
Drumburgh Castle	1½ (2.5)	4¼ (7)	86¾ (139.5)	
Dykesfield cattle grid	2¾ (4)	7 (11)	84 (135)	
Burgh-by-Sands church	1¼ (2)	8¼ (13)	82¾ (133)	52
Beaumont church	1½ (2)	9¾ (15.5)	81¼ (130.5)	
Grinsdale	1¾ (3)	11½ (18.5)	79½ (128)	
Eden Bridge (Carlisle)	3 (5)	14½ (23)	76½ (123)	66
M6 Linstock	2½ (4)	17 (27)	74 (119)	
Crosby church	2¼ (3.5)	19¼ (30.5)	71¾ (115.5)	
A6071 Newtown	4¾ (7.5)	24 (38)	67 (108)	76
Walton	1½ (2.5)	25½ (40.5)	65½ (105.5)	
Hayton Gate	2½ (4)	27¾ (44.5)	63¼ (102)	
Pike Hill Signal Station	1½ (2.5)	29¼ (47)	61¾ (99.5)	
Birdoswald Roman Fort	2½ (4.5)	32 (51.5)	59 (95)	91
Polross Burn Milecastle	1½ (2.5)	33½ (54)	57½ (92.5)	
Thirlwall Castle	1¾ (2.5)	35¼ (56.5)	55¾ (89.5)	
Walltown Quarry	¾ (1.5)	36 (58)	55 (88.5)	
Cawfields Quarry	3¼ (5)	39¼ (63)	51¾ (83)	
Steel Rigg	2¼ (4)	41½ (67)	49½ (79.5)	113
Housesteads Roman Fort	2¾ (4.5)	44¼ (71)	46¾ (75)	
Sewingshields Farm	1¾ (3)	46 (74)	45 (72.5)	

Location	Distance on miles (km)	Distance from western end miles (km)	Distance from eastern end miles (km)	Page
Carraw Farm	2½ (4)	48½ (78)	42½ (68.5)	
Brocolitia	1 (1.5)	49½ (80)	41½ (67)	137
Walwick	3 (5)	52½ (84.5)	38½ (62)	
Chesters Roman Fort	¾ (1)	53¼ (85.5)	37¾ (61)	
Heavenfield	2½ (4)	55¾ (90)	35¼ (57)	
Portgate	3¼ (5)	59 (95)	32 (51.5)	155
Halton Shields	2 (3)	61 (98)	30 (48)	
Vallum Farm	2 (3.5)	63 (101.5)	28 (45)	
Harlow Hill	1¾ (3)	64¾ (104.5)	26¼ (42)	
Iron Sign	1¾ (2.5)	66½ (107)	24½ (39.5)	
Rudchester	1 (1.5)	67½ (108.5)	23½ (38)	
Heddon-on-the-Wall	1½ (2.5)	69 (111)	21 (34)	170
Newburn Country Park	3½ (5.5)	72½ (116.5)	18½ (30)	
Lemington Community Centre	1¾ (3)	74¼ (119.5)	16¾ (27)	
A1 Denton Dene	¾ (1.5)	75 (121)	16 (26)	
Newcastle Quayside	4 (6)	79 (127)	11 (18)	185
St Peter's Marina	1¾ (3)	80¾ (130)	10¼ (16.5)	
Segedunum Roman Fort	3¼ (5)	84 (135)	7 (11)	199
Tyne Tunnel A19 bridge	2 (3.5)	86 (138.5)	5 (8)	
Albert Edward Dock	1¼ (2)	87¼ (140.5)	3¾ (6)	
North Tyne Ferry landing	1¼ (2)	88½ (142.5)	2½ (4)	
Shield Ferry journey	½ (.5)	89 (143)	2 (3)	
Arbeia Roman Fort (South Shields Metro station*)	1 (2) (2 (3.5))	90 (145) (91 (146.5))	1 (1.5) (0)	203

* From Arbeia to South Shields Metro station via Little Haven Beach for the ceremonial dipping of the boots in the sea

Sewingshields Crags from King's Wicket (Stage 6)

INTRODUCTION

Housesteads Crags from Cuddy's Crags (Stage 6)

HADRIAN'S WALL: INSPIRED AND INSPIRING

The creation of Hadrian's Wall was the masterstroke of Emperor Hadrian Aelius, who thereby achieved two things all rulers dream of – contemporary acclaim and lasting renown. Hadrian had come to power in AD117, inheriting a volatile situation at the northern edge of his empire. After failed attempts to conquer Scotland under Governor Agricola, Rome established a frontier road between the Tyne and the Solway Firth; two important forts at Corbridge and Carlisle were linked by road (the Stanegate), and additional forts were built along its east–west route.

Hadrian's startling idea was to construct a wall from coast to coast. Predominantly of stone, this linear divide would run 80 miles (128km) from the tidal River Tyne at Newcastle in the east to the Solway Firth, west of Carlisle. Such a monumental departure from existing Roman thinking was quite simply inspired. He may have seen, and been influenced by, the great pyramids of Egypt; but he is unlikely to have known that the Emperor of China had lighted upon the same solution to quell Mongol tribes to the north of that great empire some four centuries earlier.

The Stanegate was thus replaced with a physical frontier – a defensible line of control that interrupted the erratic movement of the Pictish tribes which so troubled the Romans. As Tacitus, Hadrian's biographer, put it: 'the Wall was to separate the Romans from the barbarians' (the term 'barbarian' comes from the Greek for a primitive and uncivilised people).

The Wall appeared to be the perfect 'grand scheme' to enhance Hadrian's standing at the helm of the Roman Empire. However, as the only stone-built frontier in the history of the empire, it also represented a seismic change in thinking – as the usual timber structures of an expanding empire were replaced by a permanent frontier suggesting a policy of inward-looking containment.

Such tacit acknowledgement of the end of the hitherto limitless expansion of the Roman Empire was not Hadrian's intention. To him, the Wall was a statement of authority, not an admission that the empire had reached its limit ('limit' comes from the Roman word *limes*, meaning 'a frontier'). It was also a way in which he could express his delight in architecture; he was greatly influenced by the Greeks – a factor that led him to grow a beard rather than remain clean-shaven in the typical Roman manner. Hadrian was indeed a trendsetter.

Hadrian's Wall defined the northern edge of the province of Britannia but not the extent of Roman Imperial influence in the north. For over 300 years, from the early second century AD to the early fifth, it was the focus of life for those stationed upon it and those living alongside it.

After this time people continued to live in the shadow of this former monumental frontier, even though no money ever came again from Rome to maintain it. For generations to follow, the Wall was both a source of stone and a mystery of a time gone by; people remembered the Romans but they had become confused as to why the Wall had been built.

Over the centuries the requirement for farmland led to the Wall's destruction by the plough. Today only a portion of it remains visible – mostly in the central sector – and much of that was restored in the mid-19th century or consolidated between the 1930s and 1980s. It was the conservation of one such section of Wall in 1974 that led the author Hunter Davies to comment that it was 'a living wall, not just for the local inhabitants, but for tourists and archaeologists, a living, breathing, expanding, growing wall'. Over 40 years on, that 'living wall' still breathes, grows and evolves.

NATIONAL TRAIL

In 1987 the cultural significance of Hadrian's Wall, the finest surviving frontier work from any part of the classical Roman Empire, was recognised when it was inscribed on the UNESCO World Heritage List. From 2005 it became part of the transnational Frontiers of the Roman Empire World Heritage Sites and in 2003 a designated National Trail was opened.

The romantic notion of establishing a continuous trail along Hadrian's Wall had been an aspiration since the 19th century, as scholars, the inquisitive and, later, a more leisured society rediscovered this relic from classical times. They wanted to visit it, to sense and to see the monument in its entirety and in the fullness of its wonderful landscape setting.

The establishment of a similar trail accompanying the later Saxon divide of Offa's Dyke in 1971 did nothing to hasten the arrival of its northern counterpart. However, Hadrian's Wall Path National Trail was opened some 30 years later in May 2003, marking a harmony of purpose between Natural England and English Heritage. It stretches a total of 84 miles (135km) from Bowness-on-Solway (Maia) in the west to Wallsend (Segedunum) in the east.

Great efforts have been made to keep the Trail close to the line of the Wall itself. There are a few short steep gradients in the central Whin Sill section – some have stone-flag steps, as do places where the Path briefly crosses marshy ground. At either end the Trail is composed almost exclusively of unforgiving tarmac, but the predominant surface is a greensward. Throughout, the gradients and nature of the Path

The Trail approaches Beck Farm (Stage 4)

Roman bathhouse complex Cilurnum (Stage 7), seen from across the North Tyne

encourage a flowing stride, making this an excellent exercise for anyone of normal fitness and a fine warm-up for something more adventurous.

No charge is made to walk the Path, which takes the walker past a string of fascinating Roman and later historic sites, each in turn furthering one's understanding of the context of the walk.

Throughout the walk you will encounter intriguing 'born-again' Roman names on modern road signs for various sites, such as Segedunum and Vindolanda. The original Roman names of most sites along the Wall have been deduced and brought back into currency. If only we knew what they called the other constituent features – the milecastles, turrets and so on – we would have an even better understanding of the frontier from a Roman vernacular perspective.

One magical window on the past has been revealed in the Vindolanda 'Writing Tablets', which alone make this site an absolute must-visit place. The tablets give a glimpse into the daily conversations of the Roman garrison and their families in the period leading up to the building of the Wall (AD80–122).

PRESERVING THE HERITAGE

The World Heritage Site

In 1987 Hadrian's Wall became a UNESCO World Heritage Site. The first principle of designation is to foster peace in the minds of men and women by sharing an appreciation of the diverse heritage of cultures that make up our world, and the author is proposing that the Wall be granted WHS Peace Trail status.

The site is not only the best preserved of all the Roman Empire's frontiers, it is also the most complex. As well as encompassing the remains of Hadrian's Wall itself (namely the stone structure, with its forts, milecastles and turrets) from Segedunum in Wallsend to Maia at Bowness-on-Solway, the site includes:

- Arbeia – the coastal fort at South Shields at the mouth of the River Tyne
- numerous structures and features, including the Wall ditch, the vallum and the counterscarp mound
- civilian settlement sites (vici)
- Roman quarry sites (such as Combe Crag)
- the Stanegate (which came into being around the mid-80s AD, from which date there was a continued Roman presence in the area), with its attendant forts south of the line of the Wall – most famously Vindolanda
- outpost scouting forts such as Fanum Cocidii at Bewcastle
- various defences down the Cumbrian coast by Maryport, as far south as the Roman port of Glannoventa at Ravenglass.

English Heritage sites

Along the Trail, English Heritage owns Prudhoe Castle, Aydon Castle, Chesters, Corbridge Roman Site, Housesteads, Birdoswald, Lanercost Priory and Carlisle Castle; Newcastle Castle Keep belongs to Newcastle City Council; Segedunum and Arbeia belong to

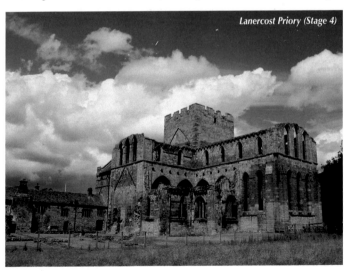
Lanercost Priory (Stage 4)

Tyne & Wear Archives & Museums (which has also created the Great North Museum, incorporating the marvellous Roman collections within Newcastle University's Museum of Antiquities); Tullie House Museum belongs to Carlisle City Council; and Vindolanda and Carvoran are privately owned.

There are charges for entry to all these sites (an English Heritage membership card is valuable). Sadly, the advent of a single day-ticket to visit a variety of sites under the custodianship of various bodies seems as far off as ever.

TAKING CARE OF THE TRAIL

The arrival of the Trail is but one more instance of change for the Wall, which over the past century has seen its close environs more than cosmetically changed in service to the curious visitor. The route is attracting many people new to the notion of walking a long-distance path, and the pressure of myriad boots upon a vulnerable archaeology has the obvious potential for adverse impact.

For generations people have wandered freely along the Wall. However, the number visiting the area today means it is necessary to protect the immediate vulnerable environment – hopefully without sullying the experience for visitors. In recognition of the fact that this is a World Heritage Site route, which requires a different approach from a normal National Trail, there is a

passport scheme (see 'National Trail Passport Scheme', below), and walkers can obtain the special Passport Booklets to use during their coast-to-coast walk. The scheme operates from 1 May to 31 October, and offers walkers the opportunity to stamp their passports sequentially as they walk.

To stem erosion – the greatest enemy of this vulnerable monument – avoid walking in single file and be careful to veer round the wooden 'tank-traps' and green stakes

Ray Purvis, one of the dedicated volunteer trail lengthsmen, with litter-picking bag on patrol

EVERY FOOTSTEP COUNTS

'Every Footstep Counts' – a voluntary code of practice for walkers and other visitors to this World Heritage Site – has been devised to protect the Trail and the Wall itself. Hadrian's Wall is the only World Heritage Site in the UK to have such a code. National Trail walkers can contribute to the conservation and general well-being of Hadrian's Wall by following the points below.

- During the wet winter months the ground becomes waterlogged and the risk of damage to the monument from walkers' feet is at its greatest. When this is the case, please respect the archaeology. Instead, consider visiting a Roman site or walking one of the many shorter circular walks along the Wall's corridor.
- Help to care for the Path and its buried archaeology. Walk side by side, and avoid walking in sections of worn path – simply walk alongside. Remember, every footstep counts.
- Keep off the Wall. The one exception to this rule is a public right of way on top of the Wall in Housesteads Wood (Stage 6), although even here an alternative path winds more sympathetically through the pine coppice.
- Help to take pressure off the Wall itself by exploring one of the excavated Roman forts. Such forts have facilities and excellent interpretative displays.
- Only walk along the signed and waymarked paths, and please oblige the Trail's field staff if you come across devices and notices asking you to avoid an area under repair.
- Please refrain from camping in milecastles and beside the Wall – use proper sites.
- Keep your dog on a lead wherever loose stock are near the Trail, and heed National Farmers Union/Ramblers Association advice about letting go if you feel threatened by cattle.
- Take your litter away with you and never light fires.
- Close all gates behind you unless it is clear that the farmer needs the gate to be left open.
- Hadrian's Wall is a Scheduled Ancient Monument. Play your part in ensuring that it remains intact for future generations to appreciate and enjoy.

Milecastle 33 (Stage 6) with vulnerable walling – hence the decking

Bath-house reconstruction at Segedunum viewed from Hadrian's Way

temporarily set on worn sections of the Path. By so doing you allow the grass sward to recover, thereby protecting the latent archaeology.

Over the first decade of the Trail's life meticulous management kept it in good order. The Trail manager, David McGlade, supported by his two full-time lengthsmen, Alan Gledson and Richard Thomas, set a gold standard. Although these dedicated lengthsmen have gone, they have left a legacy of good practice. The challenge for the Trail Partnership, with diminishing manpower and fiscal recourses, must be to uphold the greensward Trail into the future. Volunteers are no substitute for full-time professionals; path maintenance is as much about developing good relations with local people and landowners as it is about timely intervention to avoid damage getting out of hand.

TACKLING A COAST-TO-COAST WALK

Too many people who contemplate walking Hadrian's Wall Path overestimate their capacity and underestimate the task. The key word here is **planning**. The Trail may be only 84 miles long, and for much of its course passes over comparatively gently contoured country, but there are major pitfalls for anyone new to walking successive days on a tight schedule.

No printed guide can ever keep pace with month-by-month changes, nor rival online sources; hence for the latest information your first port of call should always be Natural

England's National Trail website (www.nationaltrail.co.uk/hadrians-wall-path), which is managed by Walk Unlimited. This is not only the place for gathering pertinent information on the Trail, including accommodation, but it is where you should channel feedback on your observations and concerns – an important and vital communication link with the Trail Officer.

See Appendix E for a comprehensive listing of websites and contact details that may prove invaluable in the planning and enjoyment of your visit.

START AND FINISH POINTS

Where to begin? In the west, Bowness-on-Solway – where the Wall met the sea – is an obvious starting point. Walkers with a pioneering spirit may also relish the adventure of starting at Maryport and tracing the maritime frontier, although the Cumbria Coastal Path falls some considerable degree short of National Trail standards.

In the east the focus inevitably tends to be on Segedunum in Wallsend, being the formal Trail terminus. However, Arbeia (pronounced R-bay-A) at South Shields – a Roman supply port and fort at the mouth of the Tyne – has much to reward the visitor and thoroughly merits consideration, facilitating a proper coast-to-coast expedition. The majority of walkers inevitably are content to set their sights on the National Trail, primarily because of time constraints.

Since Wall scholars, largely from a Newcastle perspective, determined that the frontier was built east-to-west, they set in stone a numbering system for the milecastles and turrets that followed suit and the habit 'set in' to walk west. However, the modern wise owl walks east! The prevailing weather is at one's back, the sun over

West gate reconstruction at Arbeia

one's shoulder makes for better photography, and the journey ends where public transport excels – enabling a swift return to 'civilian' life off the frontier (in other words it's so much easier to get home).

Whichever way you opt to walk, this guide gives you the tools to accomplish your goal, with reliable two-way navigation, supplementing the Trail's white acorns and distinctive signs.

Getting there

Carlisle Lake District now operates daily Loganair flights connecting Carlisle with Southend (London),

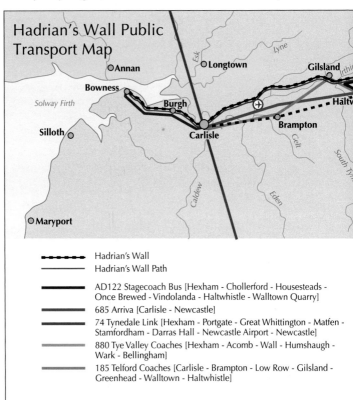

Dublin and Belfast, www.carlisleair port.co.uk.

For Bowness-on-Solway
Stagecoach runs bus service 93 from Carlisle bus station via Burgh-by-Sands, Bowness and Anthorn, although it is not the best schedule in the world for Trail walkers. Best advice: use a Carlisle taxi!

For Arbeia
Tyne & Wear Metro operates to South Shields from Newcastle Central Station, with a 28-minute journey time.

For Segedunum
Tyne & Wear Metro operates to Wallsend from Newcastle Central Station, with a 9-minute journey time.

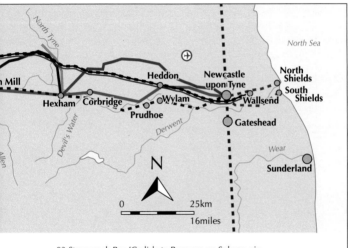

—————— 93 Stagecoach Bus [Carlisle to Bowness-on-Solway, via Burgh-by-Sands]

▪ ▪ ▪ ▪ ▪ Carlisle/Newcastle (Northern Rail) [via Brampton - Haltwhsitle - Bardon Mill - Hexham - Corbridge - Wylam]

—————— West Coast Mainline (Avanti) London Euston/Glasgow, via Carlisle

▪ ▪ ▪ ▪ ▪ East Coast Mainline (LNER) London King's Cross/Edinburgh Waverley, via Newcastle

▪ ▪ ▪ ▪ ▪ Tyne & Wear Metro Newcastle Central [via Wallsend to North Shields and South Shields]

Further information

For information about local bus services in Cumbria and Newcastle respectively, go to www.stagecoachbus.com or www.travelinenortheast.info. Train information for all areas can be found at www.nationalrail.co.uk (tel 08457 48 49 50). Appendix C contains detailed information about how to access Hadrian's Wall Path on foot from nearby railway stations; Appendix D features the names and contact details of local taxi services, as well as details of the buses that service the route; and Appendix E includes details of the region's public transport providers.

ACCOMMODATION

For accommodation, some walkers (the more hardy type) opt to camp or use camping barn facilities, and each year the number of private hotels with barns is increasing. So although at present there is a paucity of this type of accommodation, the situation is improving. The majority of walkers choose the greater comforts of B&B, savouring the good food and wider scenic delights of the area. Again, there are stretches with insufficient B&B accommodation to meet the high-season demand, and walkers who set out without pre-booking can find they have unexpected taxi bills as a result of getting to and from a more distant lodging.

Remember you are here for pleasure, to sense the magic of walking coast to coast with history at your very feet. Why not include a circular walk; take a proper look at nearby sites and towns; or, this being a Trail of two cities, make time to really

The Keelman (Stage 9)

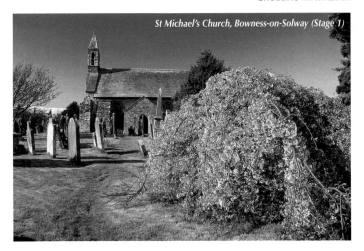
St Michael's Church, Bowness-on-Solway (Stage 1)

explore Carlisle and Newcastle. Too many walkers treat the sections from Bowness to Gilsland as two-day marches because of apparent deficiencies in the chain of accommodation; this is most unfortunate and probably unnecessary if you undertake a bit of forward planning.

The best overall approach, on the basis that most walkers embark at a weekend, is to start on a weekday. The benefits of this strategy become clear when you reach the middle section of the route, where competition for beds is most intense. You will be a day or two behind the bulk of walkers and therefore stand a better chance of finding that much-appreciated pillow. One of the problems of a hugely popular route with finite accommodation options is that, to ensure solid bookings, many B&Bs tie in with tour operators and block-book, making it almost impossible to find an impromptu bed for the night near the Path in high season.

See Appendix B for a section-by-section list of accommodation providers – including youth hostels and camping barns – and their contact details, and Appendix E for useful contacts, including tourist information centres.

CHOOSING AN ITINERARY

The common itinerary for the Trail is for a seven-day traverse (which can be done in many different ways), but I would be falling short of my praise of this historic and scenic corridor if I were to recommend anything less than nine to ten days as the most rewarding plan. A sensibly measured

THREE POPULAR ITINERARIES

The author's preferred schedule for walking the National Trail is described in the ten sections of this guide. Below are the three most popular daily walking schedules (reversible for westbound travel).

FIVE-DAY
Bowness to Carlisle . . . . 14½ miles (23km)
Carlisle to Gilsland. . . . . 18 miles (29km)
Gilsland to Chollerford. . . . . 21 miles (34km)
Chollerford to Heddon . . . . 15 miles (24km)
Heddon to Wallsend (Segedunum) . . . . . 15 miles (24km)

EIGHT-DAY
Bowness to Carlisle . . . . 15 miles (24km)
Carlisle to Newtown . . . . 9 miles (14km)
Newtown to Gilsland . . . . 9 miles (14km)
Gilsland to Steel Rigg . . . . 9 miles (14km)
Steel Rigg to Chollerford. . . . . 12 miles (19km)
Chollerford to Portgate . . . . 5 miles (8km)
Portgate to Heddon. . . . . 10 miles (16km)
Heddon to Wallsend (Segedunum) . . . . . 15 miles (24km)

TEN-DAY
Bowness to Burgh-by-Sands . . . . 7½ miles (12km)
Burgh-by-Sands to Carlisle . . . . 7 miles (11km)
Carlisle to Crosby-on-Eden . . . . 5 miles (8km)
Crosby-on-Eden to Lanercost . . . . 8 miles (12.5km)
Lanercost to Greenhead . . . . 7½ miles (12km)
Greenhead to Housesteads. . . . . 9½ miles (15km)
Housesteads to Chollerford. . . . . 10 miles (16km)
Chollerford to East Wallhouses . . . . 9 miles (14.5km)
East Wallhouses to Newburn . . . . 9½ miles (15km)
Newburn to Wallsend (Segedunum) . . . . 11 miles (18km)
(The extension to South Shields Metro station adds 7 miles (11km))

10-day schedule, that will reward you long after the experience itself is over, is listed below. This schedule is not a fixed plan – you must do the walk your way. As a further valuable device, in support of sustainable tourism, determine to stay a minimum of two nights at each lodging, using a taxi for continuity.

DAY-WALKING THE TRAIL

Some 12,000 people annually walk the Trail, but a vastly greater number walk it in parts or in modest portions, aiming to gather up the whole Trail over the course of time and often achieving their goal in 'there-and-back' sections or as part of circular walks. More indulgently, the two-car trick is often employed – a mutual arrangement whereby friends park at the end of the section to be walked and convey forward to walk back.

This guide enables whole chunks of the Trail to be walked using access routes from railway stations; see Appendix C for detailed guidance. If you are likely to be coming on a regular basis to the National Park part of the frontier, you should consider buying an annual permit for their metered car parks.

WHEN TO GO

Mindful of your boots' impact on the vulnerable archaeology, and for sheer personal comfort, you would be wise not to stray outside of the core walking season – April to the end of October (see 'National Trail Passport Scheme', below).

As the spring warms so the facilities, cafés, museums, AD122 bus and guesthouses open their doors for active visitors in time for Easter. School holiday periods bring greater numbers and pressure on accommodation. Whichever time of year you

Looking west over Whittle Dene Reservoir and broad areas of ripe wheat from Harlow Hill (Stage 8)

NATIONAL TRAIL PASSPORT SCHEME

The passport scheme, operated through the Northumberland National Park, runs strictly between 1 May and 31 October. This schedule is based on Met Office data, which says that in a 'normal' year the Wall's soils are saturated, or at field capacity, between the end of October and the end of April. Of course, some years spring is late, or it might rain incessantly the whole year long (as in 2012), and at such times the Trail maintenance rangers have to work more intensively, fighting to sustain the greensward path surface. Always remember that you can play your part in sustaining the Trail by avoiding treading in soil-exposed sections – spread the load. Passports can be bought from Segedunum in Wallsend and the King's Arms in Bowness-on-Solway, or online at www.trailgiftshop.co.uk. You can get them stamped at seven locations along the way, and once you have completed the Trail, a fully stamped passport makes you eligible to buy a certificate of completion at either of the end points. A list of stamping stations can be found in Appendix A.

Birdoswald outdoor stamping station

choose, don't bank on wall-to-wall sunshine – expect generally cooler and wetter conditions than you might find on trails further south in England.

BE PREPARED

While an army may march on its stomach, a long-distance walker relies on their head – thinking in advance about what might be needed when far from base. The Roman scouts had to be protected against the uncertainties of the northern climate, and you should be similarly prepared for exposure to wind, rain and intense sun.

Walkers should be aware that comfort facilities are frequently unavailable en route – there are considerable stretches where one would have to leave the Trail to find toilet facilities, drinks, food or shelter. Walkers need to carry their own resources in order to avoid such discomforts, and in this day and age there are lightweight options available. Drinks are the only unavoidable weight.

Two pieces of advice for the first day, whichever coast you begin at: wear lightweight boots or trainers; and allow yourself the chance to get into the pattern of walking day after day. Start steadily – the early stretch of the Trail, both on the Solway Plain and through Tyneside, has considerable stretches of sole-tiring tarmac. While some folk, used to hard surfaces, may think nothing of it, I suggest the majority will rue their folly should they not pay attention to any developing soreness. Be prepared, at the first hint of pain, to slip on a barrier plaster or different socks or footwear, placing the emphasis on a different area of your foot. If you allow your feet to form blisters, they will spoil the whole walk.

MAPS

This guide features all the mapping you will need to navigate the Trail, but if you wish to take or consult other mapping for fuller enjoyment of the route, the following maps are available in print:

- *Hadrian's Wall*, Ordnance Survey (Historical Map & Guide) – a classic, suitable for casual visitors and keen monument-hunters alike. Out of print but available on eBay and in second-hand bookshops.
- *Map of Hadrian's Wall*, Ordnance Survey, 1972 edition – only found (all too rarely, as they are treasured) in second-hand bookshops; this is the best map for studious walkers with an eye on landscape history
- Current Ordnance Survey maps covering Hadrian's Wall Path

The dolerite rock at Limestone Corner (Stage 7)

- Landranger (1:50,000): 85, 86, 87, 88
- Explorer (1:25,000): OL43, 314, 315, 316 (all this mapping is included in the booklet with this guide)

USING THIS GUIDE

Hadrian's Wall Path is presented in detail from west to east in 10 sections. At the eastern end of the National Trail two distinct routes have been included to embellish the frontier walking experience. Hadrian's Toon Trail intriguingly shadows the ghost of the frontier through urban Tyneside, while Hadrian's Cycleway makes the coast to coast connection to the mouth of the Tyne.

An information box at the beginning of each stage gives the day's start and finish points, along with walk distance (miles/kilometres), average walking time (you will have to calibrate this against your own pace as you go), places along and close to the route that offer refreshment, and places where you may find accommodation. This is followed by a short introduction to give you a feel for the day's walking.

The route description combines step-by-step directions and background information about places and features of interest along the way. Overview maps at a scale of 1:100K are included in each stage for planning purposes, with significant locations en route shown in **bold** in the route description. A more detailed map of the Path is supplied in booklet form, at a scale of 1:25K, at the back of the book. A description of walking each stage east-to-west is given in summary at the end of the route description of each west-to-east stage.

The route summary table gives two-way distances between the start and locations en route; Appendix A contains a list of passport stamping stations and details of how to use them; Appendix B is a stage-by-stage accommodation guide (including youth hostels and camping barns); Appendix C provides detailed instructions on how to access the Path on foot from a number of nearby railway stations; Appendix D lists the names and contact details of local bus and taxi services; Appendix E is a wider directory of useful contacts, including tourist information centres and public transport providers; and Appendix F features a comprehensive reading list for those wishing to immerse themselves in the history and culture of the Wall.

BUILDING THE WALL

With typical Roman military directness, Hadrian's Wall forms an almost straight east–west divide, crossing the narrowest neck or isthmus of the most northerly Roman province, Britannia, from Segedunum in Wallsend (NZ 301 660) to Maia at Bowness-on-Solway (NY 221 626).

Building the Wall was no mean feat, as some two million tons of stone had to be cut, hauled and laid in order

The Rudge Cup, centred on Birdoswald Roman Fort alias 'Banna' (picture credit: Peter Savin)

In the collection of the Duke of Northumberland at Alnwick Castle, this Roman-made memento, small enough to be held in the cup of one's hand, tells us something unique about Hadrian's Wall: it shows us what the Wall actually looked like. The design reveals regularly spaced crenulated features representing the turrets, milecastles and forts along the line of the stone frontier. These were built, like the bridges, in advance of the curtain wall, which was making strident progress westwards from Newcastle when it was decided the work could be speeded up if the 10-foot gauge was narrowed to 8 feet. That simple act was further endorsed by the in-practice realisation that crenulations and the wall walk were also unnecessary, as the regular interval towers provided all the surveillance they needed.

ROMAN WALL FEATURES

Broad Wall The original 10ft-wide stone Wall sketched out by Emperor Hadrian in his construction master plan.

Narrow Wall The 8ft-wide Wall that was later introduced to make a modest but significant saving in masonry, even though a foundation had been laid and Broad Wall wings attached to milecastles and turrets as far forward as the River Irthing.

Turf Wall The original frontier constructed as a layered bank of regular turf divots set upon a cobbled base, from west of the River Irthing crossing at Willowford to Bowness-on-Solway, built out of turf rather than stone because of its remoteness from any source of suitable building stone or lime for mortar and the need to meet the Emperor's deadline.

Milecastles Small fortlets, a mile apart, incorporating gateways through the Wall linked by a military supply road to the primary forts.

Turrets Small towers built into the Wall, spaced a third-of-a-Roman-mile apart.

Vallum A flat-bottomed ditch flanked by mounds running to the south of Hadrian's Wall at varying distances, defining a military exclusion zone.

Vicus The unplanned civilian settlement that grew up beside each fort to service extra-mural needs.

to create a curtain wall of stone, with turf and timber sections also being built on the west of the River Irthing. Concentrated in a 10-year period from AD122, the main work was undertaken by three legions: XX Valeria, VI Victrix and II Augusta.

Specifications for the Wall underwent various modifications during the 10 years it took to build. At the outset the plan was for a stone wall some 10 Roman feet thick and perhaps 15ft high (known as the Broad Wall) to run from Newcastle to the River Irthing, with a turf wall completing the journey to the coast at

Bowness-on-Solway. The turf wall was 20 Roman feet thick at its base, set on a stable bed of cobbles, and was a solution to the logistical problems of hauling stone some distance and to the lack of lime available for mortar. Later, the turf wall was replaced by a stone wall.

The Wall had integrated forts approximately every five miles, garrisoned by cavalry or foot soldiers. There were also frontier post gates at every mile, built into what are now termed milecastles (there is no record of their Roman name, nor of how each was distinguished – hence

Brunton Turret 26b (Stage 7)

the latter-day sequential numbering system for the milecastles). A small detachment of auxiliary soldiers would have been billeted at each milecastle to perform border control duties. Observation towers featured every ⅓ mile (Roman mile) between milecastles.

The milecastles were set at 1620-yard (1480m) intervals; without the aid of cartography, Romans must have judged distances by marching from one place to another. The Roman mile (Latin *mille*) was equivalent to 1000 marching paces (double-steps).

On the south side of the Wall a Military Way or supply road ran close by, and a double-banked ditch (the vallum) was created at varying distances to the rear of the Wall. A 'v' ditch was constructed immediately

north of the Wall, and so the area from this Wall ditch to the vallum became, at a stroke, an exclusive military zone separating the civil order of the empire from the 'barbarian' territory to the north.

DIVIDE AND RULE

Movement north and south through the Wall was regulated; tolls may have been exacted; and groups or individuals passing through the frontier were possibly forced to exit some distance east or west of their point of entry, thus further disrupting established patterns of movement. The Wall was like a motorway driven through an ancient wood, suddenly 'cutting off' animals from their established territory and disrupting their social patterns; the

31

Celtic Brigantes tribe experienced a similar dislocation.

The logistics of building a 10ft Broad Wall appear to have caused a rethink. An early change, narrowing the basic wall from a width of 10ft to 8ft, was undertaken partly to save time – as the construction process was carried out amid the constant threat of terror raids from not unnaturally disgruntled Picts. While the Wall foundations and lookout turrets were being set in place, the process of westward wall-building changed at Planetrees on the east side of the North Tyne Valley; here we see the start of the 8ft-wide Narrow Wall.

The Wall has often been portrayed with a crenulated parapet walk on top to match those on the forts, milecastles and turrets. This seems unlikely, as the forts and milecastles had viewing towers, which quickly rendered even the turrets obsolete. The Rudge Cup (illustrated) in the Duke of Northumberland's collection in Alnwick Castle gives us perhaps the clearest indication of what the Roman Wall looked like. It shows crenulated towers representing turrets, milecastles, forts (as two bridges) in a regular pattern around the tiny bowl, resting upon a plain (uncrenulated) wall. This confirms the view that when the wall construction was narrowed, the fussy crenulations and wall walk dispensed with and a far more substantial barrier erected.

The linear ditch of the vallum appears to have been an early invention to broaden the area of military control; however, like the turrets, which were uniformly demolished, it seems to have quickly lost its value, and crossings were constructed over it, negating its original function.

Where the Wall crossed major streams and rivers fine bridges were built, and were later enhanced with what might be termed 'chariot ramps' to service the speedy movement of cavalry and marching men.

The many subtle details of the Wall frontier – its phases, along with the various individual layouts of the forts, milecastles and turrets, and the daily life of garrisons and auxiliaries – are not given here as they are generally well displayed either on site, in nearby museums or in the excellent publications of English Heritage and others (see Appendix F).

Fifteen thousand men from three legions – XX Valeria, VI Victrix and II Augusta – were employed on the task of building the Wall, and no doubt there was a certain rivalry between the legions. The building of the Wall, milecastles and turrets was strictly standardised from the outset, although interpretation of the rules allowed for a certain level of individuality. Inscribed stones were built into the Wall at regular intervals to indicate which legion or cohort had built that section – they were simultaneously a tribute to the honour of the empire and an indication of pride in a job well done.

Some indication of 'who built what' can also be deduced from the size of the various milecastles. Studies suggest that the following three legions constructed the majority of milecastles:

- XX Valeria (milecastles 18, 19, 22, 29, 30, 44, 45, 53, 54)
- VI Victrix (9, 10, 23, 27, 33, 34, 35, 36, 39, 40, 50)
- II Augusta (13, 14, 17, 37, 38, 41, 42, 43, 52).

PILFERING AND PRESERVATION

Although the frontier played an active part in Roman life for nearly three centuries, once Roman jurisdiction fell away, the Wall too lost its meaning. Remarkably, the Wall remained largely intact for the next 1000 years, mainly because local buildings were predominantly timber-built. Its only enemy was the damp northern climate and the occasional monastic 'borrowing'. Later, when most buildings came to be made of stone, it was open season on the long-defunct frontier, so farmers and house-builders took the stones in cart-loads. This was the period known as the 'Great Rebuilding' which began in about 1600.

That there is any trace of the Wall remaining today is largely due to the enlightened and prompt action of one man, John Clayton of Chesters, whose estate was located some five miles north of Hexham, just west of Chollerford, where the Wall crossed the North Tyne. At the end of the 18th century Clayton's father began to turn his country seat into a fashionable stately park, in the process virtually flattening Cilurnum (Chesters) Roman

Tallest section of Clayton Wall within Milecastle 37 (Stage 6)

Fort. However, upon inheriting the estate in 1822, John Clayton began reversing this process.

His classical education served him particularly well, for he realised the importance of the Roman site in the grounds and developed a passion for the frontier with which it was associated. He then proceeded to acquire farm after farm along the line of the Wall as far as the Cumberland border (present day Cumbria), thus abruptly ending the thoughtless pilfering of Wall stone. This pilfering in the lowland sections of the Wall was by then almost complete anyway.

THE WALL TODAY

The following terms are used in this guide to describe the various states in which the Wall exists today.

- **Consolidated Wall**: sections where English Heritage has rebuilt the structure with mortar to resist the elements for long-term outdoor exhibition.
- **Clayton Wall**: dry-stone reconstruction with turf on top, conducted under the instructions of John Clayton of Chesters House in the 19th century. This Wall is prone to periodic collapse and

repair; walkers clambering onto it have been the main culprits of this decay – please, please keep off.
- **Semi-field Wall**: many instances of genuine remnant Wall linger as small base sections of field wall or as random individual stones – there's a sport in trying to spot them.
- **Rubble Rigg**: in areas where most of the good masonry has been stolen, sad linear mounds remain in situ. These unexcavated lengths still need securing for the long term and are just as important as more obvious Wall sections.

In some places there is no tangible trace of the Wall – its former existence indicated only by the line of an enclosure field wall, hedge or fence. At other times it runs across open pasture, under houses and even under tarmac! (The one saving grace is that the tarmac is protecting the foundations and could be lifted.) One of the best stretches of wall, although it does not replicate the wall and is not in situ, is that reused as part of the bounding enclosure to Lanercost Priory, Cumbria. This medieval rebuild is about one-third of the height of the original Wall.

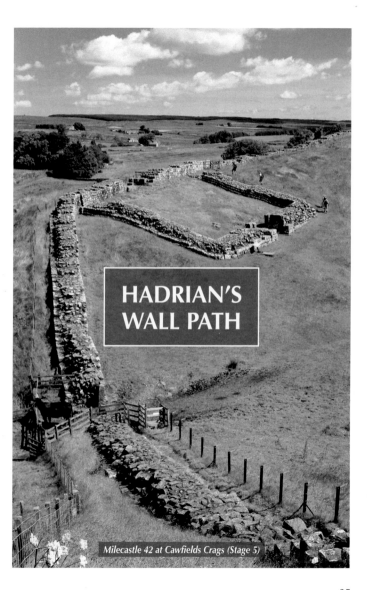

HADRIAN'S WALL PATH

Milecastle 42 at Cawfields Crags (Stage 5)

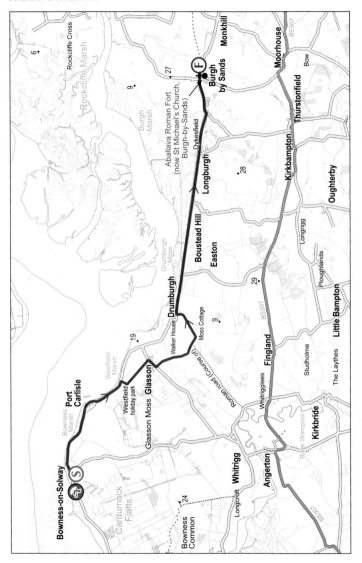

STAGE 1

Bowness-on-Solway to Burgh-by-Sands

Start	Maia Fort Visitor Centre, Bowness-on-Solway
Finish	St Michael's Church, Burgh-by-Sands
Distance	8¼ miles (13km)
Walking time	4½hr
Refreshments	Bowness-on-Solway: Maia Fort Visitor Centre, The Kings Arms (ph); Port Carlisle: The Hope & Anchor Inn, Solway Chapel self-service, Highland Laddie (ph); Drumburgh: Grange Farm – self-service refreshment bar in brick outbuilding; Burgh-by-Sands: The Greyhound Inn
Accommodation	Bowness-on-Solway, Port Carlisle, Drumburgh and Burgh-by-Sands

Within the Roman Empire, Maia Roman Fort was the furthest from Rome. As all roads are said to lead to Rome this first leg to Port Carlisle has some significance. Indeed, to start from here one may be expected to walk on to Arbeia (South Shields) and catch an imaginary boat bound for the Mediterranean – well, you will at least catch the Shields Ferry, at the mouth of the Tyne, linking North Shields with South Shields!

BOWNESS-ON-SOLWAY

The quiet community has long revolved around its church, school, pub and community centre (Lindow Hall). The main street thoroughfare, which is underlain with beck-stone cobble, sadly reveals no hint of its Roman foundation. Immediately east of the mid-town pub, encounter Midtown Farm. A major private initiative has converted it into a much-needed focal Maia Fort Visitor Centre. The centre is open all year round, providing accommodation, refreshment in the Garrison Bistro/bar and interpretation, most notably a huge scale model of Maia Roman Fort created by Bill Brown. As an introduction to the Roman Wall, this sets the mind racing, eager to track down the component parts of the frontier as they appear over coming

The Kings Arms

days. However, you won't see much on your first day's march, apart from hints of Roman rubble stone in the parish churches, both here in Bowness as well as Burgh and Beaumont and most emphatically Drumburgh Castle.

On the street-flanking side wall of the Centre see a replica stone altar dedication to Jupiter Optimus Maximus; the original, dating from AD251, was found in 1739 SE of the fort and later built over a barn door at this point. The Kings Arms, it should be stated, stands at an internal intersection of the Roman fort. There is a visitor's book in Lindow Hall (and loos) along with the all-important Trail Passport stamping station. Should you find the hall is closed (usually 8pm), then you can apply by mail order for your purple badge, requesting that the missing stamp is put in the card; this is then returned to you.

Further down the lane, beyond the churchyard hearse house of 1782 and Vallum House, is the old rectory, now appropriately called Wallsend. So, indeed you can walk from Wallsend to Wallsend.

For 1:25K route map see booklet pages 4–8.

◀ The first duty of the Wall-wide walker is to visit the Path Pavilion on The Banks. The alley approach is prominently signposted off the main street. In late winter The

THE BOWNESS ESTUARY

Should you stroll westwards out of the village, you may visit the Bowness Nature Reserve, NY 206 617, a mile west of the village. (A leaflet to a mile-long nature trail has been produced by the Cumbria Wildlife Trust.) The RSPB has a large interest in Campfield Marsh and has recently added the 200-acre Rogersceugh Farm to its estate on Bowness Common. The botanical diversity of this area of raised lowland peat bog is, without question, precious, the product of many thousands of years of development; it is a monument to protect every bit as carefully as the comparatively 'recent history' of the Roman frontier works.

En route, notice a blunt promontory from where an iron railway viaduct once spanned the estuary to Annan – an impressive feat of Victorian construction. At 5850ft (1.8km) it was then the longest in Britain. Although officially only a railway bridge, it was more than tempting on Sundays (when Scotland was 'dry') for those requiring 'a wee dram' to simply wander over; but as the bridge became unsafe, so too did this pedestrian practice, and inevitably someone did come 'off the rails'. The bridge, a crucial link between the Cumberland coalfield and the Lanarkshire ironworks, closed in 1921. Its ultimate demise came during the particularly cold winter of 1934, when ice floes fatally damaged the central pillars. It was demolished in 1936.

The estuary was also the last resting place of the Bowness church bell. In the days of reiving high jinks a raiding party from Middlebie in Dumfriesshire sneaked across and removed the bell. However, they were not rewarded, for the inhabitants of Bowness rowed after them with such vigour and in such a rage that it caused the bandits to throw the bell overboard. The men of Bowness sought reparation, and audaciously stole the Middlebie church bell. So, to this day, each new minister at Middlebie is obliged to write a futile letter requesting the bell's return – shades of the Elgin Marbles? However, the story took a new twist only a dozen years ago when Dornock church in Annan borrowed the bell for a flower festival and happily returned it to Bowness. It is now a friendship bell.

Banks are a great drift of snowdrops, and in spring, daffodils. The spot where the Wall would have merged with the northern rampart of the Roman fort has been well and truly stolen by the sea. The very Roman timber structure sits above a well and garden; this is quite appropriate, for the name derives from the Latin *papilio*, meaning

Path Pavilion – 'good luck go with you'

'butterfly tent'. There is access down onto the beach over the sea wall for that ceremonial start/finish and a long gaze over the sparkling waters, striking home the sense of being at the far-flung edge of the Roman Empire.

The **Solway Firth** means 'the ford marked by a pillar fjord'. The pillar in question is thought to be the Lochmaben Stone at the mouth of Kirtle Water near Gretna. Ordnance Survey maps suggest a boulder of Criffel granite, which marked the Scottish end of the ford, was the last remnant of a stone circle. For geologists the Solway is an interesting feature in itself: comprising the estuary of two great rivers, the Esk and the Eden, supplemented by Annanwater and the Nith, it owes its existence more to a great coming together of land masses – the same blocks that formed Ireland, although at this point the union was not completed.

The graceful mountain form of Criffel stands to the west, sheltering the mouth of the River Nith near Dumfries. Northwards there is the site of the former Chapelcross power station, opened in 1955 as a Magnox station on an old airfield site. This was closed in 2005, with the cooling towers demolished two years later, the long process of decommissioning taking a crucial turn in 2013 when the reactors were defuelled, although the site is not scheduled to be cleared until 2095! North-east is the old market town of Annan, where Thomas Carlyle, the Victorian man of letters, taught at the Academy. When lit by a late afternoon sun, the low horizon of pillow hills looks so inviting – a land of promise, not the foreboding of the Roman and Reiver ages. A coast path is being developed along the Scottish shore to Stranraer.

Leave the Pavilion by the eastern side path to re-join the village street opposite the former Wesleyan Home Mission Chapel, going left through the narrows by Shore Gate House to come alongside the foreshore road. Occasionally, you can see debris on the railings, which shows how high the tide can reach (waist high in fact). There is no option at present but the grassy verges beside **Bowness Marsh**, but the mile to Port Carlisle is a happy mix of stops and starts.

This is an early opportunity to study the **running waters**, with occasional sightings of basking shark and harbour porpoise. However, you are more likely to see the marvellous diversity of birds that use this as a conduit along the length of Hadrian's Wall to the Northumberland coast and the North Sea. Spot waders, including heron, oystercatcher, redshank and curlew, along with barnacle and greylag geese and ducks, including shelduck, as well as a variety of gulls and skua. The range of birdlife, migratory and vagrant, is quite unpredict-ably exciting.

Entering **Port Carlisle**, spot Hesket House. Above the front door lintel is a tiny fragment of Roman altar stone; the hard-to-decipher inscription, *MATRIBUS SUIS MILITE*, is apparently attributed to a mother goddess.

Hesket House was built as the Steam Packet Inn, where people bound for Whitehaven en route to Liverpool and emigration via Ellis Island to the United States lodged while waiting for their passage. The parents of **Thomas Woodrow Wilson** stayed here: he was a first-generation American citizen when he became the 28th Democratic President, holding office from 1913 to 1921. A Nobel Peace Prize winner in 1919, Woodrow Wilson was the founder of the League of Nations, although the US senate refused to support it. During his presidency he came to Britain just the once, in 1918, making a 'pilgrimage of the heart', as he put it, visiting his parents' last home in England in Botchergate, Carlisle.

Along the main street is a fine terrace of 'port' houses. Facing the old navigation basin built by the Earl of Lonsdale in 1819, now with a bowling green in its midst, is Solway House, another boarding house for erstwhile ocean-going travellers. The Hope & Anchor Inn is a more than welcome Trail-side hostelry.

Pursuing the roadway, pass the former Customs House, which became the Station House on the arrival of the railway. A track leads by a low stone building, standing on the site of the original haaf fisherman's dwelling known as Fisher's Cross – the only building in this vicinity prior to the development of the port community. ◀

Beyond the sea-lock bridge, from where a wooden steamer pier once extended, wander by cottages converted from Dandy horse stables facing directly out upon the breakwater island.

For 22 years, from 1821, the **canal** had an important commercial life when Fisher's Cross Quay became the bustling Port Carlisle. The canal ran from the vicinity of the Carrs/McVities factory in Carlisle to this spot. Shifting sands and the emergence of the great age of steam spelled an end to its commercial

Contemporary with the canal basin, this later building was originally a bathhouse to refresh passengers newly disembarked from the high seas.

fortunes; the canal was drained and a rail track installed. At a stroke Port Carlisle was no more.

This **railway line** was considered to be nothing more than a very minor branch line, subservient to the more lucrative development of Silloth – a curious town name which translates as 'sea-laith' (sea-barn) – which catered to the Victorian passion for elegant resorts and bracing sea air. The Scottish, North British Railway Company that ran to Port Carlisle ceased freight in 1899. However, the one horse-drawn coach, 'Dandy No. 1', dating from 1859, survived and remained in service until the onset of the Great War in 1914. Dandy No. 1 is currently on display at the York Railway Museum. A steam locomotive plied the line for a short period thereafter, but the tracks were lifted and Port Carlisle duly lost all rail connection, the track bed becoming either farmland or a haven for wildlife and a reed bed.

▸ Coming upon a container, housing a lovely, little oared boat, the Bowness Belle, you can slip right by the hand gate to visit Solway Methodist Chapel. In the summer season this offers refreshment for Trail walkers (honesty box). On its walls see some fabulous old photos showing the railway viaduct that crossed the estuary to Scotland, some haaf-netters and the horse-drawn Dandy standing at the station with a throng of people. You may also relish picking up one of the painted stones available at the chapel to carry to another suitable place en route, an ancient custom charmingly rekindled here. A cosily confined path leads on beside the reeds in the canal-cum-railway section, with sneak views left of the open tidal estuary. The Trail crosses the road to come to the entrance to **Cottage & Glendale Holiday Park**, bearing left within a green lane to **Glasson** – an Irish name that would appear to mean 'the green homestead'. Barracks House, immediately right of the pub, is constructed of red sandstone blocks to Roman Wall specification.

Solway Chapel offers summer-season refreshment for Trail walkers, with a field campsite adjoining.

As a place for en-route refreshment, the **Highland Laddie** serves the walker well. The Jacobite Rebellion rings in the pub name: reputedly it was near here that Bonnie Prince Charlie stepped off English soil for the last time, headed for Scotland.

Follow the village street south to find a kissing gate left, then advance in the pasture, with a hedge close right, to a double kissing gate. Bear half-left to another kissing gate and follow along the edge of a field, latterly paved, to a footbridge. Continue by **Walker House** on a gravel track in a quiet farm lane, keeping left where a lane from **Moss Cottage** joins from the right.

The great expanse of **Drumburgh Moss and Whiteholme Common** is difficult to see. It is one of the last remaining raised mires, or peat bogs, on the Solway Plain – a mosaic of peat, birch woodland and grassland. This National Nature Reserve accounts for two per cent of the total area of this lowland moss habitat in England; it contains 13 species of sphagnum moss, as well as the carnivorous sundew and a wealth of cotton grass. Lizards and adders find a comfortable haven, as does a wonderful diversity of birdlife, from red grouse and curlews to redshanks, short-eared owls and grasshopper warblers. Huge winter flocks of geese are a speciality. The rare large heath butterfly and the impressive day-flying emperor moth frequent this special place; Hadrian would have approved of the presence of the latter! Evidence of the peat cutting in the parish waste is identified by the bracken growth.

The name Drumburgh (pronounced 'drum-bruff') contains Celtic and Old English terms and means 'the flat ridge with fortifications', alluding to the Roman fort of Congavata, set unusually close to the Wall-end fort of Maia; the Roman name is enigmatic.

Stand and admire Drumburgh Castle: a farmhouse with panache; witness the Wall in a new form.

In his 1539 itinerary, the poet and antiquary John Leland referred to **Drumburgh Castle** as follows: 'Drumburgh ys in ye mudde way betwixt Bolness and Burgh. At Drumburgh the Lord Dacre's father builded upon old ruins a pretty pyle for defence of the country. The stones of the Pict Wall were pulled down to build it.' So there you have it – straight from the folklore of the time. In 1307 Edward I granted a royal licence to crenellate the older building, which explains why the farmhouse is called 'Castle'.

A fine flight of stone steps leads to the main door, replacing the original wooden ladder that could easily be withdrawn, thereby making the accommodation awkward for invaders. This is a high-status bastle house – bastles were usually of a far more modest scale. The castellated west end of the roof is a viewing platform commanding a magnificent prospect over the Solway, and south to the Lakeland fells.

The wall beneath was in danger of collapse, so in 1978 it was meticulously rebuilt, removing the internal floors and inserting concrete blocking to the

Drumburgh Castle

45

inner wall, thus making it secure for another 1000 years at least! Notice the painted Roman altar and a second one below – artefacts gathered in times past from the site of Congavata. Above the door the decaying stone coats of arms of the Dacre family, griffins with spread wings, are perched; they once included the initials 'TD' for Thomas Dacre. The same family built Naworth Castle near Lanercost.

The hamlet of **Drumburgh** is otherwise less memorable. Walkers will be pleased to know that Grange Farm has set up a self-service stop for their refreshment – most particularly welcome for westbound walkers, after the section along the marshes road. The facility is located on the left after Lowther House (former pub, hence Spirituous Liquors over the door); coincidentally, The Old Post bungalow was once a clay-dabbin house tight to the road. Go up the lane, forking left before Grange farmhouse to the brick farm shed. Notice the large erratic of Kirkcudbright granite removed from an adjacent field.

The road crosses the flood bank and line of the old canal/railway as the Trail begins the three-mile traverse of Burgh Marshes. At the Easton junction the sign includes the intriguing name Finglandrigg, which means 'the finger-shaped long ridge associated with a Viking ting or assembly'. There is a cattle grid where Fresh Creek, draining the meadows to the south via Grass Dike, slips through to the join the Eden. It is amazing the distance from which one can hear vehicles crossing the far-off cattle grid at the Dykesfield end.

The road rises up short ramps at the **Easton** and **Boustead Hill** road junctions. Easton means 'eastern farm', as in east of Drumburgh, while Boustead means 'farm with a store house'. ◀

The cattle grid marks a transition point. We leave behind the free-roaming cattle and marshland horizons; hear now the discordant chatter of rooks from the tall trees in the vicinity of Dykesfield House as we embark on the farmed landscape of the Solway Plain. The minor road leading right to **Longburgh** crosses a metal parapet bridge.

Boustead Hill has many distinguished farmhouses and cottages from its development as a colony of merchants connected with the canal.

WARNING: TIDES, FLOODING, AND DOGS

Signs stating potential flood depth along the road might look like petty scare-mongering, but they are there because at times the salt marsh is inundated as far as the flood-bank up to the various depths indicated. This tends to occur when spring high tides coincide with heavy rainfall in the hills and a strong westerly wind. Advice on tide levels is readily available: there is a signboard at Dykesfield, tidal information leaflets at local B&Bs and TICs, and information on Natural England's website: www.nationaltrail.co.uk/hadrianswall. Indeed there is no excuse to be caught out – just remember to allow one hour either side of high tide for your marsh-side march.

At two points, signs direct visitors to the distant foreshore with the necessary warning: danger from fast-flowing tides and quick sands. The tidal Eden comes within view only latterly, so most of the diverse birdlife will be encountered as it flies overhead. The marshes are a Site of Special Scientific Interest, a bird reserve of major importance, so please keep this in mind should you be in a large party or exercising your dog.

Take a look – the lower portion of the stone walling is curved with signs of rope wear on the east side, a legacy of its life as a **canal**. It was constructed in 1823 (11¼ miles/18km long) and connected Carlisle with coastal trade shipping. The adjacent cottage was built with the canal; there was evidently much heated resentment, for the property was burnt down in 1823 and the culprit never discovered, despite the handsome reward of one shilling and six pence! Interestingly, the property has always remained in the same family.

Despite the spelling, **Burgh-by-Sands** is pronounced 'bruff'. It is a village with a highly developed sense of community purpose and vitality. On the way in from the west there is little hint of anything remotely Roman, excepting 'Vallum', the house on the left just before the footpath to Watch Hill. After the new house 'Stackyard', with its name harking back to the days of corn- and hay-ricks, is a particularly handsome pale green house down a drive to the

The Greyhound pub is a mainstay for refreshment in the village for Wall-walkers. Admire the handsome bronze statue of Edward I, erected to commemorate the 700th anniversary of his death.

right with an architecturally intriguing outbuilding. Note the giant sundial on an early 20th-century house.

◄ As the village street narrows, note Cross Farm's cruck symbol nameplate, hinting at the clay-dabbin barn which survives still and can be glimpsed through the archway into the backyard. Somewhat obscured by a tall hedge opposite is Lamonby Farm, a substantial white-washed clay-dabbin dwelling with a comparatively new thatch roof. Fauld Farm almost opposite the pub – the village post office (01228 791541) – is also of clay-dabbin construction, dating from the mid-15th century. These were the characteristic dwellings of the Solway Plain from Caldbeck to Burgh since the Vikings settled in the area from Ireland. At their core they were cruck-framed structures, with quick-build walls of clay bound with straw; lime-rendered inside and out for weather-proofing, they were set on a boulder plinth to resist rising damp. The roofs were thatched with either turf, heather or

reed, invariably now replaced with corrugated iron sheets. A superb scaled-down reconstruction was built in 2016 at the RSPB's Campsfield reserve at North Farm, west of Bowness, initiated by the Solway Wetlands Landscape Partnership. Being a landscape of glacial till, the Solway Plain has always had plenty of clay and pebbles to compensate for the absence of bedrock for building material, which led to this inventive building technique. Sadly, the number of clay-dabbin houses and barns has drastically reduced in the area over the last century.

After this, on the left, spot a thatched cruck house; another exists 100 metres up the Sandsfield road. These are increasingly rare examples of vernacular architecture.

At the village crossroads note the brown sign pointing left along the Sandsfield road to the **King Edward I Monument**.

Known as the 'Hammer of the Scots' and instigator of the major stone-built castles in England and Wales, this is a king who reigned down with a passion. He died of dysentery on Burgh Marshes on 7 July 1307 after he had instructed his army to carry his body into action to make yet one more assault on his most hated foe, Robert the Bruce; instead, the army turned back. It is a little ironic that Robert's father was born at nearby Holm Cultram Abbey.

Edward's body was carried to the church at Burgh to lie in state before transfer via Lanercost Priory to his last resting place at Westminster Abbey. Probably the ablest soldier king England ever had, Edward left a legacy of the most terrible border warfare.

Fort House, short of the churchyard, is a reference to **Aballava Roman Fort**. This house, along with others, reveals the red-and-white-chequered diaper brickwork distinctive of the Carlisle area.

Edward I's statue in Burgh-by-Sands

ST MICHAEL'S CHURCH AND ABALLAVA ROMAN FORT

A visit to St Michael's is almost obligatory; a metal hand gate gives entry into the churchyard, a timeline of stones drawing you to the church door. For best effect go round to the south side and observe the red and grey sandstone blocks of genuine Roman masonry.

The church was largely built in the 13th century, perhaps a foot or two higher than the Roman Wall, but what you see is a 'living reincarnation' of the Wall that once ran up to, and from, Aballava Roman Fort, which was situated in this immediate vicinity. (There is evidence of three forts in the Burgh area.) The fort name, referring to 'an apple orchard', may seem unlikely, but it has been calculated that average temperatures in Roman times were five degrees higher than today – even with global warming. When the Romans came, only crab apples grew in Britain. Hence, we must deduce then that

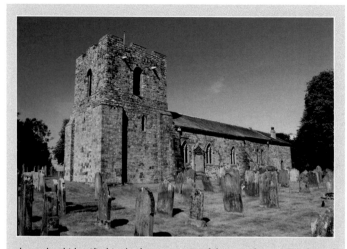

the orchard identified in the fort name was of the succulent variety derived from the east. What did the Romans ever do for us? Well, they certainly brought tasty apples, relished by active Romans and modern trail-walkers as handy nourishment on the move!

St Michael's is not just a church; it is a social-history record from times when there was a greater fear than the fear of God. Following the death of Edward I, the entire Anglo-Scottish border erupted into violence, and people sought every means by which to protect their lives and property. When the folk of Burgh fortified their church, they were in such haste that some parts collapsed during the process. Hence, with Roman Wall stone still abundant in the vicinity, they raised a stoutly buttressed tower with arrow slits, the only access being from within the nave via a 'yatt' or iron gate. Medieval bands of thieving, pillaging and murdering Border Reivers met their match here.

The church merits a careful look: inside, on the east wall of the chancel is the carved head of a Roman pagan god, and the most beautiful feature of the entire church is the series of stained-glass windows in the north aisle, depicting St Cuthbert with Durham Cathedral, St Aidan with the ruins of Lindisfarne, St Kentigern with St Asaph Cathedral, Edward I with Burgh Church, and St Ninian with the ruins of Whithorn Abbey. St Michael's is one of the East Solway Churches with Bowness and Beamount, Kirkbampton, Great Orton and Aikton, projecting the long-standing heritage and life of these communities. See www.eastsolwaychurches.org.

WESTBOUND: BURGH-BY-SANDS TO BOWNESS-ON-SOLWAY

From **Burgh Church** (see boxed text, above) follow the road through the village. It's a tarmac mile to **Dykesfield** and a further three more beyond the cattle grid, traversing the low-lying Burgh Marsh, wedded to the open road. The Trail-walker may stick with the road or its verge, or even the tidal bank up to the left if encounters with lumbering loafing cattle would be considered unwelcome – particularly an issue when you are accompanied by a dog. (See 'Warning: Tides, flooding and walking with dogs' above)

The open road remains the unfailing guide across the marsh to **Drumburgh**. Pass up into the village, turning left with the lane signed 'Whiteholme'. This opens into a broad droveway on a gravel track; keep right where a cattle grid intervenes, with Drumburgh Moss NNR signboard adjacent. Follow the gravel lane to **Walker House**, passing on by the farm buildings to a small plank bridge and hand gate. Stone flags minimise the potential for mud along the edge of the field. After a kissing gate bear half-left to a double kissing gate beside a cattle holding pen. Advance with the hedge to a kissing gate onto the road.

Turn right into **Glasson**. Opposite the Highland Laddie go left with the lane to reach the entrance to **Cottage & Glendale Holiday Park**, then turn right with the access road. At the T-junction go over and through the hand gate, following the narrow path beside the old canal, sheltered from the estuary by trees. Passing Solway Chapel, proceed via hand gates; keep to the shore path and cross the bridge over the former sea lock from the old canal basin to join a roadway which draws back onto the open road leading out of Port Carlisle. This road is an unerring guide to **Bowness-on-Solway**, a little under a mile-long estuary-edge saunter beside Bowness Marsh, with attention transfixed on the great tidal swathe of the Solway.

Expect no great fanfares on entry into this quiet, historic coastal village (see 'Bowness-on-Solway' and 'The Bowness Estuary' above). Turn right opposite the Wesleyan Home Mission Chapel, along an alley leading to The Banks – a modest promenade centred upon the Path Pavilion and the formal western end point of the Trail. The continuing path leads back into the village street, turning right to reach the King's Head junction. This is many walkers' last port of call – although the 'call' is more likely to be that of real ale or sparkling water than port!

STAGE 2
Burgh-by-Sands to Carlisle

Start	St Michael's Church, Burgh-by-Sands
Finish	Eden Bridge, Carlisle
Distance	6¼ miles (10km)
Walking time	3½ hr
Refreshments	Burgh-by-Sands: The Greyhound Inn; Grinsdale: drinks cabinet (honesty box); Carlisle: café at Tullie House, Carlisle Cathedral café, Cakes & Ale Café, Bookcase, The Sands Centre café, plus a wide variety of hotels, pubs, cafés and shops throughout the city
Accommodation	Plenty of choice in and around Carlisle
Railway link	Carlisle

Maritime influences are forgotten as the trail accompanies the ghostly line of the Wall through pastures and by shy villages upon the Solway Plain. Coming upstream with the River Eden, we enter the parkland heart of Carlisle.

Despite riverbank erosion having taken a lovely wooded section of path beyond Beaumont from the expedition, the walking is consistently relaxing and pleasing to the eye. Although the Trail may deliver greater visual riches as the days unfold, you will enjoy the verdant face of the Great Border City – a landmark end to the West Cumbrian passage of the journey.

For 1:25K route map see booklet pages 8–11.

◀ The Trail exits the village, avoiding the narrow road by slipping through a kissing gate and entering a pasture. It keeps close company with the roadside hedge, emerging at a further kissing gate to rejoin the road at a lay-by. It soon escapes the road's clutches when ushered into pastureland at a further kissing gate, to be fence-confined to the footbridge spanning Powburgh Beck. ◀

Over the road to the right the eroded trough banks of the old canal/railway.

From the line of ageing, aesthetically pleasing ash trunks, look north to **Burnswark**, the distant hill. This table-topped mesa, the vent plug of a 450-million-year-old volcano, lies close by Ecclefechan – as the place name suggests, a late Roman Christian site – the hill being the site of a ballistic siege camp, the only one identified in Roman Britain.

Beyond the pasture advance within a farm lane, precisely aligned with the Wall, to **Beaumont**.

It was an interesting evolution – as the Wall followed good ground, the adjacent **Military Way** continued to be the link between the emerging communities of Burgh and Beaumont. The Wall stone was pilfered for Burgh church, leaving the simple trackway with enclosure; this was lined with hedges, although curiously aligned slightly north of its original line.

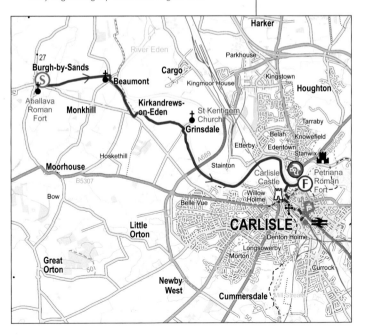

BEAUMONT VILLAGE

This village (whose name is pronounced 'bee-mont') is of hamlet proportions, hence its happy marriage with Kirkandrews. The village grew and was sustained because it lay close to an age-old River Eden ford used by cattle drovers, who accessed the Cargo shore above the high-tide point – hence the Drover's Rest public house at Monkhill, a valued port of call for Trail walkers (although the eight-minute walk suggested by the advertising board frequently perched on the triangular green is ambitious).

Many a walker will have sat happily on the tree-base seat and gazed at the high-set St Mary's, the only parish church to stand precisely upon the line of Hadrian's Wall. In the 11th century a motte-and-bailey castle was erected on this natural mound, taking advantage of its extensive outlook, the bailey extending over the area of the present triangular village green. The village name is a direct reference to this and translates as 'hill with a beautiful view'. Indeed, you can see the squat square hill Burnswark to the north across the Solway, scene of a Roman ballistic attack in AD140.

The late 12th-century church is built upon a Norman motte/mound set upon Turret 70a, palpably using recycled Roman Wall stone. The Norman castle might have been timber-built. You'll enjoy surmising which might be Roman stones in the outer fabric of the church.

At the road junction beside the salt box, attracting ivy growth and not a second glance from passing walker, find the inscribed stone LEG XX to the

Centurial Stone in Beaumont (with RIB drawing)

Twentieth Legion (see photo). It is impossible to judge from what Roman structure it was derived, certainly not the Wall itself, more likely from Aballava.

The original route above the wooded riverbank is no longer accessible due to irrevocable landslipping, so the replacement route reaches **Kirkandrews-on-Eden** by road. ▶

After the converging road junction, pass the Manor House and bear left with the lane by The Croft. Find a kissing gate to the right. After the slabs advance beneath the high bank, on top of which the Roman Wall ran and after climbing a flight of steps, from a reed-filled pond, continue following the bank-top fence along the line of the Wall, itself set some five paces from the edge, by kissing gates to cross the Sourmilk Gill bridge. Continue on beside the field-edge track to an unusual raised 'sidling' stile at a galvanised field gate. As you proceed along the open track, noting the retaining wall, you will spot a fragment of Eden cobble herringbone walling, known in Cornwall as Curzyway.

St Andrew's Church was demolished in the late 19th century; the vicarage and churchyard tombs are testimony to this charming village's merger with Beaumont.

The River Eden at Grinsdale

The village name derives from 'Grimnir's valley'.

Approaching farm buildings, slip through the kissing gate to the right, where a confined path leads into **Grinsdale** village street. ◄

It is all too natural to plough on along the Trail and ignore **St Kentigern's Church** – a haven of peace, secreted in a spinney to the north above the river bend. This charming retired church, alternative name St Mungo, was built in 1743 by Joseph Dacre on 12th-century foundations and has the most Arcadian feel. A green lane leads from the head of the village street to the embowered churchyard – although on a hot day perhaps the greater allure is the 'drinks cabin' prominently sited in the street.

Leave the street along the line of Hadrian's Wall. At a kissing gate cross a meadow to the footbridge, the gill chocked with Himalayan balsam. The non-tidal **River Eden** is a good companion henceforward. Continue above the riverside meadow, soon upon a tree-shaded, stepping-down-stepping-up path that copes safely with

The old Waverley Line Bridge

the **A689 Northern Bypass** by threading a sunken underpass via hand gates.

After Knockupworth Gill a profusion of power pylons cast their shadows over the Trail. The path descends steps beneath the near arch of the old Waverley Viaduct, built in 1861. The railway connected Edinburgh with Carlisle, ultimately developing a link that transformed Silloth into a Scottish golfing resort. ▸ Pass by the blocked southern end of the old Waverley Viaduct – a stone-arched river-bridge opened in 1861.

Well hidden, close by Engine Lonning, are a locomotive turntable and engine sheds – evidence of a once-busy railway siding. A local group of enthusiasts has plans to restore the turntable.

The **railway** closed in 1969 despite considerable opposition. Interestingly, work is now progressing to re-lay the tracks on the first 30-mile section south from Edinburgh back to Galashiels, with aspirations to reconnect the line to Carlisle. Of no less importance, it is fervently hoped that the bridge itself might open again purely as a bridleway with enormous local recreational value. Hopes that this might be realised within the next few years are quietly yet confidently held.

After passing a former coal-fired brick electricity power station, dismantled in 1982, with its industrial semi-waste, **Willow Holme** begins. The route slips beneath the West Coast Main Line, destination Glasgow, then passes Sheepmount Stadium and sports grounds. You enter Bitts Park by crossing the River Caldew. In Roman times this tributary ran close under the high bank, where the Norman castle was built, thus the Roman Wall crossed just the Eden from the vicinity of Edenholme cricket ground. ▸

Born high on the southern slopes of Skiddaw, the Caldew may be traced by following the 70-mile (112km) Cumbria Way – a stunningly beautiful walk that stretches the length of Cumbria, starting at Morecambe Bay.

Entering Bitts Park, take an early glance at a hitherto invisible Wall by diverting off the roadway half-left to inspect the dredged collection of 97 Roman bridge stones among the trees close to the river.

The massive walls of **Carlisle Castle** tower over the main walkway through Bitts Park, with 'The Sauceries' playground at their foot to the right of the drive. Only the most ardent hiker will pound on without giving the castle

Carlisle Castle | and the historic city the benefit of a few hours' exploration (see detour below).

THE CITY OF CARLISLE

Known as both the Great Border City and the 2000-Year-Old City, Carlisle stands on a battle line. It has faced the slings and arrows of a long, turbulent relationship with the land we now know as Scotland. Indeed, during the 10th and 11th centuries Carlisle and the countryside down to the River Eamont lay in Scottish hands, and was wrested back by Rufus only in 1092.

After the Romans there followed six centuries with scant record, although it is plain that Carlisle continued. It is even said that this was the seat of Coel Hen – the 'Old King Cole' of nursery rhyme fame and the earliest ruler of the British kingdom of Rheged. In the seventh century Rheged was taken over by the Christian Angles of Northumbria, who founded a monastery to St Cuthbert which came under the Diocese of Durham until the foundation of the Carlisle Diocese in 1133. In the ninth century – probably Carlisle's blackest hour – the Danes sacked the largely timber-built city, with fire completing the destruction.

Turning thoughts back to Roman times... in their quick movement up the country, the Romans established York (Eboracum) as their legionary base.

Hence, the north of the province, up to and beyond the Wall, came under its jurisdiction. Yet in forging their military roads, the Romans soon saw the importance of holding an east–west line in the neck between the Tyne and the Solway, as evidenced in the construction of Stanegate (a medieval post-Roman name which simply means 'the stone road') from Coria [previously known as Corstopitum] (Corbridge) to Luguvalium (Carlisle).

The Romans were adept at negotiating with the natives; so for all their lack of a map, they soon learnt the 'lay of the land' based on local knowledge. They often adapted existing trackways, although some of their routes, such as the Stanegate, must have been original.

The Roman Wall fort of Petriana lies beneath Carlisle's Stanwix district, which can be easily accessed from Bitts Park. There is some doubt concerning the fort name, for Uxelodunum, meaning 'the high fort', is also considered a possibility. Whatever its name, this was certainly a most important fort. Covering 9.3 acres, it was the largest along the Wall and it was here that the most senior officer on the Wall was stationed.

The name Stanwix means 'stone walls', alluding to the residual walls of the fort in the Dark Ages. Between AD126 and AD400 the fort accommodated up to 1000 cavalry – the largest body of cavalry anywhere in the empire. Such a complement suggests that the need for swift defence, over the western portion of the Wall, was deemed essential from the outset. Should you make a detour to explore this area, don't expect to find much evidence, although there is a tiny section of the north Wall core and three chamfered blocks tucked into a brick enclosure in the far corner of the Cumbria Park Hotel car park. The rounded corner of the fort can be traced in the tall garden wall at the junction of Well Lane and Brampton Road.

Detour to explore historic Carlisle

Approach Carlisle Castle via the gatehouse and portcullis – once the headquarters of the King's Own Border Regiment. Enter the castle through the English Heritage reception area/shop and enjoy a tour of the keep.

Out of all the sensations, doubtless the chill of the **dungeons** will linger longest. It was here, in the rout after the Jacobite Rebellion, that the followers of Bonnie Prince Charlie were shackled before being hanged by the Duke of Cumberland on behalf of the king.

'Ye tak the high road and I'll tak the low road, and I'll be in Scotland before ye': this well-known emotional Scottish ballad, composed after the Rebellion, refers to the Highlanders who died in Carlisle Castle. Their spirits travelled underground (the 'low road') back to their clan homes so were faster than the few that were released and returned overland.

Mary Queen of Scots was held in detention here in 1568. Her diary documents the first recorded mention of the game of football played on the Sauceries, when some of her entourage and local lads kicked a bladder ball – Carlisle United 1, Queen of the North 0!

Mary was keen on golf and got her cadets to carry her clubs, from which derives the term 'golf caddy'.

Walk down the steps and through the passage below Castleway. It is laced with artefacts, indicative of the city's history: from the Cursing Stone bearing a curse from the Bishop of Glasgow, to a paved way engraved with all the Border Reiving names, to the boots of Jimmy Glass, the 'on-loan' goalkeeper who scored a goal in injury time and thus saved Carlisle United from being relegated from the Football League in 1999.

The castle rests on part of the city's second Roman fort, **Luguvalium**. Excavations to create the Millennium Gallery in Tullie House Museum and the underpass beneath Castleway, between the castle and the museum, unearthed considerable archaeological evidence, including a hoard of armour – although it seems that, sadly, much stonework has been 'mislaid'. The relationship between Luguvalium and Petriana (the fort now buried beneath the nearby community of Stanwix) is not properly understood, although the former seems to have had more civil functions.

Climb the steps at the other end and enter Tullie House Museum for a feast of heritage, culture and food, all located in the modern expansion of the original Jacobean house – the oldest domestic dwelling in the city.

Take time to explore within, as the exhibits reveal the fascinating background to this area of Cumbria. The new interactive Roman Gallery is a highlight and is especially recommended; it provides activities, information and a collection of Roman remains to captivate all ages.

Walk into the garden to view a sunken native shrine – one must presume it was located close to, but not within, the Roman fort. Wander left into Abbey Street and through the Abbey Gatehouse to enter the Cathedral Close, a remarkably peaceful haven.

The Cathedral is a gracious, inspirational monument to the genius of ecclesiastical architecture. Its history is fascinating, being as much influenced by its time under Scottish ownership as during its later medieval English

Carlisle Cathedral

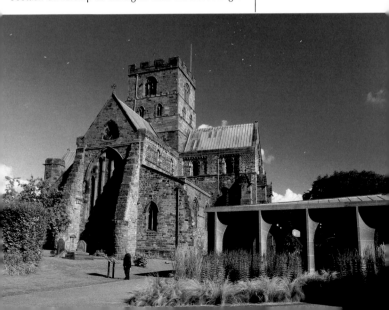

period. Take time to examine its many fine features, including the beautiful, highly colourful nave ceiling, its diverse collection of Green Men, the stained-glass windows, and the Treasury dedicated to Willie Whitelaw – former Deputy Prime Minister and MP for Penrith and the Border. To round off your visit, The Fratry – the former Chapter House under-croft beside which stands a modern, sympathetically stylish café – will doubtless hold great appeal.

Having left the Cathedral, continue through the close and turn right onto Castle Street to visit the pedestrianised Market Square, which was probably a market in Roman times too. Note the Guildhall Museum, a unique survival from the medieval city. The neighbouring Old Town Hall (now a tourist information centre) is an eye-catching building, and the square in front of these buildings is frequently a scene of cultural activity, complete with bandstand and buskers.

Wander up English Street to admire the twin barrel towers of The Citadel (a Victorian replacement of the city's late medieval bastion south gate, built for Henry VIII by Stefan von Haschenperg in 1541) and the fine Tudor-style Citadel Railway Station, built in 1847. Backtrack via Castle Street to regain the route.

The Trail follows the tree-lined municipal walkway to Eden Bridge, with the unprepossessing 1960s Civic Centre looming to the right above the great traffic roundabout. (To its credit, the interior is splendid and belies the exterior.)

As you stroll through Bitts Park, there are two landmark features worth perusing: first, the imperious **monument to Queen Victoria**. Newcastle upon Tyne was largely the product of the British Empire, Carlisle far less so; nonetheless, this monument exhibits the sense of civic pride felt during her reign and illustrates her place at the helm of an empire that was even larger than the limitless bounds of Roman rule. At the far eastern end of

Roman Eden bridge stones dredged from the river, on display in Bitts Park

our coast-to-coast journey stands an equally imperious statue in front of South Shields Town Hall.
The big difference? The British Empire lasted perhaps a third of the time of the Roman Empire and
allowed some semblance of self-rule to its constituent nations.

The second point of interest lies within
Hardwicke Circus, where the **'Peace Garden'**,
dedicated in 1986, is sited at the hub of the busiest
roundabout in the city – which makes it anything
but peaceful. However, pedestrians may pause
amid the hubbub and read two thought-provoking
plaques. One is dedicated to the Peace Garden
itself, with a quote from Martin Luther King: 'We
must either learn to live together as brothers or we
are going to perish together as fools.' The second,
strikingly set against the rather gross architecture
of the Civic Centre, is found on the monument of
James Creighton, and displays this late-Victorian
mayor's citation on the honourable cause of service
to the community.

Slip through the passage beneath Eden Bridge and stride along the tree-shaded municipal drive through Bitts Park to reach the Caldew Bridge. Enter Sheepmount Stadium car park and stay on the continuing track – there is a riverside path too, but this is prone to flooding when the river is swollen. Go under the two concrete railway bridges (you may catch a red-flash glimpse of an inter-city Avanti train on the electrified West Coast Main Line).

The Northern Bypass spanning the River Eden

Pass by the old brick power station, ascend steps in passing the old stone-arched Waverley Viaduct, and follow the Engine Lonning. Steps, a footbridge and kissing gates lead on along the edge of the pasture above the river, where once ran Hadrian's Wall.

After crossing Knockupworth Beck the Path, regains pasture level. Kissing gates now lead to an underpass simplifying the Trail's progress beneath the new **A689 Northern Bypass**, and then further steps and a footbridge over Boomby Gill lead on via kissing gates to a pasture-edge path leading, by a gated footbridge, to the street into **Grinsdale** at a kissing gate. Go right (drinks cabin at hand) and find a hand gate on the left after 50m, where a confined path is signed off the street. At the end another hand gate gives access into cattle pasture.

Sourmilk Bridge with walkers

Follow the open track, rising by trees to go through an unusual raised 'sidling' stile at a galvanised field gate. Cross Sourmilk Bridge, with its cattle watering place. After kissing gates descend the bank by a flight of steps and advance by a pond to reach a green lane. Keep within the lane, passing The Croft, to reach the village street in **Kirkandrews-on-Eden**. Go right with the footway by the Manor House and keep right as the road forks, following the road signed 'Beaumont'. The Trail has been obliged to follow the road to **Beaumont** due to the loss of the Path through landslipping in the steep, wooded bank above the River Eden. (See 'Beaumont Village', above.) At the T-junction at the top of the rise go right, passing below the church, then bear left at the triangular green and take the first lane to the left. The green lane, lying on the exact course of Hadrian's Wall, leads to a kissing gate exiting into pasture. Follow on beside the line of aged ash trees to cross the Powburgh Beck footbridge, the fenced path leading to a kissing gate onto the road.

Go right, and at the lay-by slip through the kissing gate (with its drinking water notice – welcome news in hot weather), following the roadside hedge to exit at a corresponding kissing gate and advance into the village of **Burgh-by-Sands**.

STAGE 3
Carlisle to Newtown

Start	Eden Bridge, Carlisle
Finish	Newtown
Distance	9½ miles (15km)
Walking time	5hr
Refreshments	Carlisle: wide variety of hotels, pubs, cafés and shops; Crosby-on-Eden: The Stag Inn, High Crosby Farm refreshment cabin (honesty box); Wellbeck Snack Shed (honesty box) en route in Newtown
Accommodation	Linstock, Crosby-on-Eden, Irthington (off-route)
Railway link	Carlisle

The third stage of the Trail is initially influenced more by the Stanegate, the pre-Hadrianic road, as it sets sail through the riverside park of Rickerby and comes onto the bank of the broad Eden, decked with wildflowers in summer. Joining the street in Crosby-on-Eden, precisely upon the line of this Roman Military Way, the hollowway approaching High Crosby Farm is indeed the Stanegate. A green lane, then a quiet by-road marking the line of the Wall, leads to a sequence of pasture paths along the Roman frontier up to the Brampton/Longtown road.

For 1:25K route map see booklet pages 11–15.

◀ From Eden Bridge the Trail passes The Sands leisure centre (café/Trail Passport stamping station), with its frontier heritage installations, stepping down to follow a grass path upstream, skirting the Swifts golf course, on the site of the old Carlisle racecourse. At a T-junction it becomes a tarmac path leading to and across the **Memorial Bridge**.

The Memorial Bridge, a grey-painted suspension bridge erected in 1922, spans the **River Eden** beside the confluence with the River Petteril, which has flowed some 25 miles from Greystoke to this point. By contrast, the Eden's greater volume is due to its

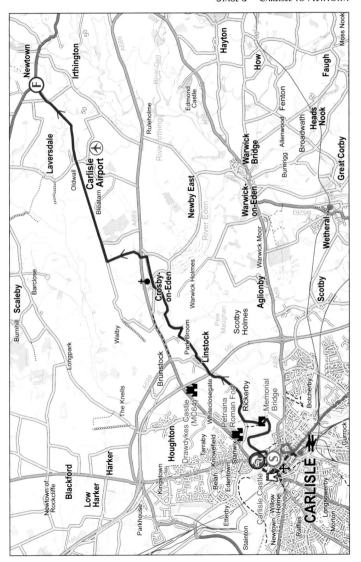

War memorial in Rickerby Park

wide catchment, embracing the streams flowing off Spadeadam Forest, the western slopes of the northern Pennines and the eastern Lakes – notably Ullswater – on a 64-mile journey. Interestingly, it is the only English river to flow north.

Repeated mid-July floods in the last decade have prompted the annual Cumberland Show to be transferred from Rickerby Park (its original home was Bitts Park).

Once over the River Eden follow the tarmac path traversing the open **Rickerby Park** – bought by the Citizen's League in 1920 and now a popular riverside open space for exercising limbs, young and old – to meet the open road near the exit from the park.

The late-18th-century Rickerby House is well screened; it was built by William Richardson, who made his fortune in the City of London. The miniature Grecian lodge has the air of a temple; to the left, in a field, stands the Bull Pen – a tall octagonal folly tower. (Rickerby could be said to ally with the author's name as it means 'Richards' place'.)

Within the old estate buildings, note the step-gable towers to the old stable yard, now largely converted into the bijou homes of Rickerby Gardens by the renowned local entrepreneur Fred Story. Tower Farm even has a tiny mock tower as a novel garden feature.

A cycleway leads to The Beeches – a beautifully proportioned brick residence. Following the road, cross the bridge over the **M6 motorway**, which was opened here in 1971. Looking north, see the next motorway flyover, which lies between the course of the vallum and the Wall. Also in view is Drawdykes Castle – a decorative 14th-century defensive peel, a legacy from the days of Border Reiving. This lies to the left, adjacent to the site of Milecastle 64.

THE BORDER REIVERS

The calm that has pervaded the Anglo-Scottish border for many centuries was wrought from a cursed age. From the late 13th century until the early 18th century, a fearful cocktail of blood-feuding tore the heart out of a huge region, from the Tweed and the Tyne to the Nith and the Eden. Spine-chilling tales of reiving raids are a legendary legacy of these violent times, when careless murder, theft and pillage were everyday professions. Retribution and reprisal made no one safe; lies and deceit were the lethal currency.

Skeletons are to be found in the cupboards of many families whose names persist in the local phone book – Armstrong, Bell, Charlton, Douglas, Elliot, Graham, Irvine, Kerr, Maxwell, Nixon, Ridley, Robson, Scott, Storey and many more. Reiving lawlessness was eventually stemmed in 1707 by the Act of Union bringing Scotland and England under one crown. However, the term 'reiving' persists in the word 'bereavement'; and from this time too comes the term 'blackmail' – a payment extorted for not disclosing a secret. For more information on the reivers, visit the Millennium Gallery at Tullie House, Carlisle, or best of all read *The Reivers* by Alistair Moffat.

As you look south, the large blue motorway sign heralds Junction 43, the junction with the Military Road (A69) constructed in the immediate aftermath of the Jacobite Rebellion in the 1750s, while on the west side is a petite brick lodge with fine architectural features and only the birch thicket shielding it from the clamour of the motorway. There are days when the motorway's heavy drone can be heard three miles east at Wallhead!

Keep right as you enter **Linstock**, with its pleasing mix of old and new red brick. ◀ The motorway sound begins to fade as you wander along the suburban road, which leads by Linstock Cottage, a handsome stone dwelling and adjacent brick barn on the left, with its trail refreshment cabinet and seats under the yard canopy, to a lane. The tall, ridged building before the farm buildings is Linstock Tower.

Refreshments:
Linstock Cottage
(honesty box) en
route in Linstock.

> **Linstock** means 'enclosure where flax was grown'
> – flax being a fibrous crop woven into linen.
> The tower is an adapted peel, the country home
> of the Bishop of Carlisle until the mid-13th cen-
> tury when, inexplicably, the bishop moved to
> Rose Castle, some eight miles south of the city –
> although this far grander residence has now been
> sold and the current bishop's residence is a more
> modest one in Keswick. One must presume the
> medieval city was not an environment conducive
> to the dignity of this office!
>
> Linstock Castle is a dairy farm with a differ-
> ence: Alistair Wannop, the pioneer farmer, has
> turned the proximity of a pylon power line to
> impressive advantage. His anaerobic biodigester
> installation turns maize silage and dairy herd slurry
> into methane, powering a massive generator that
> feeds 1GW per year of electricity into the grid.
> Green energy or watt (sic)?

Follow on with the green farm lane (the recent diver-
sion at Park Broom is no longer applicable, as the riverbank damage does not impede the trail). Bear right to

The Stag Inn, Crosby-on-Eden

the riverbank, wandering upstream beside the Eden, pass-ing Eden Grove – a handsome, single-storey, porticoed sandstone lodge with bayed lawn and mature sheltering beeches alive with rooks.

The Trail skips over a small bridge to regain the river-bank before veering left via a hand gate into a suburban road, Green Lane, leading into the village of **Crosby-on-Eden** (Low Crosby). Joining the main street, pass The Stag – a walker-friendly pub – then a nursery, a primary school and the handsome sandstone parish church of St John the Baptist, standing regally among tall trees. ▶

The road through the village is a rare instance en route when you are actually walking on the Roman Stanegate.

Approaching High Crosby Farm, notice a hollowway in the trees to the right, in season resplendent with blue-bells; the pre-Hadrian's Wall military frontier thorough-fare intact. High Crosby Farm not only has a refreshment chalet set between the fenced Trail and the farmhouse, but half a dozen smart glamping pods, ideal for a cosy overnight or two.

Crossing the **A689** farm bridge, bear right with the farm lane and then left on Sandy Lane, with plenty of evidence of 'sandy' in this green droveway. Reconnecting with the frontier, turn right to wend your way along the quiet back road leading to Wallhead, holding to the course of the Roman Military Way and tight to the line of Hadrian's Wall.

Two bridleways run north from this byway lane, crossing Brunstock Beck and converging at the moated **Scaleby Castle**, which was built unashamedly of Severus' magic Wall stones (bearing in mind that east of the River Irthing Hadrian's original wall was built of turf 20ft wide at its base). The castle has its place in the Picturesque Movement as Rev William Gilpin (1724–1804) was born here. He observed that the aesthetics of ruins and rugged landscape form had a peculiar kind of beauty when set within hand-held frames, hence his term 'Picturesque'. His first writings, published in 1768, include pen-and-wash drawings.

The apparent turf causeway is the base of Hadrian's Wall; maps suggest it was just the Roman Military Way, but it will have been both.

As the road bends right, go forward with the farm roadway. This concrete track swings left, but continue straight ahead to a kissing gate entering a long pasture. ◄ Pass by the reed- and bullrush-filled Blea Tarn, whose the name means 'blue pool' and in the local vernacular is pronounced 'blitteren'. Bleatarn Park, overlooking the tarn to the south, has been handsomely restored, with self-catering accommodation a recent addition. Stepping into a tiny paddock, find a potted history and 'Stall-on-the-Wall' honesty refreshment box – just the ticket! Exit the paddock and bear left with the short green lane to step up to the next kissing gate. ◄ Follow on with the hedge and the Wall ditch.

Bleatarn Farm has installed a much-needed portaloo – an interesting twinning, given the high-sided slurry tank over to the right!

Reaching the Laversdale road at **Oldwall**, there is the option of wandering right with the road for half a mile to inspect the Solway Aviation Museum, sited at the edge of Carlisle Airport and open weekends April–October.

In this vicinity you will hear and see the occasional light aircraft lifting into the sky, the end of **Carlisle Airport** runway being close by.

Old Wall Cottage is a charming vernacular single-storey dwelling, its garden rampant with floral pleasure. Via gates, advance along a narrow, hedged lane and emerge into pasture at the first of a sequence of kissing gates. If refreshment is required, you may follow a bridleway down to Irthington for the welcome enticement of The Salutation Inn. ▶ The Trail, however, pursues the Wall ditch, which shows its age by the presence of bluebells – a species associated with ancient woodland.

Approaching **Newtown**, switch sides of the adjacent fence to emerge onto the road at a kissing gate. Keep forward along the village street and beside the open green to reach the main road.

Old Wall Cottage – a 17th-century dwelling, surely built of Wall stone rubble

Irthington's village street is set upon a sinuous section of the Roman Stanegate, which sliced through the middle of the airfield via Buckjumping.

73

WESTBOUND: NEWTOWN TO CARLISLE

Leave the road at the left-hand bend via a kissing gate. Soon after the next kissing gate the Trail switches sides of the fence, now with further kissing gates, and advances with the Wall ditch close by to enter a hedge lined green lane. Pass **Oldwall**, going through gates to reach the Laversdale road. Go straight over via the kissing gate (bus stop) and advance by a series of pasture fields, faithfully keeping the hedge close right. Keep resolutely to the field-edge path, via kissing gates.

Further kissing gates lead by a small enclosure. Entering pasture, advance with the lake close left, upon the faint bank foundations of Hadrian's Wall. At the far end a path leads on from another kissing gate, promptly joining the concrete roadway from Highfieldmoor. Advance onto the road at Wall Head and keep forward.

The quiet byroad leads to a left-hand turn into Sandy Lane, a green droveway. Nearing the **A689**, watch for the right-hand track turn leading

to a farm bridge crossing of the busy road. The Trail is confined on either side as the bridge is occasionally used by dairy cattle and farm tractors. The refreshment cabin may be much appreciated. Hand gates lead onto the road; go right with the footway into the village of **Crosby-on-Eden**.

After The Stag Inn, fork left along the side road. A kissing gate at the end leads onto the banks of the River Eden – the water's edge may be difficult to reach as the banks are delightfully

Church of St John the Baptist, Crosby-on-Eden

River Eden, Park Broom

clothed in a dense mantel of wild flowers. The Path is forced to the right by an entering stream; cross a small bridge to regain the riverbank way via an open track.

The Path then veers right off the banking, following the track as towards **Park Broom**, but it bears left into a farm lane that leads below Linstock Castle Farm into the village of **Linstock**. As you walk through this charmingly suburban community, spot the refreshment facility at Linstock Cottage on the right. Soon the reverberating sound from the **M6 motorway** becomes all consuming, especially as you cross Linstock Bridge.

After The Beeches (private residence) join a cycle path adjacent to the road. The fenced cycle path leads to a gate into **Rickerby Park**; bear left, traversing the open park on a tarmac path to the Memorial Bridge spanning the Eden. Once across, go right downstream, still on a tarmac path. At a path T-junction continue on a grass path skirting the Swifts golf course, leading to steps up by The Sands Centre café/Trail Passport stamping station and ultimately reaching the Eden Bridge underpass. (See 'The City of Carlisle', above.)

STAGE 4
Newtown to Birdoswald

Start	Newtown
Finish	Birdoswald Roman Fort
Distance	8¼ miles (13km)
Walking time	4¾ hr
Refreshments	Walton: tearoom (closed January), Old Vicarage Brewery bar; Brampton: Off The Wall coffee shop, Mr Brown's café; Haytongate: refreshment cabin (honesty box); Lanercost: Lanercost tearoom (off-route); Birdoswald: café on-site at fort
Accommodation	Walton, Banks
Railway link	Brampton

Anyone who has traced the Anglo-Saxon frontier of Offa's Dyke will feel a sense of déjà vu here. Throughout this section you accompany the faint earthwork of the Wall as a vague shadow in the rolling landscape. Soothing to the eye and gentle on the muscles, this is pastoral England of a former age.

The actual 'Roman stone' has been spread like peanut butter into the surrounding countryside and repurposed for buildings such as Scaleby Castle and Lanercost Priory, which are entirely composed of Severus stone. Only after the Roman retreat from the Antonine Wall was the frontier strengthened in stone, with suitable sandstone and lime for mortar being laboriously hauled considerable distances to build a uniformly imposing structure to the sea.

For 1:25K route map see booklet pages 15–20.

◀ The hamlet of **Newtown**, with its open green, has its peace punctuated by traffic on the Brampton/Longtown road (A6071); be watchful as you cross this busy thoroughfare. The community hall lies over to the left, and community pride is conveyed in a gallery of four plaques recording the Cumbria in Bloom Best Hamlet and Best Small Village awards.

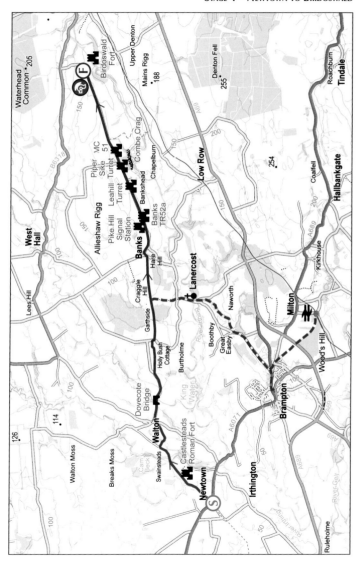

Walkers and sheep near Cam Beck

From here the Trail is set fair and square on the course of the Wall. The path squeezes between a tall bungalow fence and a corrugated barn, passing a vegetable patch via kissing gates. Skirt a horse paddock and paling-fenced lawn at Heads Wood to descend a flight of flagged steps in harmony with the Wall. Pass to the left of the dilapidated barns at The Beck Farm to reach a kissing gate; enter a fenced passage beside a deep beck to get to a footbridge.

The term 'cam' derives from the Celtic and means 'comb-shaped', as in a winding stream. Note, then, the comb-shaped weir at hand.

Continuing, with the hedge on your right, go through the farm buildings at Cambeckhill then via kissing gates through pasture fields to a footbridge spanning **Cam Beck**, where recent excavations have revealed the site of a hitherto unsuspected Roman watchtower. ◀

Though not pertinent to the course of the Trail, you can follow the footpath by Cambeck Bridge, crossing parkland pasture east of **Castlesteads** to reconnect with the Trail at the gate near the cattle watering place at Sandysike. This gives you a remarkable view of the great house, built in Adam style in 1779 by a wealthy merchant from the East India Company. Castlesteads' secret walled garden rests upon Camboglanna Roman Fort, which describes the fort's location 'at the bend (bow) of the crooked stream'. Note that there is positively no public access.

Step along the flags before ascending the pasture to join a farm track. Go through the field gate, passing **Swainsteads** farm buildings, to reach the cattle grid. Turn right with the gravel lane as to Sandysike. The Trail, however, breaks left and enters woodland. Weave through the wood, with stone flags and bark chips aiding where the ground is susceptible to dampness, to emerge at a cattle watering place where you join the track beside the young hedge, heading north-east.

The hedge-side path comes by a lane via a kissing gate into **Walton**, whose name, not unsurprisingly, means 'farmstead on the Roman Wall'. The road junction sports an unusual signpost and parish sign. ▶

Follow the minor road signposted to Lanercost Abbey (sic). The road bends beside the popular Florries on the Wall Bunkhouse at the site of Milecastle 56. Descend to **Dovecote Bridge**, perhaps taking a moment to glance into the paddock left where a turfed-over section of sandstone Wall confirms the line of the frontier.

This section of the Wall was excavated in 1983 and then concealed after 20 years when it became apparent that the **red sandstone** could not survive permanent exposure to the elements. The condition of much of Lanercost Abbey betrays this frailty too.

Keep to the road, winding up by High Dovecote Farm and Low Wall, reuniting with the line of the Wall opposite **Holly Bush Cottage**. Go up the steps and into a fenced passage – which might be muddy – passing the invisible site of Milecastle 55. Follow on with a sequence of kissing gates, crossing the access lane to Howgill Farm. ▶ Dip into a marshy hollow with stone flags to keep the boots dry.

A brief detour to the left reveals a charming tree-lined green, in the midst of Walton. Occupying the old school house, the Reading room café is open Wednesday to Sunday 10–4.30pm, closed January. A great addition to the village is the Old Vicarage micro-brewery, adjacent to the parish church, with bar and beer garden.

You might divert right with the farm access lane to find, in the in a low sandstone building in the yard facing the main farmhouse, a roughly inscribed Roman stone. This is thought to record work on the Roman Wall in the fourth century by the Catuvellauni, a native British tribe from southern Britain, whose name was Latinised.

Switch through the hedge line and rise to a kissing gate in the fence, then angle part-left to a kissing gate and flags onto the minor road near **Garthside**. Go right and then left at a kissing gate beside a holly bush. Flags are initially needed in this rush-filled pasture. After the second kissing gate, heed the field boundary close left. ◄ Early on, notice the curious section of formal Wall base stones, presumably a medieval estate adaptation, first identified by the eminent archaeologist Sir Ian A Richmond.

This is composed of Wall core – a rare survival that was thankfully consolidated and protected in 2014.

Cross the Burtholme Beck footbridge, go over a track and continue up the hill, crossing the access lane to Haytongate. Picnic tables give a clue to the existence of the Haytongate Hut – a refreshment resource – and iTrod clothing, both accessed via a hole in the bushes. Perhaps of greater importance is the presence of a toilet: go right with the access road to find the hygienic portaloo secreted in the bushes to the left.

This is the prime moment to break from the Path to visit Lanercost Priory, by taking the lane that leads directly right.

The garth entrance, Lanercost Priory

LANERCOST PRIORY

Part romantic ruin, part serene parish church, Lanercost Priory ('Lanercost' derives from the Welsh *Llanerch*, meaning 'glade') stands within a parkland setting in the Irthing meadows. The walls of the priory were built unashamedly of plundered Wall stone – from military device to the duty of God seems a fair exchange. The roadside wall of the priory garth is bounded by regular Wall stone too.

The adjacent vicarage features Edward's Tower, where King Edward I convalesced for six months from the discomforts of dysentery. Hence, from late 1306, Edward, along with his 200-strong court, governed the nation from this spot and the monks duly became impoverished! An inverted centurial stone can be seen on the tower.

Among the revitalised farm buildings stands Lanercost Tearoom, which uses excellent locally sourced ingredients for their sumptuous home-made refreshments: a touch of class.

The nearby Abbey Bridge is also worth visiting: the graceful twin-arched structure spanning the confluence of Quarry Beck with the River Irthing, no doubt indicative of the desire of the Earls of Carlisle, at nearby Naworth Castle, to impress travellers. While on the far side of the Priory find the circular Lanercost cricket ground, where you can witness a fine English summer sporting tradition in action.

Completely unsuspected, and totally unseen from the vicinity of the Priory to the south, is the amazing stronghold of Naworth Castle – 'the new work'. Crenellated by Ranulph of Dacre in 1335, to this day it is the seat of the Earls of Carlisle, a branch of the Dukes of Norfolk.

Continuing upon the Trail from Haytongate, ascend **Craggle Hill** – whose name means 'hill frequented by cranes'. ▶ At the top of the rise enjoy a wonderful all-round view stretching north to the Langholm hills and south to the Pennines and Lakeland fells.

The Trail runs on within a lightly fenced lane, keeping right of Hare Hill, via a metal gate; flagstones crowded by nettles on the muddy upper field edge lead to a kissing gate onto the road. Descend the access road, taking the opportunity to inspect the eye-catching ragged Roman Wall lurking behind a beech hedge.

The Great European crane is thought to have become extinct in Britain 400 years ago.

Victorian rebuild of Hadrian's Wall at Hare Hill

Hare Hill is a veritable tower by comparison with the rest of the Wall, being the tallest section on the entire frontier. William Hutton, striding along his merry way in 1802, said: 'I viewed this relic with admiration… I saw no higher'. Only the lowest courses are original; the main structure was rebuilt as a romantic ruin after Hutton's time – and thank goodness it was too. The most important stone is found on the north face at head height and is inscribed with the initials 'PP' (Primus Pilus), referring to the principal centurion in a legion. The stone is clearly suffering from exposure to the elements and must surely be reaching a point where it is preserved and a replica inserted.

`While researching for this guide, the author had to report gross weathering of this stone to English Heritage; sadly, it is in a sorry state. The lower portion of the Wall was excavated and studied during spring 2004.

At the foot of the lane go left and then take the first right through the dingle, rising through the hamlet of **Banks** – whose name means 'up the banks from Lanercost'. This little community has changed less than most over the years.

Opposite Riggside, glance across the field northwards to the woodland of **Noble Hott**. This intriguing name contains the old word for woodland, revealed in place names such as Hotbank and Haltwhistle. While Noble is a local surname. It is thought that a Roman lime kiln lay in here.

Just out of the hamlet, find a wall stile on the right, which takes the Path off the road along a gravel path to re-emerge at **Banks Turret 52a**. ▶ Pass through the car park – a favourite viewpoint across the Irthing Valley to Cold Fell, the northern outpost of the Pennines chain.

Notice its thin north wall and chamfered mid-course to repel the rain, as well as the chunk of preserved masonry 'frozen' where it fell.

Banks Turret 52a

83

To the right of Cold Fell are Tarnmonath, Simmerson, Talkin Fell, Hespeck Raise and then the scarp of Cardunneth Pike, collectively encircling the wild King's Forest of **Geltsdale**, an RSPB Nature Reserve; while across the road to the north, well screened by trees, is an old lime kiln with Gothic arch, in sterling state. Reputedly, this saw active use for only six years due to the expense of local coal.

A narrow fenced passage now leads to **Pike Hill Roman Signal Station**, a superb viewpoint.

Degraded by road excavation in 1870, the remains of the **tower** rise some four feet up from the modern roadway. The tower belonged to the earlier Stanegate communication system and, being angled on a south-west–north-east axis, was askew and amalgamated awkwardly with the Wall. The doorway, facing friendly country, looks over the Irthing valley to the distant Blencathra and Skiddaw fells of northern Lakeland.

Slip through the kissing gate and follow on along the pasture shelf to rejoin the ridge-top road at a wall stile short of **Bankshead**.

Here are two separate **dwellings** – the first is a farm, the roadside byre commendably converted into a camping barn, while from 1924 the second was the home of the famous Cumbrian artists Ben and Winifred Nicholson. A considerable proportion of these buildings is composed of reused stone from Milecastle 52 – a classic case of farming continuity, generation after generation, finding succour and shelter from this elevated location. The road is a natural ridgeway; perhaps some form of track existed here before the Romans came and they adapted it to serve the Wall. It continues to be used today, forming a heritage trail for pedestrians and cars.

Turret 51b

The Trail slips into a field-edge passage opposite a 19th-century lime kiln, although you may be reasonably tempted to stay on the road, watchful of traffic, to inspect the two turrets beyond Lee Hill Farm with its traditional red byre doors.

Lea Hill Turret 51b and **Piper Sike Turret 51a**, in common with most turrets, were occupied only until the end of the second century AD, when such structures became redundant. They lie exactly one-third of a Roman mile apart; measure the 333 double steps (Roman marching paces) and master for yourself precisely what this distance feels like – you'll get no better opportunity.

Arriving at the Comb Crag Farm road junction, look left (north) along the facing road, as down the barrel of a gun, to the distant, if a trifle obscured, Gillalees Beacon, pinpointing the tiny mound of the Roman signal station. This was the fast-reaction warning system from Roman scouts stationed at Bewcastle for the Wall garrison at

Birdoswald. It is better viewed from the entrance to the Roman fort; make a point of looking again.

Turn right, passing the farmhouse to bear left into the woodland in harmony with the vallum.

The continuing path leads to the impressive **Combe Crag ridge and gorge**. This annexed portion of the Geltsdale Bird Reserve (RSPB) is a quite sensational place to explore, with evidence of Roman quarrying as well as scenic drama, the River Irthing running through a rock-ribbed bed. A further continuing footpath leads through to Chapelburn, accessed by a suspension bridge, where St Cuthbert's church stands on a tangible Stanegate fort.

The Trail exits the woodland and follows on with a fence to skirt round the grassy earthworks of **Milecastle 51**. Don't be tempted to short-cut through the monument. This is a significant spot in terms of the construction of Hadrian's Wall as the Severus stone Wall ran on with the modern road, while the turf Wall from the original Hadrianic phase ran on through the pasture ahead towards the tall beech trees in Wall Burn.

The farm name Lanerton presumably means 'the farm associated with Lanercost'.

The Trail is contained close to the road to avoid contact with cattle; cross a plank bridge over Wall Burn to join the Lanerton track. ◀ Note the beech tree roots entangled like a jazz pianist's fingers, then go right then left up the steps to the hand gate beside the turf Wall.

English Heritage excavated the Wall at the end section, close to Wall Burn, revealing that the **turf Wall** was no hastily contrived mound. Although there was a standard Roman size to their sods, here they were not so regular – possibly because of the poor source material. When set in layers upon a firm cobbled causeway foundation, the turf made a remarkably stable structure.

Unlike the vallum, which remained a substantial earthwork, it appears that the Romans disposed of the bulk of the turf Wall, hence only the ditch betrays its course. The only portion of the turf Wall to have survived to any height is to be found closer to the High House track, soon to be encountered.

Cross a sequence of fields by kissing gates in harmony with the north ditch of the turf Wall. A permissive path has been installed after High House Wood hand gate as an escape route to the road to avoid contact with cattle – a valuable safety valve for dog walkers. At a wall stile at the top of the rise, with Birdoswald in view ahead, bear left following the field wall to accompany the roadside wall, which becomes consolidated Roman Wall. ▶ Continue, via hand gates, to slip through the spinney and emerge onto the road beside **Birdoswald Roman Fort**.

Spot Turret 49b and the generous drains in the Wall base; the field before you get to the fort was the site of the Roman vicus (civil settlement).

THE BIRDOSWALD ESTATE

Operated by English Heritage and centred upon Banna Roman Fort, this is a peerless historic site. For many first-time Wall visitors it provides all they may need to gain a sense of the Roman Frontier. As Cumberland's principal Roman Wall exhibition fort, it is a flagship for the county's many Roman sites, rivalled for sheer drama only by Hardknott Roman Fort with its stunning setting. Should you sense the magic of the place, know that you are not alone. The impressive stretch of consolidated Wall running east from the fort is the longest anywhere on the Roman Frontier. In 2018 English Heritage

Birdoswald Roman Fort

refurbished the visitor facilities at the fort to include a descriptive map of two circular heritage country walks from the site (coincidentally prepared by the author).

By bringing their Wall onto the north side of the Irthing gorge, the Romans gave themselves room for fast, reactive movement into hostile territory. They could have set the Wall close to the Stanegate – in effect closer to the current line of the Carlisle–Newcastle railway – and put a real obstacle in the way of any incursionaries.

The high ground westwards to Craggle Hill mimicked the Whin Sill, giving good vision both north and south. Birdoswald cleverly combines the parkland essence of Chesters with the impressive wildness of Housesteads; it may be the sense that this consciously romanticised farm steading only thinly disguises evidence of a long and turbulent history that makes a visit to Birdoswald special.

Across the yard from the café and toilets find the entry reception and shop for the site, from where the visitor is drawn into the barn museum, with its life-sized, burly, Barbour-jacketed model of Mr Birdoswald himself – the archaeologist Tony Wilmott, who has brought his own refreshing vigour and rigour to archaeological research at Birdoswald. People love to know that archaeology is alive and kicking – and staid exhibitions pale beside the occasional revelation. At the time of writing this edition, we are at the midpoint in a four-year programme of excavation on the vicus on three sides of the fort, with great discoveries of a bathhouse and precisely why the stone wall runs to the north wall of the fort: to allow for a great expansion of the vicus settlement on both sides of the fort. Tony's previous excavations expanded understanding of the Dark Age life of the fort, following Roman withdrawal. Certainly, there are several examples of the continuity of the agricultural use of Roman structures along the Wall, the farms at Willoworld and Birdoswald being clear proof.

For all that, during the next 1000 and more years Saxons and others reverted to timber as the primary building material, and the Roman walls in the widest sense were used as the basis of settlements and farm estate boundaries as well as buildings. Wander around the fort area with the interpretative panels as guides.

A visit to the southern plateau edge above the Irthing gorge, with the curling thread of the river far below and a huge sand martin colony on the nearer banks, is strongly recommended. Beyond the meadows lies Upper Denton, and the great green slopes lead the eye to the Tindale Fells overtopping the plantation on Denton Fell.

WESTBOUND: BIRDOSWALD TO NEWTOWN

Pike Hill Roman Signal Station

Either follow the adjacent off-road paths or the ridge-top road to Bankshead. Then keep to the roadside pasture path to **Pike Hill Signal Station**, continuing within the passage to the car park. The option of either road or confined path continues to the hamlet of **Banks**; now follow the road, forking right at the junction. At the next road junction bear left a short way to ascend the access road to **Hare Hill**.

At the top of the road, short of the farmyard, go left through the kissing gate upon a flagged path beside the farmhouse garden. Join the ridge-top droveway and advance to Craggle Hill, where there is a great open view. Follow alongside the wall set upon the Wall, descending by Haytongate, where there is a refreshment cabin and the opportunity to visit Lanercost Priory (see above).

From the picnic tables, via further kissing gates, reach and cross the footbridge over Burtholme Beck. Ascend the pasture, going through further kissing gates to reach the minor road after a flagged section. Turn right, passing two pine trees, then go through a kissing gate to the left and follow the field-bounding fence.

Slipping through the hedge line below the old pine growing from the foundations of Turret 54b, cross a flagged bridge and head on to cross the access lane to Howgill Farm, via kissing gates. Keep beside the line of the Wall, entering a fenced passage beside a pony paddock before stepping down onto the road at **Holly Bush Cottage**. Follow the road downhill over **Dovecote Bridge** and on up into the village of **Walton** (refreshments available). Leading on from the road junction, after a line of three bungalows, the Path departs along a short lane to access pasture at a kissing gate. A green track runs beside a young hedge to the left of the pasture.

Coming down towards a field gate, bear right by the cattle watering place and enter the woodland via a kissing gate. Weave through to emerge via a kissing gate onto a gravel lane from Sandysike Farm. Go right then left at the cattle grid on the bend. Follow the track past the entrance to **Swainsteads** farmyard; where the field tapers at the end, go through the field gate and bear left to a kissing gate.

Descend the pasture beside the remnant Wall ditch to reach a kissing gate. Stone flags lead to a fine footbridge spanning **Cam Beck**, and then a sequence of kissing gates leads to Cambeckhill. Go between the farm buildings with the adjacent hedge replicating the Wall. A footbridge and fenced passage leads to a kissing gate and past the rather dejected-looking stone barns at The Beck Farm.

Continue along the hedge to a kissing gate; a flight of stone-flagged steps leads up the bank to a hand gate. Skirt round Heads Wood garden to a kissing gate, advancing by a vegetable patch then a narrow passage between a tall fence and corrugated barn to emerge into the street at **Newtown**. Gingerly cross the A6071, passing on from the green to leave the road where it bends left at a kissing gate into pasture.

Walton from Craggle Hill – the field wall runs upon the line of the Roman wall

STAGE 5
Birdoswald to Steel Rigg

Start	Birdoswald Roman Fort
Finish	Steel Rigg
Distance	9½ miles (15km)
Walking time	6hr
Refreshments	Gilsland: House of Meg Tea Rooms, The Samson Inn, The Bridge Inn, Bait Box pop-up café (www.greencroftonthewall.com); Greenhead: Greenhead Tearoom, The Greenhead Hotel, Roman Army Museum café (entrance fee for museum); Cawfields: The Milecastle Inn; Haltwhistle (off-route): Pillar Box café, Centre of Britain Hotel, The Black Bull (ph), La Toot Tearooms, Kasteale coffee shop; Twice Brewed (off-route): Twice Brewed Inn; Once Brewed (off-route): The Sill café in Northumberland National Park Centre
Accommodation	Gilsland, Greenhead, Cawfields, Twice Brewed, Once Brewed
Railway link	Haltwhistle

From Birdoswald you enter five-star Roman Wall Country – a west–east county and regional divide (Cumberland–Northumberland, North-East England) where you can even hear the linguistic changes, yet in following the Trail you are reinventing a cohesion unique to Roman rule, as before them the native tribes will have been just as fragmented as modern culture and jurisdiction.

This phase of the journey follows notable stretches of standing Wall and includes hills composed of the hard volcanic dolerite known as Whin Sill, resulting in more physically demanding and energetic walking.

Take a minute to 'stand and stare': lean on the field gate opposite the fort entrance and gaze north to view the Maiden Way Roman road stretching away, crossing the skyline and Gillalees Beacon ridge to reach the outpost fort at Bewcastle (Fanum Cocidii). The initial course of the Roman road is not that of

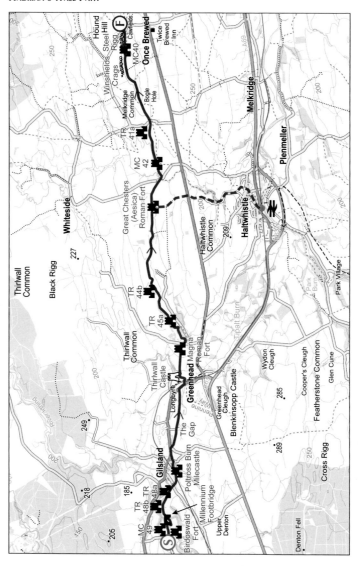

the bridleway, as it wisely skirted the marshy hollow of Midgeholme Moss, keeping right to the modern road before switching left to regain the bee-line left of Slack House Farm.

Then turn half-left to catch a glimpse of a slender ruined peel tower, Triermain Castle. Just discernible to the right, in the hazy distance of Dumfriesshire, is the distinctive table-topped hill of Burnswark – the scene of a battle in AD140, when a legion attacked the native hill fort with lead and stone ballista, making an awesome statement of advance as Emperor Antonius Pius sought to expand his empire. Subsequently, a new frontier was built in the Forth-Clyde isthmus, what we now call the Antonine Wall. Although it must be said that this lasted only 18 years before his successor retreated to reconsolidate the frontier upon Hadrian's Wall.

▶ Depart from Birdoswald via the hand gate at the north-eastern corner of the fort. One should first stand by the broken Wall-end at the road bend to admire the view towards the craggy scarps at Walltown Crags, due east. ▶

The Path runs on within the pasture alongside a famous stretch of Roman Wall; keen eyes may discover several engraved stones – rather too many have become weathered since this length was uncovered in the 1950s. There are two phallic carved stones 'warding off the evil eye', and two centurial stones. The first phallus occurs some 120ft (36m) after the Wall appears to set down beneath a southern ditch; a further 30 paces on, a brown centurial stone on the top course is inscribed: 'Julius Primus of the VIII Cohort "of an unspecified unit" was responsible for building this legionary length.' Then, as the Wall ends, spot a protruding drain; three paces further is a second phallic stone, and beneath this is a stone marked with a Roman mason's mark cross.

After the kissing gate step over the low walls of **Milecastle 49** on Harrow Scar. ▶ Follow the track downhill to the right towards Underheugh. Near the foot of the

For 1:25K route map see booklet pages 20–25.

Please, please, resist the temptation to step onto the inviting wall-end and walk perilously along the top: this causes damage to the monument.

The movement of the river has eroded the bank to such an extent that it has left a considerable wooded cliff immediately east of the milecastle.

Roman Wall and Wall ditch farm access track from Willowford Farm

bank watch for the flagged path signed left; this contours along the base of the bank to a hand gate through a hedge before crossing the elegant **Millennium Footbridge**, erected in 1999. The rusty metalwork is actually part of the preservation process, not a design flaw; it is the same material that has been used in Anthony Gormley's 'Angel of the North' sculpture.

Bear left and advance via kissing gates to an enclosure containing features of Roman bridge abutments. The flood channel is a sign that the river altered course, as well as the bridge being subject to the major modification of a chariot-way and tower. ◄ Keep to the left of this fascinating feature, following a confined path up a flight of steps by hand gates. Cross in front of Willowford Farm entrance. (The farm's name is a corruption of 'Wall ford' – willows being quite uncommon along the Irthing.)

Pause to look at the centurial stone and the English Heritage plaque on the adjacent barn wall. The stone's

This tower probably had a corresponding tower on the turf Wall's west side, now lost to river erosion.

94

inscription translates as: 'From the fifth cohort the century of Gellivs Philippus (built this)'.

Centurial stones were a common feature of the Wall. They were inserted every 45ft (13.5m) as a form of hallmark device to confirm the proper completion of a section of Wall under the stated centurion. Only a few have survived, which suggests they may have been attractive targets for stone robbers, especially as they were sited at head height in the Wall – a layer invariably long stolen.

Leave the farm track (which continues within the deep Wall ditch) at the platform by **Turret 48b** and keep to the right of the re-emerging Wall. ▶ At a second hand gate rejoin the farm track and advance by **Turret 48a**, with its Broad Wall wings proving that the construction of the turrets went on apace, well ahead of the original construction of the Wall. Across by the cattle grid, emerge into the street in **Gilsland**, with its primary school on the right.

This fence-confined passage runs beside a most impressive stretch of consolidated Wall up to eight courses high, with the Broad Wall foundations up to two courses high.

GILSLAND

In its heyday Gilsland was a 'spa resort' in regional terms, on a par with Bath and Harrogate, with the railways bringing large numbers to partake of the sulphur spring. The old Spa Well was built in 1740, its development hindered until then by the lawless nature of the area. It is located just below the Gilsland Spa Hotel, prominently sited to the north of the village, overlooking the Irthing gorge. This hotel was built in 1859 following a fire that destroyed its predecessor, the Shaws Hotel. The present well-patronised hotel belongs to the North Eastern Co-operative Society. Of the many who have known and appreciated these waters – in spite of the fact that sulphur springs smell like rotten eggs – Sir Walter Scott was perhaps the most famous. Sir Walter came here in 1797, stayed at Wardrew House and met his future bride, to whom he proposed at the Popping Stone in the gorge.

The setting may have had many similarly romantic moments since then. An analysis of local mosses has indicated that the air here is the purest in England – the perfect ambience for romance? Indeed, couples were in the habit of chipping chunks off the Popping Stone and putting them under their pillow when they became betrothed! The Romans also used the waters, and a most unusual altar, which referred to the health of the empress, was found in 1685. While the modern Gilsland Spa Hotel does not trade off its mineral assets, nearby Bush Nook Guest House goes some way to replicate the luxury of a Roman Spa with its own hydrotherapy hot tub.

Around here the River Irthing is as black as pitch – not because of coal, but from peat erosion. It drains the huge mires of the 65,000-acre Spadeadam Forest, itself part of the 250-square-mile Border Forests tended by the Forestry Commission. Gillalees Beacon ridge is the location of a dry-bombing range – hence the midweek 'treat' of low-flying jets.

The village is currently engaged in a worthy campaign to re-establish the railway station, putting Gilsland right at the heart of Hadrian's Wall Country and making it a superb destination for non-car-borne visitors.

You may wish to visit the **House of Meg** in Hall Terrace down to the left. Formerly 'Mumps Ha', it was referred to in Sir Walter Scott's novel *Guy Mannering*. In the 17th century the proprietress was known to board brigands, and such 'free-booters' made the village a place to be avoided. In striking contrast, Mumps Ha now includes this lovely café-cum-social centre, which welcomes walkers – ring ahead on 01697 747 777 for opening hours and to ensure your refreshment needs will be fully met.

From the cattle grid the Trail goes right, ushered off the road at a kissing gate between the school and the car park. The flagged path leads to a fence corner where you bear right to cross a simple plank over the ditch and swing left, crossing the pasture to ascend a ramp up to the Newcastle–Carlisle Railway.

BEWARE!

When crossing the railway line you must 'Stop, Look, and Listen' before you cross – from the left, a curve brings a speeding train without warning, while the line stretches away into the distance to the right.

The succeeding fenced passage leads to Arthur's Stables – a classic example of how folklore, recognising old ruins, hazards an explanation based on a fabled king rather than known fact.

> Despite being damaged during the construction of the railway, enough of **Milecastle 48** has been salvaged to show a near-complete picture of the internal features of a large milecastle – arguably the best on the entire frontier system. The barrack blocks, the so-called stables, were large enough to house 30 men. Of most interest, perhaps, are the low steps onto an internal walkway estimated to have been 15ft above ground level. The north gate was partially walled-up; see also the ovens in the north-west corner.

The Trail descends a flight of concrete steps to cross Poltross Burn. (With the Irthing, north from the Bridge Hotel junction, this forms the Northumberland border – hence, the milecastle lies in Cumberland, as does nearly half the village; yet for practical purposes it is treated as a Northumbrian community.)

Ascend the corresponding steps. The confined passage leads up to a fading 'The Spa on the Wall' heritage

Poltross Burn Milecastle, Gilsland

The gravel strips in the adjacent paddock are lingering evidence of the old stock pens from the September sheep auction mart, last held in 1989.

board; turn right. (Ahead, through the old station car park, is The Samson Inn – a hostelry popular with Trail walkers.)

Go right via the kissing gate, rising by the fence, then go left at the hand gate. ◄ Cross the road and the subsequent recessed stile to advance within the Wall ditch; where this 'opens', angle down the slope to a ladder stile into a garden. Follow the path round to a hand gate and through the small paddock to a kissing gate onto the road at **The Gap**.

> The name **'Gap'** for the farm is appropriate, for in this vicinity the Path crosses over the Tyne Gap and the watershed of England – although the name probably refers to a gap in the old Wall. The Path is now set irrevocably on course for the Tyne and the North Sea; hitherto all the waters have drained via the Solway into the Irish Sea.

The name Chapel House indicates that the farm was once a Primitive Methodist meeting house.

Go right, cross the ladder stile to the right of the bungalow, and from a gravel strip rise up the bank ahead, continuing with the field wall to the right. Traverse an intermediate wall by a hand gate en route to another ladder stile into a farm lane. ◄ Go forward, slipping through an annexed garden at Green Croft, where you may very well encounter Art in the Barn and refreshment facilities, including a green toilet, a most welcome innovation.

Follow the hand gated pathway, signed 'Longbyre', crossing a gated footbridge. The turf path turns left above the stream and advances to a kissing gate, now with the well-evidenced Wall ditch and bank to the left, and on the right a field wall set upon the foundations of the Wall.

> In two places the **ditch** holds water like a moat, and an active badger sett near a solitary thorn bush disturbs the bank. All along this section the ridge of the north ditch is distinctly higher than normal; here the excavation material – normally dispersed by the Romans – was heaped up and has, remarkably, remained intact.

As the ditch falters the Path steps in, wending down via a plastic causeway to cross a footbridge. Go through the subsequent kissing gate then traverse the next field to a ladder stile beyond the old railway wagon, continuing down to a ladder stile and steps onto the road. To the left is Balmoral House – a handsome farmhouse with a tall barn.

Turn right and walk along the verge, noting the abutment-like vestige of Hadrian's Wall on the bank. Advance to the little red-brick terrace, built in 1907 for the captains (managers) of Barn Colliery; the colliers' terraces are at nearby Longbyre. (Considering the Industrial Revolution's commitment to coal mining in the area, it is remarkable that the residual surface evidence is so low-key.)

At this point the **Pennine Way** – the first National Trail in Britain (opened in 1965) – joins Hadrian's Wall Path via Haltwhistle Golf Course. The trail leaves the road at Thirlwall View. Keen eyes can find a centurial stone set in the low garden wall, facing the road at ground level, first spotted in 1980. Crudely incised, it translates as 'of the Sixth Cohort, the century of Lousius Suavis (built this)', apparently the most prolific cohort on the Wall. The author drew the householder's attention to its presence, as they, like most passers-by, were oblivious of its existence. Advance in front of the terrace to facing kissing gates, taking care when crossing the railway – remember 'Stop, Look, Listen'.

Go over the footbridge at the watersmeet of the Pow Charney and Tipalt burns, from where a confined path leading right connects with **Greenhead**. ▶ Follow the Tipalt Burn to a hand gate opposite the access to Thirlwall Castle and make the short climb to ponder this splendid site; its restoration is the largest of its type undertaken by the Northumberland National Park Authority.

The adjacent cluster of cottages is known as Duffen or Doughan Foot – the whereabouts of Duffen Head is unclear. Presumably, there have been dwellings here for a long time, providing shelter and serving the needs of the masters of the early 14th-century

Fanciful tales that this was Saint Patrick's birthplace are tenuous at best, but the link with the post-Roman era and figures like King Arthur and St Patrick will always tantalise.

Thirlwall Castle

castle, now an imposing romantic ruin. The name **Thirlwall** means 'hole in the Wall': did the castle builders exploit an existing breach in the Wall or create one by recycling the all-too-handy stones for their stronghold? To the most casual eye every last stone looks Roman, and it is worth noting that even in the 1600s most Roman structures still existed to around their original height.

The medieval barons, the de Thirlwalls, lived in troubled times but were clever enough to plunder more than they ceded – hence the tale of the Golden Table guarded by a Black Dwarf. Reputedly, he gave Scottish raiders the slip by throwing the table and himself down a well!

Go right, crossing the footbridge at Duffen Foot via the lane by Holmhead.

An **inscribed Roman stone**, *CIVITAS DUMNON*, inserted into the kitchen wall at Holmhead, is visible to B&B guests. This authentic graffiti relates to Dumnoni slaves – Celts from near Exeter in the south-west of England, who would have been marched up to repair the Wall close to Magna Fort. It was unusual for natives to work in their own land; the Romans mastered the principle of divide and rule, bringing a 'united nations' workforce from all around their empire to do service in Britannia.

Swinging round behind the house, take a moment to look at the low out barn and note two stone pillars inserted into the facing wall, indicating the original line of the Roman Wall. The track hairpins up to a gate/stile and now the Wall ditch is strikingly evident, the Trail ascending the pasture to its left. At the top, cross a ladder stile above a swollen bank and look right to the shallow banks in the sheep pasture, which hint at the outline of Magna Roman Fort. Complete the ascent to a stile onto the road. Go right to enter the Walltown Quarry car park, but before you do, take the opportunity to visit Carvoran Roman Army Museum in the adapted farm buildings beyond the car park to the right. ▶

Owned and run by the Vindolanda Trust, the museum gives a remarkable insight into garrison life on the Wall and includes an inspirational film.

MAGNA ROMAN FORT

The faint earthworks of Magna Roman Fort, levelled by farming, lie in the field 900ft (275m) to the south-west of the museum. Magna, 'the rocky place', does not fit with the logic of the Wall, although it must have come to play some significant role. It was built well before Hadrian's time, marshalling the Roman road system at the point where the southbound Maiden Way met the Stanegate. Magna was excluded from the military zone defined by the vallum.

In Hadrian's time the fort was associated with the first cohort of Hamian archers, the crack bowmen of their time brought here from Syria – very much the forerunners of the yeomen of England.

Passing the pond (a haven for mallard), take the central, partially fenced path up to the south-eastern corner of the landscaped enclosure. Pause to look at the hexagonal metal tubes simulating the dolerite columns of the cliff above. A more useful simulation would be a reconstruction of the Roman Wall to full height, as exists at Segedunum, tracing the quarried line of the original mural feature through the quarry.

The working life of the 40-acre Walltown Quarry ended in 1978, the dense rock prized for more than road-building purposes.

Hadrian's Wall on Walltown Crags

Wander through the Walltown Quarry car park, passing the shop and a toilet block.

Leaving the quarry enclosure at a kissing gate, turn left and rise beside the quarry boundary wall to connect with the remnant Roman Wall. Turn up right to go along this wonderful section of consolidated Wall over, and through, outcrops of Whin Sill.

This **scenic stretch** dips then rises to Turret 45a, adapted from an earlier Roman signal station associated with Magna – hence the odd angle of the structure in relation to the converging Wall. The whinstone quarry may give drama to the view now, but unfortunately giant chunks of Wall rubble were removed, as this portion of the frontier did not receive the keen attention of John Clayton's workforce (see Stage 6 for more information).

Follow the undulating ridge beyond the older quarry. Keep right; the single strand of barbed wire affords minimal protection on a considerable cliff. ▶ Cross the grassy platform of Milecastle 45 and descend into Walltown Gap, the site of the so-called King Arthur's Well.

The **spring** is associated with the baptism of King Edwin, who ruled the Deira division of the Kingdom of Northumbria in the early seventh century. The ceremony, conducted by the monk Paulinus in AD627, marked Edwin's conversion to Christianity. The Wall has mesmerised romantics from many a century, so it is little wonder that King Arthur has found his place in this setting too. Conversations with locals suggest they take it for granted that he was here – or why else would Paulinus choose this spot?

Cross the farm track onto the following ridge above Walltown Farm – historically the home of the Ridleys, infamous Border Reivers (like many in this area; after all it was simply their way of life, and maybe they had no choice).

The **wild chives** growing on the bare whinstone slabs behind the farm are thought to have been brought over by the Romans. Now under a protection order, they are clinging perilously on the edge of extinction on this and one other local site.

Look forward to a little knoll crowned with trees: a pleasing subject for the camera.

Walkers are beseeched to keep right so as to avoid treading on the rubble rigg and adjacent eroded patches.

Note that rock-climbers have been known to use this detached portion of the quarry – hence the metal loop to which they attach top ropes.

Turret 44b, looking down on Walltown Farm

Periodically, 'tank traps' are positioned in this area, gently guiding walkers onto a new, more appropriate grassy line. Climb some 300ft (90m) by the sensational **Turret 44b**. One can almost sense the Roman patrol keeping their ghostly watch.

Mucklebank Crag, the highest part of this ridge, is a **superb viewpoint**. The name appropriately means the 'big hillside'. From here one can see Skiddaw Little Man and Skiddaw over the shoulder of Talkin Fell down to the far south-west horizon; Cross Fell at the head of the South Tyne valley; Gillalees Beacon to the north-west, and the great dark skyline of the Border Forests across the northern arc of the view.

The Path slips through a depression and over a second ridge, going down by a ladder stile within the ninth of the Nine Nicks of Thirlwall. In deference to the archaeology, keep off the spine of the ridge where the rubble rigg persists. Contour to a ladder stile with a tantalisingly long view ahead of the Wall's progress along the Whin Sill ridge of Cawfields and Winshields Crags.

From this point to Cawfields the ridge shrinks, although initially the Wall has more substance beneath a modified field wall on the inaccessible north face. Cross the grassy bank of Milecastle 44; the ditched effect is the result of stone-robbing with the infill cast aside. ▶

The gravelled Path leads through to an open pinewood and via a ladder stile into the pasture in front of Cockmount Hill, which translates as 'the lekking ground of woodcock'. Keep faith with the line of the Wall by field walls and two ladder stiles, drawing close to **Great Chesters** (Roman Aesica) beside a considerable rubble rigg.

Immediately short of the plantation glance left at the field gate and note the distinctive Roman milestone now recycled as a sturdy gatepost. It is thought to have been transferred from the Military Way.

AESICA (GREAT CHESTERS) ROMAN FORT

The situation of the fort is odd, being only three miles from Magna. It seems to have been a later addition, albeit as the Wall was under construction. In purely practical terms there was a problem: a natural water supply was non-existent. Roman surveying guile was tested in bringing a head of water some six miles along a serpentine aqueduct on a slight gradient from Fond Tom's Pool, located only two miles distant in Caw Burn.

Coming upon the fort from the west, you can see a couple of low ramparts, an unusual feature. (If you want to see a Roman fort with ramparts then

West gate of Aesica Roman Fort

the unexcavated Whitley Castle (Roman Epiacum) near Alston is remarkable – hold a visit in store for another day.)

Enter the fort by the north-western corner guardhouse. Down to the right, intriguing walling includes the partially blocked west gate. Walk along the southern edge and note traces of barrack blocks in the grass bank. An altar at the south-east corner gateway attracts modern votive offerings of coins; notice the crude relief of a Roman soldier holding a shield at arm's length on the adjacent block.

Many walkers will be attracted to the central fenced arch – remains of the headquarter building's cellar strongroom. Sheep, cattle and horses graze this site, daily challenging the survival of this precious antiquity. Clambering over the ladder stile as you leave the fort enclosure some 60ft (18m) left of the farm buildings (which encroach into the fort area), note a rudimentary plan giving a clue to the layout.

This was the site of a Roman watermill for grinding corn; today, amid the alder carr, the streamside flowers bloom.

Beyond the fort, follow on by a series of ladder stiles with a grand view ahead to the whinstone scarp of Cawfields Crags, the Wall ditch a striking foreground feature. Pass Burnhead Cottage and proceed via a wall stile step onto the road to cross Haltwhistle Burn. ◀

Within a mile of this spot is the greatest concentration of **Roman marching camps** anywhere along the frontier – ten at least are identified on the Ordnance Survey map. Downstream, where Caw Burn becomes Haltwhistle Burn, and on the surrounding slopes behind the Milecastle Inn, both Roman and later bell-pit shafts were sunk to exploit the excellent quality coal found close to the surface. The Inn, named after Milecastle 42, was once known as the North Jerry (a 'jerry' being a beer house – the ale will have been served in jugs for the navvies building the Military Road as well as for later travellers).

Haltwhistle lies in the South Tyne valley just two miles from here.

Recycled Roman milestone

The town's proud boast is that it is the '**Centre of Britain**', and the centre for the Wall it most certainly is. Some visitors have construed the name to mean a place for whistle-stop visits, but local hoteliers are not too keen on that perception, stressing the true meaning of the town name to be 'the wood at the meeting of streams' – which is not as much fun.

Turn left, enter **Cawfields** Quarry car park (toilet facilities and water tap) and follow the path beside the quarry pool. The chilly waters of the deep dark pool add sparkle to the dramatic scene backed by the impressive quarried peak. Watch out for six-foot black frogs – as frogmen frequently use the site for scuba diving training. (Book through National Park Rangers should you be interested!)

Successive kissing gates lead to Hole Gap, the first one announcing that you are entering the National Trust's Hadrian's Wall Estate. ▶ Before you bear up left to get close and personal with **Milecastle 42**, you should first clamber up the steps to the right of Hole Gap to study this strikingly sited milecastle from the crest of the 'peak'.

The Trust is the biggest single landholder along the Whin Sill and has a proud record for its care.

The natural weakness in the Whin Sill was purposefully blocked, forcing carts to plod through this steep control. The **milecastle** might look jaunty to modern eyes, set on an awkward slope, but doubtless the auxiliaries and native Brits will have used a different adjective!

The north gate masonry is substantial – notice the guidelines etched on the top surface of the stones. A great tower stood over this gateway, making this quite a landmark; it appears that the fort and milecastle towers were the 'crows' nests' of the frontier, which explains why the turrets were removed.

This is an excellent spot from which to survey the course of the vallum, which forms a striking component of the view east along the dip slope towards Shield-on-the-Wall Farm.

At Thorny Doors (ignore the hand gate), just before the ridge makes a sharp upward step, the Wall momentarily stands an impressive 14 courses high.

Interestingly, Bogle Hole, which means 'the goblin's hollow', betrays the local cultural superstition that it was the haunt of evil little folk.

Ascend beside the fine stretch of Wall along the rising ridge of Cawfield Crags with its lovely mantle of native trees clinging to the cliff face. ◄ It is rare to wander this way and not encounter rooks and jackdaws, their chattering antics and rasping call a characteristic sound, giving rise to the name of the crag and the farm, Cawfields, 'open ground frequented by crows'.

Advance via stiles, passing **Turret 41a** and a lovely stretch of consolidated Wall to cross the Caw Gap road by facing kissing gates. The roller-coaster ridge climbs and dips beside the semi-field wall, by the north-facing combe of **Bogle Hole**. ◄ Pass the earthen platform of Milecastle 41, the adjacent thick Wall for all intents a Clayton Wall minus a turf cap. At a dip in the ridge a wooden sign indicates a short-cut footpath down the dry valley to Winshields Farm – a useful campsite for self-sufficient walkers.

Complete the ascent to the Ordnance Survey pillar on the top of **Winshields Crags** – at 1132ft (345m) the highest point on the Whin Sill and therefore on the entire walk.

The hill name **Winshield** means 'the windy summer shelter'. In the immediate country to the north, below this great scarp, lie a dozen farmsteads which originally would have been summer shielings – spread out, in typical Scandinavian fashion, equidistant across a broad, low moorland vale. From this spot the sense of being above, and yet within, a living, breathing landscape is profound.

Some 20 years ago a telescope stood here, giving the energetic visitor the opportunity to gaze at a marvellous panorama; its removal an undoubted loss. The view stretches from Cross Fell – the highest summit in the Pennine chain within the North Pennines Area of Outstanding Natural Beauty – down to the south, and extends to the northern horizon, limited by the Border Forests of Wark, Spadeadam and Kielder (although The

Roman Wall along the top of Winshields Crags

Cheviot is plainly in view). Westward, gaze into Scotland to Criffel, which rises across the Solway from Bowness; nearer, Gillalees Beacon is visible, upon which the Romans built a beacon to communicate between the scouting outpost fort Fanum Cocidii (Bewcastle) and the Wall fort Banna (Birdoswald).

Heading on, all eyes will be transfixed on the remarkable view ahead, of the scarp edges traversed by the Roman Wall from Peel and Highshield to Hotbank Crags and the more distant Sewingshields Crag.

Pass a further stretch of consolidated Wall; as this falters a narrow Wall foundation persists beside the replacement field wall on the easy descent.

From **Milecastle 40** – the adjacent fenced gap a clue to its position – proceed by a hand gate, noting the small platform of the unexcavated site of a medieval shepherd's shieling. From a gate/wall stile the slope gently declines to a kissing gate onto the road, with **Steel Rigg** (National Park) car park close left.

The Sill

To visit Northumberland National Park's Landscape Discovery Centre, otherwise known as The Sill, go down the hill and bear right on the verge path to enter the grounds after cautiously crossing the Military Road, a notorious traffic hazard. The eye-catching building includes a state of the art Youth Hostel and daytime café facilities, the adjacent independent business, the Twice Brewed Inn, with its micro-brewery, offers refreshment throughout the day and evenings.

WESTBOUND: STEEL RIGG TO BIRDOSWALD

Crossing the minor road via the staggered kissing gates, begin the steady ascent to **Winshields Crags**, highest point on the National Trail. Proceed via a gate/wall stile, followed by a hand gate higher up, after which the ground eases to the Ordnance Survey column on the summit. A field wall replacement for the Hadrianic structure acts as your ridge-top guide via a hand gate in a dip, then, shortly after passing through the hollow of **Bogle Hole**, descend sharply to the Caw Gap road.

Cross by facing kissing gates and follow on with the base Wall via a fence stile, stepping down at Thorny Doors to keep close to a particularly handsome stretch of consolidated Wall. Slip through the kissing gate at Hole Gap and quickly through a second, leading by the old quarry pool into **Cawfields** car park.

Exit, bearing left to cross the road bridge over Caw Burn. Step over the wall stile, passing up by Burnhead Cottage. Ladder stiles lead to **Aesica Roman Fort** (see 'Aesica (Great Chesters) Roman Fort', above), which you traverse, continuing by two ladder stiles to pass Cockmount Hill and enter open woodland at a further ladder stile.

Emerge at another ladder stile, noting on the right the Roman milestone recycled as a gatepost. The field wall runs upon the line of the Wall, rising to yet another ladder stile. Skirt the crest of Mucklebank Crag to the left, crossing a wall stile and bearing up onto the ridgetop with its Wall rubble spine. After the next crest descend by the impressively sited **Turret 44b** into the gap behind Walltown Farm, and then go via a wall stile to the next edge, leading to the single-strand fence-protected quarried edge and **Turret 45a** – a pre-Hadrianic Roman signal station.

Follow the Wall weaving through the Whin Sill outcropping until it abruptly ends at a wall by Walltown Quarry. Go left and down to a kissing gate, entering the Country Park, then skirt round the pond to enter the car park, passing the café/toilet block to reach the road. (See 'Magna Roman Fort' above.)

Go right, then go left via a hand gate into the pasture just before the cattle grid and advance to a ladder stile, admiring a fine long view west. Cross and slip down the bank, keeping the Wall ditch close left. At the foot of the slope cross the wall stile/gate and enter a green lane winding down to Holmhead.

Cross the Tipalt Burn footbridge at Duffen Foot; **Thirlwall Castle** can be accessed right. Turn left at the hand gate, following the fenced stream-side path and crossing a footbridge. With the utmost care, cross the railway by facing hand gates, from where a short confined path by a brick terrace leads to the road.

Go right, watching for the embanked relic Wall on the left, then climb the roadside bank by steps and cross a ladder stile, rising to a kissing gate beside Wall End Farm. Traverse the next pasture to a kissing gate and plank bridge, then ascend the bank by the groove of the Wall ditch.

Continue via further kissing gates and a plank footbridge to emerge into a farm lane at Green Croft. Keep forward, taking the next ladder stile at the right-hand bend, following on by a hand gate and then a ladder stile to join a minor road at Gap Farm.

Roman signal station Turret 45a at Walltown Crags

From the next kissing gate advance to tiptoe round the border of an industriously worked cottage garden vegetable plot. From the exiting ladder stile traverse a pasture bank to emerge at a hand gate onto the minor road in **Gisland** (see 'Gisland' above). Keep straight on, going via kissing gates and following a fence on the right, towards the railway.

Centre of Britain Hotel, Haltwhistle

At an information panel go left within the confined path, descending via concrete steps to cross the Poltross Burn footbridge, and arrive at **Poltross Burn Milecastle** (King Arthur's Stables). The continuing confined path leads to a further crossing of the railway; **take care** as the trains are swift and can be almost silent, so pay attention and Stop, Look, Listen.

Descend the ramp to a kissing gate and traverse the pasture to join a flagged path to another kissing gate onto the road between the school and the village car park. Bear right to the cattle grid and kissing gate, where the track to Willowford Farm is joined. As the track switches right, keep forward beside the consolidated Roman Wall, tightly fenced from the pasture.

Step off the decking at the farm and from the facing kissing gate descend a flight of stone steps beside the consolidated Wall to reach the Roman bridge abutment. After the corner kissing gate the Path is ushered left to cross the handsome **Millennium Bridge** spanning the River Irthing.

The Path leads on via a hand gate and then up a bank onto a track, completing the ascent to **Harrow Scar Milecastle**. Step over its low walls in leaving the track to reach a kissing gate. Advance within the pasture beside a grand parade of consolidated Wall to **Birdoswald Roman Fort** (see 'The Birdoswald Estate', above).

STAGE 6
Steel Rigg to Brocolitia

Start	Steel Rigg
Finish	Brocolitia Roman Fort
Distance	8 miles (13km)
Walking time	5hr
Refreshments	Vindolanda Roman Fort café (off-route – entrance fee for fort); Bardon Mill (off-route): village store and tearoom, The Bowes Hotel; Housesteads Roman Fort – coffee/tea machine and snacks in shop
Accommodation	Housesteads, Grindon, Carraw
Railway link	Bardon Mill

This next stretch of the Wall, to Housesteads specifically, is the most popular of all. The Wall runs along a rousing crescendo of crags, roller-coaster fashion, with one fabulously sited fort and various other Roman relic features – and of course wonderfully scenic outlooks to the north and south to inspire the imagination. After Sewingshields Farm the scarp melts away and the frontier constricts, with the Wall ditch and vallum a matter of yards apart on the comparatively level rough pasture to Carrawburgh.

The incessant footfall through this section puts a strain on the path surface, hence the need for stone flags in various critical places to alleviate wear on the largely hidden archaeology. Such stone additions bring with them the confusion between Roman relic and modern recreational civil engineering.

▶ Heading for the Wall, the National Trail crosses the road by the staggered kissing gates, now accompanying the first example of Clayton Wall via a hand gate – uniting with visitors from the car park – and for the first time we encounter Clayton Wall in its basic form.

For 1:25K route map see booklet pages 25–29.

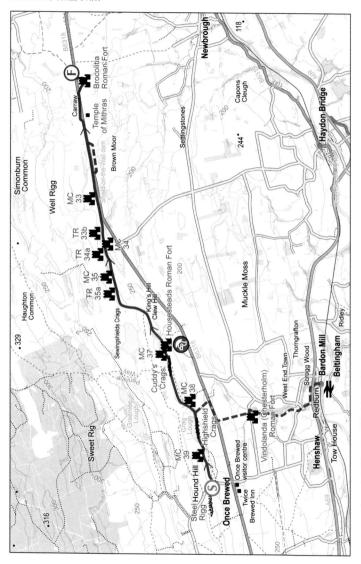

John Clayton of Chesters House devoted every Monday of his professional working life, as a lawyer and Town Clerk in Newcastle, to the Wall. He employed William Tailford as his foreman for Wall excavation and reconstruction tasks; that we have Roman stone walling here at all is due to this one man's classical education and passion.

Notice how the Wall occasionally steps in and out; a curious detail, possibly done just to affirm the work of Tailford's team – although equally it might be correctly observed from the original construction.

The name Steel Rigg translates as 'pointed ridge' – descriptive of the short tapering spur of pasture ahead. Inevitably, as the gravel path ends and the Wall swings down to the right, you will pause to comprehend the most handsome view ahead.

The dolerite cliffs of **Peel Crags**, sometimes used by rock climbers, make a striking subject for your camera. This landscape was fashioned by the irresistible, abrasive progression of an

Sycamore Gap from the east

eastward-moving glacier forcing through a weakness and creating Peel Gap; tapering the low ridges such as Steel Rigg; creating hollows below the crags where the loughs (natural lakes) have collected; and gnawing at the dolerite, thereby creating this impressive cliff line with its distinctive dolerite columns and coarse scree.

As you descend into Peel Gap, an inviting hand gate up to the right leads to the road beside Peel Bothy.

The Bothy, a Landmark Trust holiday let, was opened after renovation by Her Majesty the Queen Mother in 1989, the connection being that it had formerly been in the possession of the Bowes-Lyon family, from Ridley Hall. It is an unusual survival from the age of Border Reiving, the name suggesting that a former defended dwelling stood here, or that the present building was adapted from one – this being a continuity of watchfulness in the Gap, where the Romans had placed a turret watchtower too.

Interestingly, the debate as to whether the Wall was castellated gained strength from evidence of such a feature in the rubble of the turret here. Contemporary thinking has swung back in favour of castellation after a period of serious doubt. A Wall-top walkway does seem logical and therefore a parapet a natural accompaniment, although it just might be that only some strategic sections of the mural barrier had Wall-top walks.

Stone slabs have been inserted to minimise the impact of the great many walkers who come this way down through the Gap. Continue up, passing through two narrow squeezes – one through a low wall stile, then the Sill – and go up the steep bank, where the Wall once ran to the brink of Peel Crags, to reach a recessed hand gate.

Follow the Clayton Wall along the ridgetop. Cute eyes are needed to locate the swastika stone – an ancient symbol

Swastika Stone

of good fortune, now matched by the luck in finding it on the lowest undisturbed course of the Wall (see photograph).

Dipping by a ladder stile at the Cat Stairs nick (the name an allusion to wildcats, long fled), the Path now continues, initially by a Wall rubble bank, to come upon one of the most iconic views of Hadrian's Wall, overlooking Castle Nick, sweeping around **Milecastle 39** – very much a square peg in a square hole. ▸ One might reasonably ask why Milecastle 42 was not placed similarly snugly in its notch of the ridge.

The low walls within the milecastle are remnants of 16th-century cattle byres.

Proceed to the next stepped rise in the ridge – Mons Fabricius, named in 1928 in honour of the eminent German frontier scholar Ernst Fabricius.

Note the outline of two 16th-century **shielings**. These shepherds' shelters would not have been occupied in the winter, as the flocks were moved back into Tynedale. The humble herdsmen needed the hilltop site and the substantial Roman Wall as double indemnity from sheep thieves: the moss troopers were as likely to kill as to rob!

Milecastle 39 (Castle Nick)

A steep flight of stone steps descends to Sycamore Gap, named for the presence of the stately tree.

Standing upon a massive quantity of tumbled Wall rubble, the tree may well yield valuable information in the event of its eventual demise, doubtless fuelled by the discovery of a coin hoard, from the AD330s, in the vicinity. Many visitors call it **Robin Hood's Tree**, after this spot featured in the adventure movie *Robin Hood, Prince of Thieves*, starring Kevin Costner. The replacement sycamore, in the round walled pen, is finding it hard to establish itself – the attention of visitors a greater threat than the elements.

Cross over the Wall in the gap and look at the consolidated north face of the Wall up to seven courses high, which includes dark dolerite stones – an unusual use of the immediate bedrock.

Whin Sill rock was used only in the lower courses because it was too hard to quarry; hence, only easily obtained surface rock found a place in the Wall. The overwhelming majority of the stone was quarried, cut, and drawn some distance to the site by horses with wagons or sledges.

It is worth mentioning that, for all the brilliance of the Whin Sill as a natural line for the frontier, the Romans would not have built here but for the presence of limestone. The local carboniferous geological succession also gave them coal to burn the limestone to create the most fundamental ingredient for the entire Wall-building process: mortar.

The Trail ascends stone steps to a ladder stile, the sturdy consolidated Wall lost once the crest of **Highshield Crags** is reached.

Imagine what the frontier Wall would have looked like running along this **fantastic clifftop**. Crag

Lough's resident swans may draw your attention far below, nesting in the marshy alder carr
fringe, while you might catch sight of fly fishermen in boats attempting to hook brown trout. The
surrounding marshes are ecologically important
for pondweed and freshwater invertebrates. The
backing moors are a haven for curlew – a bird
that features as the Northumberland National Park
emblem, although here it is sometimes rivalled in
early May by the lookalike whimbrel. The calls are
quite different – in fact the latter's name means
'whimper', while the curlew's evocative rippling
cry is quite the reverse.

There are several great lakes bearing the Irish
Viking term **'lough'** in this vicinity of the Wall.
Greenlee, Broomlee and Crag Loughs lie to the
north, while Grindon Lough is set to the south
beside the Stanegate. All were formed as a result of
the irresistible eastward passage of a great ice sheet
in the final phase of the last Ice Age, scouring the
cliffs and upland ridges to give a consistent trend to
landscape features.

*Crag Lough from
Highshield Crags,
with fly fishers in
boats below*

The walking link with Bardon Mill railway station – and route to Vindolanda Roman Fort (2km away and well worth the detour) – leaves at this point.

Ahead see the next great rise in the ridge: Hotbank Crags, drawing you on. Enter a pine wood, watching that the tangle of tree roots doesn't cause you to trip. Cross a ladder stile, then go alongside a field wall, with the alder carr of **Crag Lough** close left, to reach a farm track and Milking Gap via a hand gate. ◄

Alternative route to Vindolanda

While many visitors choose to visit Vindolanda from The Sill by boarding the AD122 bus, there is a more direct walking route that breaks from the National Trail here at Milking Gap.

Follow the track, spotting the irregular ring of boulders on the right, the remains of an Iron Age farmstead., which consists of five round houses and a walled yard. After the vallum a gate gives access to the Military Road. While being aware of traffic, go right along the grass verge, which soon becomes rank with burdock, to find a low wall stile on the left, where the vallum sweeps across the main road.

Entering the pasture, keep initially beside the vallum bank but be sure to maintain a beeline as it swings right, heading to a fence styleinto the light wood adjacent to High Shield. The footpath leads down to a tall ladder stile accessing a pasture. Descend with the fence left, crossing a further fence styleas Vindolanda Roman Fort becomes ever more evident ahead. At the foot of the hill find the Chesterholm Milestone, the only fully intact example beside the Stanegate. A ladder stile gives access to the Stanegate road, where you turn left to reach the access drive to the Vindolanda museum and thereby the fort.

Although not set upon Hadrian's Wall, **Vindolanda** sustained an important role in the practical functioning of the frontier throughout the Roman period. Nine distinct structural phases have been identified from a long-term programme of excavation and interpretation of the fort and adjacent vicus. Over the years the Birley family has nurtured and developed the site within the care of the Vindolanda

Trust. Perhaps most famous for its Writing Tablets and other personal effects, including footwear, the constantly enhanced museum is rightly celebrated.

The natural gap gained its name from the historic use of the passage by cattle herdsmen. In fact, a small **Iron Age farmstead** can be seen if you follow the track a short way south, identified by an irregular cluster of stones. Five round houses and a walled yard existed, vacated when the Romans took control of the immediate countryside, building first the vallum which is prominently seen close by.

Cross this access track to Hotbank Farm and continue via a kissing gate, following the field wall on the line of the Wall, which smartly bends north, confined by a fence on the right. Draw close to Hotbank Farm – a traditional stock-rearing farm, herding cattle and sheep in the age-old way.

Stone flagging protects the **earthworks** of Milecastle 38. Judging by pottery finds it was occupied throughout the frontier's life. Two telling inscriptions were found here during the excavations in 1935; they record the milecastle's construction by the Second Legion under the governor Aulus Platorius Nepos (Governor of Britannia) for the Emperor Hadrian, suggesting that it was within the years 122 to about 126.

The discovery of the two stones suggests that both the north and south gateways were adorned, indicated further by the survival of red paint on one inscription. (It was normal in antiquity for prominent inscriptions of this significance to be highly decorated.) These inscriptions are the one sure and certain proof that the frontier was born in Hadrian's mind, and that he promptly acted upon its genius – a firm line in the sand.

The plantation may indicate a connection with the name of the hill and farm, as the term 'Hott' meant a circle of trees.

From the exit kissing gate the Trail ascends beside a fine example of Clayton Roman Wall reconstruction, just above the round plantation that the Military Way breaks right to contour. ◀ Wander along the ridgetop of Hotbank Crags, avoiding the temptation to stand on the Wall at the top of the rise to capture the fine view west to Highshield and Winshields Crags.

The Roman Wall marches attractively on eastward, dipping and rising with a wonderful backdrop view towards the distant scarp of Sewingshields Crags and along the line of the Wall to Housesteads. The intervention of Rapishaw Gap brings a halt to your footloose freedom; dip to cross the ladder stile. Here the Pennine Way leaves the Wall, heading north into the lonely forests and far-off Cheviot Hills on the Scottish border. Veer right to avoid shattered outcropping of Whin Sill on the east side of the gap – the original Wall must have been impressive to cope with this sharp dip.

Next comes the short ridge of **Cuddy's Crags** – a name possibly derived from a local landowner (in the vernacular it was the pet name for Cuthbert). Ahead is the most cliché 'picturesque' prospect on the Wall: the view towards Housesteads Crag – best observed at the point where the stone flags break away right towards the depression. Climbing beside the Wall, arrive at **Milecastle 37**.

This is a rather special **milecastle**: the arched span of the north gate has partially survived, showing the character of these controls limiting the height of traffic – no double-deckers here, please! To the left of the gateway the Wall is 11 courses high, the highest minimally disturbed section of the original Wall on the entire frontier. The low interior walls are the remains of 16th-century stock byres. Just down the slope the Roman Military Way remains a popular thoroughfare to this day, as walkers stroll from Hotbank to Housesteads on the dip slope, avoiding the ups and downs of the ridge-top Wall and frequently using it to make a simple circular walk with the skyline Wall.

Enter Housesteads Wood at a kissing gate, a windbreak pine grove running along the brink of Housesteads Crags. Either step onto the Wall walk or thread through the trees on a bark-bedded path. On purely aesthetic grounds this is a lovely moment, satisfying an urge many people have to walk upon the Wall. For one brief moment walkers – with a head for heights – may step aside onto the top of a basalt pinnacle to feel the exposure of the clifftop setting, perhaps also experiencing a biting northerly breeze!

Upon exiting the wood, the Trail steps down left and passes the north walls of **Housesteads Roman Fort**. (John Clayton's excavators removed the original ramp from the north gate, which explains why there is such a step down in the masonry.) During 2022 one of the most magical contributions to mark the 1900th anniversary of Hadrian's only known visit to Britannia and his brainchild Wall was the erection of a temporary and hugely colourful installation replicating the north gate. The phrase that accompanied it was 'The future belongs to what was as much as what is'. Where the Wall meets the curved corner of the fort, the Trail runs steeply down the grass bank, which can be very slippery, to go through the Roman Knag Burn gateway.

Out of preference – or might that be deference – to that horrid slippery slope, you are encouraged to exit the wood right by the kissing gate and visit the site Museum, which in any case is an all-important Passport stamping station. Take this fabulous opportunity to pay the English Heritage entrance fee and inspect the impressive and hugely inspiring interior of the fort. (Be sure to purchase the site guide, too.)

VERCOVICIUM ROMAN FORT

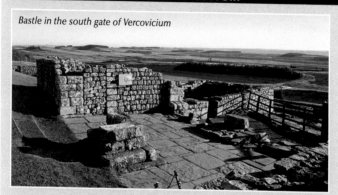

Bastle in the south gate of Vercovicium

This is the most inspirational and impressive Wall fort on open exhibition. It was garrisoned by 1000 Tungarian infantry from the modern Belgium, so they were well attuned to walking in this climate. This five-star, five-acre sloping site includes a central headquarters building (principia), commanding officer's house (praetorium), twin barrack blocks, a hospital, latrines, granaries, stout gates and watchtower features.

The south gate includes a medieval bastle (pronounced 'bassul'). Fortunately, the Roman focus of the excavators did not prevent them from keeping this adaptation, made some 1000 years later, although other elements of the medieval farm within the fort were swept away to reveal the Roman components. William Camden, visiting the area in the 1580s, was warned to keep well clear of the Armstrongs, fierce moss troopers who lived and farmed from the bastle.

The tiered central accommodation of the fort is impressive, with hypocaust confirming the commanding officer's slightly more luxurious residence. The upper building, comprising the granaries (horreum), reveals stone plinths; these held a flagged floor, encouraging ventilation in order to prevent the grain from heating up and spoiling with fungus – a practice still necessary in modern agriculture. A Roman army marched on its stomach, and bread was the basis of its diet.

The communal conclusion of all this eating, the latrines, down in the south-east corner of the fort, are remarkably complete, and quite the best example of such a functional building in Britain. 'To get the wrong end of the stick' is a phrase that comes down to us from the Roman use of personal toiletry sticks with a sponge tied to one end for the purpose of… well, I won't say quite what! The sponge was imported from the Mediterranean, while the lower orders used moss. Roman latrines did not have the benefits of a 'u' trap, so many valuables ended up in the spoils, which is good news for field archaeology. When Vercovicium was first constructed, it was thought that the Stanegate fort at Vindolanda would serve well enough. But it was soon apparent that the garrison needed to be quick off the mark – a fast-response force to react to spontaneous rebel gatherings was needed. The time and effort lost in getting up the mile of fellside was considerable and costly in terms of effectiveness. The implanting of forts bang on the Wall made the frontier a working success; Brocolitia actually rests upon the vallum, which had to be filled in to construct the fort.

Marking the 1900th anniversary in 2022, a scaffolding artwork representation of the north gate at Housesteads created by Morag Myerscough

Aesica, the next fort westward, had a major water-sourcing problem – the solution to which was a six-mile-long aqueduct snaking across the shallow slopes in what were termed 'the barbarian' lands to the north of the Wall. Clearly, preventing the sabotage of this head of water was a significant task at Great Chesters.

Most visitors arrive at Housesteads via the National Trust visitor centre, having parked in the Northumberland National Park car park. We long for the day when with others, like the Vindolanda Trust, these all-important organisations shake hands and offer the visitor a single-ticket Wall experience – it's been a dream for far too long.

Passing on by the south gate of the fort, observe the confusing mix of Romano-British, Saxon and medieval cultivation on one south-facing slope. Cultivation was probably established in the late third century to supplement the fort's store of spelt (an early from of wheat, widely available from health food shops today!) and was used at various times after. You may also note that the walls of the fort seem very irregular; this is because it was shoddily built in the first place and had to be repeatedly rebuilt during its Roman working life!

Knag Burn gateway is a notoriously damp spot. ◀ The Trail heads east up beside the consolidated Wall to a wall stile, and promptly, upon entry into the tapered end of a mixed woodland, the Hadrianic Wall is lost and replaced by a common-or-garden field wall. From the exiting ladder stile keep close to the advancing, neatly coursed field wall on Kennel Crags, whose name means 'slope clear of scrub', which is certainly true today.

Guardrooms flank the gate, which was probably inserted after the fort's north gate was closed and may have had mixed military and civilian purpose.

The ridge takes two great dipping swoops, firstly onto **Clew Hill** and then **King's Hill**. In the process the emphasis on one path is putting a strain on holding a greensward surface; walkers are encouraged to make strenuous efforts to avoid adding to the wear line, and by spreading their walking pattern, they minimise erosion and secure any hidden archaeology. The Trail is a 'braided route'.

The ridge turns north, descending past King's Wicket, thought to be a reference to King Arthur. The way through the Wall has an alternative name: Busy Gap.

This was always a sneaky **passage** – a droveway into antiquity, traversing the spongy mosses. In medieval times people of a thieving disposition entered Tynedale via this route. These 'moss troopers' were known as Busy Gap Rogues – a moss trooper being a miscreant inhabitant of this wild mire country.

Go through the hand gate in the depression and follow on, rising with the Wall where the bracken growth allows and snaking onto the crest of **Sewingshields Crags**.

This is a memorable **panoramic spot**, providing the last and perhaps finest view of the Whin Sill, and sufficiently removed from the main Roman sites to be enjoyed in comparative solitude. Broomlee Lough fills the hollow below, and in the far westward distance see Winshields Crags beyond Steel Rigg, already looking a day's march away.

The Whin Sill scarp is formed from dolerite, a dense magma that intruded as a sheet between layers of carboniferous limestone, shale and sandstone – hence the name Sill. The landmass has been subsequently tilted, creating the characteristic scarp/dip slope-rolling scenery. The dolerite came from a volcano that was active some 295 million years ago, located somewhere near the present Cheviot Hills. The rock is patterned with joints that have given rise to columns.

Northwards, a field wall falls from the scarp and runs on to form the eastern edge of Wark Forest, at which point it is known as the Black Dyke, suggesting an ancient boundary in all probability older than the Roman Frontier. The lime-washed Ordnance Survey pillar may be defunct as a triangulation sighter, but it certainly fulfils a valuable purpose in holding walkers to consider the elevated view from this windy headland. All too often great views like this are missed when people become too intent on covering the ground, rather than appreciating where they are.

> Both before and certainly after the OS column, lengths of Wall foundation impressively confirm the **historic line of the frontier**. Inspect Turret 35a and then Milecastle 35, containing traces of a 16th-century farmstead, precursor of the current Sewingshields Farm. It would seem the shieling (or shield) in the milecastle was once the abode of someone called 'Sigewine' – this being the origin of the name Sewingshields. The milecastle did not serve the usual function: a north gate was not created as the escarpment rendered progress to the north impossible; it can have been no more than a glorified watchtower with auxiliaries' lodgings.

Grave cist beside the Wall on Sewingshields Crags

Spot the medieval stone burial cist tucked up against the Wall some 50 metres beyond the milecastle – a unique

discovery revealed when the relic was excavated. Shortly after go through a kissing gate to enter Sewingshields Wood.

Pass through and continue along the declining ridge, coming close to the 'netty' (a privy outhouse) adjacent to Sewingshields farmhouse, itself entirely built from Roman stone – first upon a gravel, then a bark surface – and exit via a kissing gate. Stride on, crossing the open track and passing the lone cottage to reach the low ridge, location of **Turret 34a**. It would seem that when the turret was decommissioned, the north wall was strengthened, supporting the view that it under-pinned a wall-top walkway. (A nugget gleaned from Dr Mike Bishop, www.perlineamvalli.org.uk, in whose informed company the author walked this whole section one glorious September day.)

Go through the adjacent hand gate and stride along the pasture, the scarp diminishing with every step and traces of Wall core rubble evident as the Path approaches the sycamore-filled enclosure. The Path follows the emerging Wall ditch – seemingly strategically dug to shield the milecastle.

The clump of trees precisely footprints **Milecastle 34**, their roots doing the hidden archaeology no favours. Note the sheep creep, which gave lambs access to sheltered grazing (from the time before the trees were planted), while the wing walls provided a similar windbreak for ewes. A faded interpretative panel draws attention to the moated site north of the emergent Wall ditch, known as Sewingshields Castle.

Romantic writers have embroidered Arthurian leg-end around this **'moss' castle**, suggesting that King Arthur hid with Queen Guinevere and their entou-rage in a cave on Sewingshields Crags, waiting for ritual release from their entranced state (hence King's Hill and King's Wicket above Busy Gap). The pillow mound site of this ring-and-bailey stead-ing in Fozy Moss, complete with fish ponds and moat, was relinquished around the middle of the

16th century. Blooms of cotton grass characterise the quality of the fragile and nationally important habitat of the surrounding raised mires with their associated flora and fauna.

WARNING

The fields in this section are populated by suckler cattle. Be warned, be watchful and do not walk between cows and calves, as cows are protective of their young. This can be a particular concern if you have a dog – always be prepared to let your dog run loose to avoid inadvertently being trampled by cattle in their protective excitement.

Wander on, giving **Turret 33b** a quiet moment. It has the typical Broad Wall wings, an internal platform base, but no evidence of the door; this was blocked in the latter half of the second century. Although originally recessed into the Wall, this too was modified to strengthen the Wall and, as with Turret 34a, served to hold up the Wall walk (although this infill has now slumped).

The Path slips through the shallow Coe Sike hollow. ▸ Come up beside the field wall resting upon the foundations of the Wall, with the Wall ditch close left. Looking over the Wall, see an alder tree growing in a marsh (alder carr), and beyond, over the Military Road, **Shield-on-the-Wall dam** – a brown-trout-stocked fly fishery.

Next go up a platform, crossing the western wall of **Milecastle 33**. Looking over the fence, see that the milecastle is neatly defined by bracken growth – a plant that evidently prefers drier ground. Unfortunately, the walls of the milecastle underfoot are perilously exposed, so watch where you put your feet and stay with the defined Trail to avoid further damage to the relic.

Where the field wall merges with the Military Road bounding wall there is an intriguing option: either you stick with the Trail, shortly slipping through the Wall ditch to advance naturally east, or you cross the Military Road (with care) by the facing ladder stiles and follow the considerable bank top of the vallum – which is Open Access land, not a right-of-way as such, hence the presence of the stiles. The vallum more than matches the Wall bank here in terms of height, although it has been quarried. Knowledgeable eyes will spot several crossings in it, inserted by the Romans to negate the ditch as an impediment. A fixed metal hand gate is crossed, then after around 1000ft (320m) veer left off the low bank to a fixed field gate (in the vicinity of lost turret 33b) in the road-bounding wall. Walk diagonally to cross the opposing fixed field gate, thereby rejoining the Trail.

After 1200ft (366m) the Path goes through a kissing gate, suitably defended by stone flags against aggressive cattle poaching (not rustling – that's an altogether more unwelcome activity). A stone post with an acorn guides the Trail left before the wooded enclosure of **Carraw Farm**. ▸

Sadly, the stone flagging on the approach to the next kissing gate offers inadequate protection from the ankle-deep mud. Stone flags run along the north side of the fenced woodland, which commonly rings to the raucous sound of rooks, and on to a hand gate. From here bear

Over to the right the Military Road slices through the vallum; sadly, the 18th-century road engineers took advantage of the Wall as a road hardcore for much of the journey east from this point.

The farmhouse, once centred upon a defended peel tower, is now a valuable B&B for Trail walkers.

131

half-right to follow on down the pasture to a hand gate into a green lane.

Go right, carefully crossing the Military Road to a ladder stile, then advance via a flagged path crossing a double-flagged causeway and the shallow line of the vallum, which curiously ran under the site of Brocolitia, proving that the fort was an afterthought to fill in a long gap between Cilurnum and Vercovicium. Come into the rush-filled hollow of Meggie's Dene Burn, site of Coventina's Well.

> The rush-filled **springs** are where the Celtic deity Coventina was worshipped by the Romans. When excavated, Coventina's Well was found to hold the most enormous hoard of offerings, including 22 altars and in excess of 16,000 coins covering the full period of Roman occupation. (There were so many coins, in fact, that one local lad remembers being given handfuls of them, which he and chums used as skimming stones on Park Dam on their way home.) Coventina's original shrine stone can be seen in Chesters Museum.
>
> The well was discovered accidentally by lead miners during prospecting work in 1876. Note the officers had a masculine temple, Mithraic, while the soldier of lower rank held a feminine temple, Coventina. If nothing else, it does show the predisposition of humanity to spiritual observance.

Located in a marshy hollow, it was only discovered in 1949. Above it lay the civilian settlement (vicus), evident as the sun lowers in the sky, emphasising platform banks with shadows.

The marsh, crossed via stiles and stone flagging, glances by the **Temple of Mithras (Mithraeum)** enclosure, which attracts many visitors from the handy car park – some come to investigate its purpose, while others come to worship in their own way; hence the occasional votive offerings of coins and other artefacts that appear on the trio of replica altars. ◄

Rise by the fenced **Brocolitia Roman Fort** (gifted to English Heritage in 2020); a grass-covered earthwork, a fraction under four acres is all that can be seen. Go round the fence corner with the path that leads towards the car park. You can slip through the inviting hand gate and rise onto the grassy bank onto the fort's rampart and orbit the interior to an exit hand gate close to the car park. The only evidence of the fort stone amid the rank grass being at the west gate.

The high earthen banks of the **Brocolitia** are clearly in view over the fence, to casual eyes looking like an Iron Age encampment. The fort name means 'hill above a badger's sett' – another example of the Romans adopting a colloquial term to ingratiate the natives and suggest normality, in a situation that was anything but, being a military exclusion zone!

The fort is only 3½ miles west of Chesters and appears to have been something of an after-thought, inserted as the Wall went up – albeit after the vallum was dug – to bridge the long gap to Housesteads. You might like to know that the Roman cemetery lies under the car park, close to the parking meter; so if you're hesitating to pay, be warned that the ghosts of Romans past may very well be watching!

There are no permanent visitor facilities in the car park. Toilets would be appreciated, as in many another situation along the Trail, although it is a bus stop on the AD122 route.

AD122 bus at the Brocolitia bus stop

WESTBOUND: BROCOLITIA TO STEEL RIGG

From the car park follow the gravel path south, skirting the fort's perimeter fence and dipping into the hollow to pass the fenced **Mithraeum** enclosure via stone flags. Step over the ladder stile and cross the marsh at the head of Meggie's Dene Burn, with stone flags leading to a fence-stile, heading on with further essential stone flags to the ladder stile onto the Military Road. Cross with great care into the green lane, and within yards go through the hand gate, ascending the pasture towards the woodland at **Carraw**, guided rightwards by the acorn stone.

More stone flags run along the northern fenced edge of the woodland; proceed via two hand gates to emerge into cattle-poached pasture; hence, after rain expect ankle-deep mud. Bear half-left then advance parallel with the road via a hand gate. After 400 metres you may choose to cross the metal field gate (in the vicinity of lost turret 33b) on the left and cross the Military Road diagonally to a corresponding gate, thereby joining the vallum bank in access land.

Climb over a metal fence en route to a notably tall section of the vallum and find two facing ladder stiles, enabling you to make a warily swift recrossing of the Military Road to reunite with the National Trail – which otherwise progresses from the early departure point in harmony with the Wall ditch, latterly crossing it to come close to the roadside wall.

The wall-side path next encounters the poorly protected northern walls of Milecastle 33; walk respectfully over and avoid disturbing the remnant walls (see also the warning about cattle along this stretch of the Trail above). The Trail eventually parts company with the wall and runs on to pass the isolated turret 33b, thereafter passing on stone flags the walled copse containing Milecastle 34.

From here there is no Wall ditch; advance to a kissing gate, passing turret 34a on the right to pass a cottage. Cross an open track, pressing on to enter the woodland via a hand gate. A lovely contrast to the largely open pasture trail, the Path comes close to the outhouse walls of Sewingshields Farm before exiting the wood at a hand gate.

Follow on, climbing easily beside a series of low sections of Wall to Milecastle 35, reaching the Ordnance Survey column that marks the summit of **Sewingshields Crags**. The ridge-top path leads to a field wall and follows this down into the dip, going through a hand gate then rising by King's Wicket onto the crest of King's Hill.

The ridge-wall roller coaster continues. Please remember that the Trail is supposed to be a 'braided route'; walkers are asked to spread the load on the path by varying their walking line. Avoid following the pencil-thin path that has developed on the way down and up over the next crest of Clew Hill and on to Kennel Crags. Advance to a ladder stile into the woodland and step over the wall stile at its junction, with a fine stretch of consolidated Wall running down into the Knag Burn valley. Switch through the hand gate at the Roman gateway and rise beside the Wall to go under the walls of **Housesteads Roman Fort** (see 'Vercovicium Roman Fort', above) to a ladder stile onto the actual Wall. For the one and only time you can walk along the top of the Wall through the pine grove of Housesteads Wood, although it is kinder to the historic relic not to.

Emerging at a kissing gate, advance by Milecastle 37 and step down through the next gap to then climb the flags onto Cuddy's Crags, with its renowned view back to Housesteads Crags. Rapishaw Gap, the next notch in the ridge, is abrupt, causing the Path to veer left to find easier ground before coming back to a Wall-side ladder stile to meet the Pennine Way.

The Path traverses the gently undulating ridge of Hotbank Crags beside the Clayton-reconstructed Roman Wall, and comes down to Hotbank Farm, passing through the compound of Milecastle 38 by kissing gates on stone flags. The ensuing passage leads to a right-hand bend in the replacement

Looking west from Hotbank Crags

wall then via a kissing gate onto the farm access track in Milking Gap.

Cross the near ladder stile and continue in the company of the Wall, passing up through the conifer plantation to emerge onto the impressive top of Highshield Crags. The path zigzags down steps to slip over the Wall in Sycamore Gap and climbs the facing flight of stone steps onto the hilltop of Mons Fabricius. 'Skip down' easier steps through Castle Nick, climbing again to look back at the classic Wall scenery.

Following on with a rubble bank to a ladder stile, ascend onto the skyline of

Highshield Crags from Mons Fabricius

Peel Crags beside Clayton Wall. From a recessed hand gate descend steps via a wall stile into Peel Gap, stone flagging again ensuring dry feet, before climbing to join a gravel path to a hand gate with **Steel Rigg** car park on the right. Keep forward to a kissing gate onto the road. (See 'Once and Twice Brewed', at the end of Stage 5, for information about nearby facilities.)

STAGE 7
Brocolitia to Portgate

Start	Brocolitia Roman Fort
Finish	Portgate
Distance	9½ miles (15km)
Walking time	5¾hr
Refreshments	Newbrough (off-route): The Red Lion (ph); Chesters Roman Fort: Chesters Tearoom; Chollerford: The George Hotel, Riverside Tea Rooms; Humshaugh: The Crown Inn (ph) and village shop; Wall: Hadrian Hotel; Acomb (off-route): The Miners Arms (ph), The Sun Inn (ph), The Queen's Head (ph); Hexham (off-route): variety of hotels, pubs and cafés; Portgate: Errington Coffee House; Corbridge (off-route): variety of hotels, pubs and cafés
Accommodation	Chollerford, Wall, plenty of options in and around Corbridge
Railway link	Hexham

As the Whin Sill recedes, so the Trail revels in the level terrain and far-reaching Northumberland views. The close company of the Wall and vallum hold the theme of the walk by Limestone Corner, from where begins the easy descent to Chesters and Chollerford. A crossing of the North Tyne precedes a steady climb to historic Heavenfield, from where the plateau resumes to Portgate.

▶ The Path breaks from the fort-side fence by the car park wall (were Wall stones used in its construction?). Skirt a shallow quarried hollow with Wall stones also evident in the road-side field wall. A step stile puts the Trail onto the Military Road; carefully cross into the track entrance to High Teppermoor Farm (an enigmatic place name for which there is no satisfactory explanation – although this in itself suggests it is certainly old). Go immediately right over the light fence styleand follow the Wall ditch by a sequence of three ladder stiles.

For 1:25K route map see booklet pages 30–35.

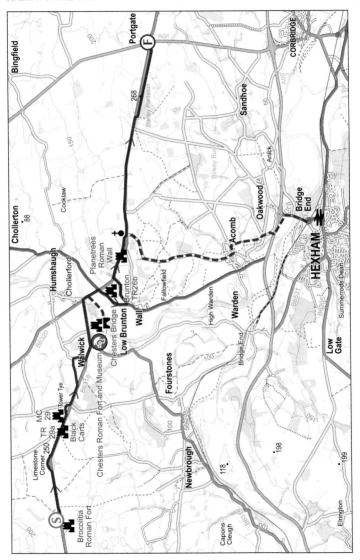

Carrawburgh, on the far side of the road, means 'defended place near rocks' – from the Welsh term *carreg*. The rocks are clearly those cast up by **Roman excavation** of the vallum; one must presume the 18th-century Military Road in this stretch runs upon the Roman Military Way.

After a further stile the Path slips through the Wall ditch, passing the rocky section at **Limestone Corner**.

LIMESTONE CORNER

This is a real misnomer, as the rock is unforgiving Whinstone (dolerite). At the centre of the ditch one particularly large rock catches the eye; spot the nine haphazardly set slots in the top, cut by Roman quarrymen attempting to prize open the massive block. You will see many large irregular stones above that did split, winched up block-and-tackle fashion onto the northern brink.

The vallum had been completed, with the rocks set up on either side of that ditch, but the excavation of the Wall ditch was halted at this point, in spite of its important defensive role. The problems must have been mounting and discontent rampant – had mutiny been threatened? When the order came forward to cease work, there must have been loud cheers and much merriment that night in Brocolitia – perhaps even the officers said their prayers in the Mithraeum at a calamity avoided. Limestone Corner is the most northerly point on Hadrian's Wall.

The view north reveals a spacious scene down into North Tynedale, with Chipchase Castle prominently in view; this Jacobean mansion was built by Cuthbert Heron in 1621 around a 14th-century peel. The eye is drawn over the spreading hills of Redesdale, beyond Bellingham to the Simonside Hills and the distant Cheviots; this is the upland heartland of Northumberland, beloved of discerning travellers, and much of this area has rightly been designated a national park.

This land is brimful of ghostly stories, black deeds, pillage and cruel blood feuds from the centuries of unchecked lawlessness. Henry VIII did not ease affairs with his eagerness to keep the 'pot boiling' among these reiver families. He instructed the Duke of Northumberland to slacken his iron hand and 'to let slip them of Tynedale and Redesdale for the annoyance of Scotland'. Not until the Act of Union in 1707 did this sad and over-prolonged embitterment mellow.

The rocks and ditch quickly abate. The Path keeps by the shallow trace of the Wall ditch, crossing a ladder stile to reach an old Ordnance Survey column amid the untidy evidence of Wall robbing – although this could equally be the result of lax works from the days of Ministry of Works contractors gathering stone for their consolidation rebuild.

Brush by the invasive gorse by two neat sections of consolidated Wall. Cross the minor road (to Simonburn) by facing wall stiles, and continue down by the fine stretch of consolidated Wall, including Turret 29a with its Broad Wall wings indicating that it was built in advance of the Wall. ◄

Notice the slots and curved groove in the slab footing, betraying wear from a heavy door hinge.

Stubborn stone in the ditch at Limestone Corner with failed notches

140

Roman Wall at Black Carts

Drift to the right-hand corner and cross the lane to Black Carts Farm by facing kissing gates. (The farm name means 'sour peaty soil', in contrast with Green Carts, which means 'sweet or fertile soil'. The term 'carts' comes from 'ceart', meaning 'rocky land'.) Keep beside the roadside wall, passing above the earthen remains of **Milecastle 29**, sorely exposed to farm stock damage.

A hand gate gives entry into a fenced passage; step through the Wall ditch and then over the stile. Continue on stone flags, keeping the Wall close right and curving round beside the conifer copse to meet the road at a verge parking space at **Tower Tye**.

Tower Tye means 'boundary peel' – the present dwelling, set plumb on the line of Hadrian's Wall, was presumably constituted from a previous rebuild of stout Wall stone. This, in turn, may have replaced an earlier timber dwelling, possibly set into the remains of Milecastle 29. This spot is the crossing of an old drove route and there are Roman marching camps immediately to the south on Walwick Fell.

A mile south of here is Carr Edge Plantation, with its memorial to Robert Baden Powell's very first Boy Scout holiday camp in 1908. Only eight years previously, during the Boer War, General Baden Powell had distinguished himself at the defence of Mafeking. The reception area at the George Hotel at Chollerford has some interesting allied pictures and letters on display.

Cross over to the ladder stile and continue in the pasture beside the Military Road. Cross a further ladder stile, and as the next field draws to an end, veer half-left by the old limestone quarry set into the field to reach a ladder stile where the Wall ditch comes through the open pasture. Follow on with the field-edge path to cross a light fence-stile, bearing slightly left to come to a projecting corner with a double-fenced horse paddock. Walk alongside the old walled garden of Walwick Hall Hotel and by the horse paddocks to a ladder stile onto the minor road.

Turn right to reach the Military Road in **Walwick** (pronounced 'wolik'). Immediately left stands Walwick House, unashamedly built of Roman Wall stone.

Anyone wise enough to own a current copy of the *Handbook to the Wall*, edited by Prof David Breeze, will have seen the illustration of a print from 1862, which shows the Wall's foundation as the road core climbing the hill, with **Walwick House** as the backdrop, two gentlemen in top hats and a walking stick considering the Wall remains – which will still be there, encased in tarmac.

The view from this spot is grand and includes both the North and South Tyne valleys and Warden Hill, crowned with an Iron Age hill fort – the largest in northern England, thought to have been something of a fulcrum retreat most actively used prior to the arrival of the Romans. The last dwelling on the left with arched windows, as you leave the hamlet, was once a smithy.

The Trail follows the roadside footway; you may now forge down the hill to pass the grand stable block (former stud) and the twin lions at the private entrance to the Chesters estate. But unless time is a concern, most definitely do not pass the entrance to English Heritage's **Chesters Roman Fort and Museum** site, as it's a fascinating site and Roman collection. (It's also a bus stop on the AD122 route.)

CILURNUM ROMAN FORT AND CHESTERS MUSEUM

Strongroom at Cilurnum Roman Fort

This is a famous spot for Wall pilgrims, with its Clayton connection. The overwhelming majority of exhibits derive from along the great Whin Sill ridge to the Cumberland border, have survived only because of John Clayton's committed, enlightened and enthusiastic preservation of the Wall.

From the site reception (official National Trail Passport stamping post), make your first port of call the purpose-built fort museum, which is full of stones and artefacts to excite the mind; the inscriptions constitute our formal records from the age of the Roman Wall. Notice the inscribed stone casually lying on the ground at the entrance: sawn from a Roman quarry face on Written Crag, Fallowfield Fell, it refers to Flavius Carantinus.

Advance along the fenced passage to make a detailed scrutiny of Cilurnum Roman Fort, its portions crisply defined by fences within a greater enclosure. Cattle graze at liberty in the park, perhaps ruminating on the paradox of humans thus corralled. The fort rests in an agreeably pastoral setting beside the tree-shaded River North Tyne: clearly in view to the south is Warden Hill Iron Age hill fort, brought under the empire's control.

In its design Cilurnum breaks the mould of Wall forts, which are normally seven miles apart in exposed situations, and is unusual in that the Wall meets the fort plumb in the middle. Its special function was to serve as a cavalry garrison – hence the appropriateness of the impressive Vanbrugh baroque courtyard block across the road from Chesters House.

In 1978 an altar inscribed 'ala aug b virt appel' was discovered, identifying a cavalry called Augusta for Valour – the first regiment to occupy the fort. The Second Cavalry Regiment of Asturians succeeded, and were stationed here for 200 years, during which time they would have lost all trace of their Spanish origins, although the fort's name Cilurnum derives from their northern Spanish tribal name, Cilurnigi.

Touring the site, one quickly recognises that the spacious interior allowed for a generosity in the proportions of the buildings. The outline of the fort is poorly represented in the reconstruction; of the central features, only the north-east barracks, the headquarters building with strongroom and the commanding officer's residence remain. John Clayton is known to have found, and promptly backfilled, other elements which appear to have included granaries, workshops and stables. The gates are the exception to the curtain wall deficiency, with both east and west exiting unusually north of the Wall (which is visible).

Descending towards the river, pass a fragment of Wall as the ground begins to swell, forming the ramp for the great bridge carrying the Military Way high over the river. The second bridge, built circa AD208 during the reign of Septimius Severus, was considered to have been the single most impressive component of the entire Wall system. It carried the Military Way, flanked by a parapet decorated with columns and altars.

Perhaps the most fascinating component of the site today is the bathhouse suite, complete with robe niches (or did the seven alcoves hold deities?) and evidence of plaster still clinging to the inner walls. There is a separately accessed platform providing a superb view across the North Tyne to the eastern bridge abutments. You may roam no further in this amiable place; backtrack to the reception and onto the roadside footway.

The footway comes to the roundabout, with the attractions of the Riverside Tea Rooms and the George Hotel to tempt you from crossing **Chollerford Bridge**; you may also be lured north into Humshaugh, where there is a village shop and The Crown Inn. The George Hotel, a former coaching inn, stands at an important fork in the way: northwards the road leads to Bellingham, Kielder, Redesdale, Carter Bar and on to Hawick and Jedburgh in Scotland, while the Military Road formed the pre-railway coaching link from Carlisle to Newcastle.

The refuges on Chollerford Bridge (Chollerford means 'ford in a gorge') are a real blessing as there is not much room for pedestrians and traffic. They also give you the chance to gaze into the river, the downstream weir ensuring a great body of water upstream of the bridge to encourage birdlife. ▶

The weir, a popular haunt of grey heron, was built to provide a head of water to power a corn mill on the Chesters Estate.

The George Hotel at Chollerford

Detour to Chesters Bridge

Immediately after the Chollerford Bridge, pass through the hand gate on the right with an intriguing, weighted shutting device. Follow the rather fussily restricted fenced approach path beside the old North Tyne Railway, which ran from Hexham to Bellingham (pronounced bell'in'jum). The Roman bridge abutments and stem Wall lie in a beautifully embowered and seldom-visited situation.

There were two bridges, the earlier footbridge superseded by a grander structure sporting a chariot way. There are two interpretative boards offering substantial information. Notable features include a Roman phallus repelling the evil eye (a common device on the Wall), and the Roman crane emplacement used to lift the massive limestone blocks with their Lewis-hole slots. Pier masonry dredged from the river lies adjacent.

Look through the trees for a view of the magnificent Chesters bathhouse across the river in the parkland of Chesters House. The river name Tyne suggests 'the forked river', like the tines of a pitchfork, from the meeting of the two main tributaries – North and South Tyne – downstream of this spot near Hexham.

Retrace your steps to return to Chollerford Bridge.

Follow the footway from Chollerford Bridge, noting the railway station on the left, converted into a private dwelling. At the Brunton Watermill crossroads turn right, keeping to the footway.

Roman Wall enthusiasts will relish the opportunity to visit **Brunton Turret 26b**, which includes a fine stretch of Wall – enjoy it now as there are precious few portions remaining east of this spot. The turret's construction suggests it was only partially built when the decision to narrow the Wall was made, and as such it was one of the last turrets to be built (bearing in mind that the turrets and milecastles were constructed in advance of the Wall).

The A6079 footway marches on towards the enchanting village of Wall, set around a green with several bastle-conversion cottages – home of the Hadrian Hotel – but at the old road lay-by, just short of the village, carefully cross the road into the byroad. This leads towards the Military Road; only paces short, bear right into the woodland strip, where dog's mercury might be found (an indicator of old woodland). At the top cross a ladder stile and continue up the pasture to a further ladder stile spanning a field wall to reach the midfield **Planetrees** stretch of Roman Wall, some 120ft (36m) long.

It was here in 1801 that William Hutton beseeched Henry Tulip, a farmer, not to take any more **stones** from the Wall for his new farmhouse. The plea went unheeded. A 600ft (183m) section, some 7ft high, was systematically dismantled, although mercifully a precious portion was left. In its midst, miraculously surviving, is the point where the initial 10ft Broad Wall changes to the 8ft Narrow Wall, and from this point westward the structure reflects Hadrian's Narrow Wall.

Planetrees 'Broad Wall' transition: the culvert in the foreground enabled the Wall's course to cope with frequent wet conditions

147

Although much of it has the Broad Wall foundations, such evidence clearly shows that these foundations were laid prior to the main building process. This point is significant as it shows how far the Wall-building process had progressed before this major time- and labour-saving decision was made.

Keep up the pasture towards Planetrees Farm. ◄ Note the circular 'gin-gang' among the farm buildings: in this device a harnessed horse walked around in a circle, with gearing transferring the power to a corn mill, which ground oats and barley for stock feed.

There is no present evidence of plane trees growing in the vicinity, these being distinguished by their height and maple-like leaves.

Find steps onto the verge of the Military Road; traverse with care, as traffic can come hurtling down at this point! Cross the fence stile immediately to the right at the old limestone quarry access. Follow the roadside hedge, via the ladder stile, and rise up the pasture to the stile beside a holly bush. Continue to a ladder stile over a wall corner, marching on to the Heavenfield Cross beside the gate access from the lay-by. **St Oswald in Lee Church** lies over to the left of an island, at the site of the Battle of Heavenfield, AD633.

ST OSWALD IN LEE

Do visit the little island church of St Oswald in Lee over the molehill-mounded open pasture. The wall and much of the church fabric was constructed from Wall stone, although the church was completely rebuilt in 1737. Take a moment to look inside and note the large family hatchment on the wall – it is black, confirming the husband died after his wife. Observe the Roman altar a little under 5ft high beside the font – the lettering has gone, but its height suggests that it belonged to an officer of high rank.

Within the anteroom there is an exhibition prepared by the monks of Lindisfarne. A hand-held board shows the content of the wonderfully expansive view obtained from the north side of the churchyard. The church, where once Roman scouts trod, is the spiritual home of the Northumberland Girl Guide Association.

The earliest church lay close to the rallying point of the momentous battle of AD635 between Oswald, the Christian King of Northumbria,

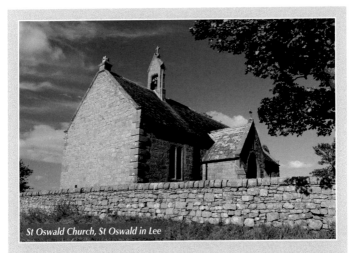

St Oswald Church, St Oswald in Lee

and Cadwallon, the heathen leader of British tribes. Prior to this event Northumbria had been divided into two kingdoms, Deira and Bernicia. Deira was ruled by Oswald's uncle, Edwin, converted to Christianity by Paulinus in AD627, while Bernicia was ruled by Eanfrid, Oswald's brother.

Cadwallon made war with Northumbria, confronting and killing Edwin, his son Osric and Eanfrid, the last two having both renounced Christianity. When Oswald became king he rallied forces and raised a rude wooden cross as a standard, confronting his adversaries south of the Tyne. The Venerable Bede refers to the act of raising the cross as being the first sign of Christianity in Bernicia. Cadwallon was chased and killed on the banks of the Rowley Burn to the south of Hexham.

Tradition holds this to have been an important moment for the flowering of Christianity in Britain: the church erected here by the monks of Hexham Abbey became the fountainhead for the proliferation of places of worship throughout the kingdom and beyond. On his death Oswald's head was placed in St Cuthbert's coffin in Durham Cathedral, thus confirming the high esteem in which he was held. A final detail – as you leave the churchyard, note the stepped horse-mounting stand, harking back to the days when the preacher and much of the congregation arrived on horseback.

*Walkers beside
the Wall ditch east
of St Oswald's*

To archeologically
trained eyes this
section is fascinating,
the Path running
over a variety of low
mounds from the
Roman excavation of
the defensive ditch.

From the Heavenfield Cross lay-by the Trail advances inside the field beside the main road to a hand gate. Pass on in front of the terrace at St Oswald's Hill (tearoom, closed on Mondays) via steps to a hand gate.

Entering the Wall ditch, slip left through the gorse-choked hollow to a hand gate. Advance within pasture close by the Wall ditch via a ladder stile beneath a stately beech tree. Continue with the Wall ditch; the Military Road is lined with fine mature beech trees on its south side, adding to the landscape's elegance. ◄

After a small ladder stile and Keepwick farm-track crossing, the ditch is shallow and marshy at first then very deep, with some fine ditch extraction mounding to be seen. Coming to the Errington Hill farm road, cross a curious field boundary bank and climb the steps to a wall stile at the farm access cattle grid.

Cross the Military Road to the recessed wall stile. The Path is clearly marked, leading to a ladder stile entering a rough strip close to the vallum. Another ladder stile puts you onto the road at a minor junction with the Military Road. Continue within a plantation, an open section initially nicely stone-flagged to a track crossing to where a track intervenes.

Here, following the ravages of the northerly Storm Arwen wind in 2022, the trail has been rerouted right with the lane. After some 180m a waymark post points left over a broken wall into the birch woodland of Stanley Plantation. The new route weaves through a delightful ground foliage of bilberry and heather. The path comes by a cleared and replanted section to reach a gate into pasture. Turn left with the wall to a hand gate, with the vallum ditch ahead, partially beset in gorse. However, keep immediately right by a second hand gate and follow the fence by two gates to the minor road. Turn left and right by the green gate/ladder stile, with the diminished vallum ditch beside a fence. Two further ladder stiles lead into the car park of Errington Coffee House at Portgate.

The **pub**'s name derives from the local landowning family whose Victorian Gothic home was Beaufront Castle, above Hexham. Several years ago it was seriously damaged by a fire; refurbished, it makes a lovely haven for travellers and Trail-walkers alike. The pub provides wonderful food and real ale – you can eat on the premises or avail yourself of the service for fast-moving walkers (ring ahead on 01434 672 250 to collect made-to-order sandwiches).

Errington Coffee House, from the site of the Roman gateway arch

151

PORTGATE

The A68 follows the line of a major prehistoric trade route, far older than the Roman Dere Street. This meeting place became known in Saxon times as 'the port gate' because of its regional importance as a place of barter. It was later the site of Stagshaw Fair, the largest open-air livestock market in England. Where the roundabout now stands, the Romans built a great fortified gate; out of kilter with the tidy order of Wall structures, it was designed specifically to marshal this convergence of age-old roads.

Writing in 1732, John Horsley stated that the Roman fortified gate in the Wall was still in situ. To what forlorn height it had languished by that time we have no record, but it is yet another stark reminder of the cruel loss of an important component of the Wall's structure. It was located in the space between the inn and traffic roundabout; this was a significant Roman control on what in later years was termed Dere Street.

This arterial military road stemmed from York, the northern command base for the Roman province. It strode north, entering the frontier zone at Corbridge (Roman Coria, until fairly recently known as Corstopitum) some three miles south of this spot. Advancing from here, it proceeded northbound for Risingham, High Rochester and Chew Green, where it then crossed the Cheviot Hills bound for Melrose (Trimontium).

Anyone who has admired the famous 'Scott's View' will know of the Eildon hills above that town, reflected in the Roman name for the fort (Trimontium means 'place at the three hills'). Why, one might reasonably ask, was Halton Chesters (Onnum) Roman fort not installed here? This is a far more strategic spot, in stark contrast to the fort's actual location, which overlooks and to modern eyes appears to command nothing.

WESTBOUND: PORTGATE TO BROCOLITIA

Depart the Coffee House car park over the ladder stile and head up the field, precisely upon the shallow course of the vallum, crossing two ladder stiles to reach a minor road. Turn left to reach a gate on the right. Now advance with the field-bounding fence to the right, passing through a second galvanised field gate to reach a hand gate. Immediately turn left through the adjacent hand gate and follow on with the wall right to reach a gate into the wooded enclosure of **Stanley Plantation**. Advance beside and then through the gorgeous birchwood to reach a green lane and turn right.

Bear right and follow on with the roadside wall; the Path is in almost permanent shadow, hence expect the ground to be slippery in places. Crossing a track, the Path resumes as a fenced passage to duly cross a minor road by facing ladder stiles. Advance via a further ladder stile to reach a recessed wall stile, and then carefully cross the Military Road.

Step over the wall stile left of the cattle grid, where the open access road to Errington Hill Farm departs. Descend the abrupt flight of steps and stride west beside the Wall ditch – it's quite deep after the ash tree. As the Wall ditch dwindles in a marsh, cross a track then a ladder stile and continue to a further ladder stile sheltering under an aged beech.

Trail threading delightfully through the birch wood adjacent to Stanley Plantation

After the next hand gate, veer left; gorse engulfs the Wall ditch. Pass via a second hand gate, through a kissing gate and onto the verge in front of St Oswald's Tearoom. The next hand gate gives access to the pasture; continue in harmony with the road to the wooden cross at Heavenfield. St Oswald's Church rests on an island in the pasture and can be accessed by the open track (see 'St Oswald in Lee', above). The Trail keeps forward to a ladder stile then goes down by a fence-stile, now in a pasture, to a ladder stile over a wall; follow the field-edge path to a fence stile at an old quarry lane access. Carefully cross the Military Road, stepping down into the facing field below Planetrees Farm. Turn right to pass an important remnant of Hadrian's Wall, which shows the transition from Broad Wall to Narrow Wall.

Descend the pasture via a ladder stile to enter the woodland strip at a low ladder stile. Meeting the road at the foot, go left, following the minor road towards the village of Wall. On meeting the main road, cross to follow the footway right, to the crossroads, turning left (still on a footway) beside the Military Road leading to **Chollerford Bridge**, which spans the River North Tyne. From the roundabout bear left by the Riverside Tearoom, following the footway, and pass the entrance to the English Heritage **fort and museum** (see 'Cilurnum Roman Fort and Chesters Museum' above). Keep with the footway, rising to the hamlet of **Walwick**.

Mithreum in the Meggie's Dene Burn valley at Brocolitia

Directly after Walwick House go right with the minor road, seeking a ladder stile directly after a private entrance to horse paddocks. Follow the field-path, passing an old walled garden; as the fence ends, veer half-left to a fence stile and advance to a ladder stile with the Wall ditch ahead. Drift leftward in the pasture to come beside the roadside wall, rising to a ladder stile at a staggered crossroads. Turn right, cross to the verge parking and follow the path from the step, signed 'Black Carts' (with a Green Carts B&B sign).

The Path, which includes some stone flags, leads to a fenced crossing of the Wall ditch beside Milecastle 29. Follow the roadside wall to cross the access track to Black Carts Farm via facing kissing gates. Rise to come beside a fine length of Roman Wall and cross the minor road by facing wall stiles. Continue with further instalments of taller Roman Wall, brushing through encroaching gorse to pass the Ordnance Survey column.

Cross a ladder stile and pass the unfinished Limestone Corner section of Wall ditch (see 'Limestone Corner', above). After the fence stile continue beside the Wall ditch; there are three further ladder stiles, then at a fence stile enter into the access lane to High Teppermoor. Go left and carefully cross the Military Road. Stepping down into the pasture, go right to reach **Brocolitia** car park and Roman fort site.

STAGE 8
Portgate to Heddon-on-the-Wall

Start	Portgate
Finish	Heddon-on-the-Wall
Distance	10 miles (16km)
Walking time	6hr
Refreshments	Wallhouses: The Tea Room on the Wall, Vallum Farm, The Robin Hood Inn (ph); Wylam (off-route): The Fox and Hounds (ph), The Boathouse (ph); Heddon-on-the-Wall: The Three Tuns (ph), The Swan (ph), Spar garage
Accommodation	Wallhouses, East Wallhouses, Matfen, Newton, Stamfordham, Harlow Hill, Ovingham, Wylam, Heddon-on-the-Wall
Railway link	Corbridge

Still in cahoots with the Military Road, the Trail cuts through an undulating fertile countryside with only the Wall ditch for company – although the stage ends on a high with a fine length of exhibition Wall.

▶ From Portgate the Path crosses the A68, passing the old garage and following a footway on the tapering verge from the roundabout to step down a ladder stile into the pasture on the right. Proceed via a fence stile to a flag-footbridge and ladder stile; ascend with the small plantation on the left, coming along the edge of an arable field to a ladder stile to enter the **Halton Chesters** enclosure, placidly grazed by sheep.

For 1:25K route map see booklet pages 35–40.

At your feet, the shallow undulations hint at unidentified underlying features of **Onnum Roman Fort**, which lay either side of the Military Road. If you think there's not much to see, then take a look at the geophysical survey illustrated in the current

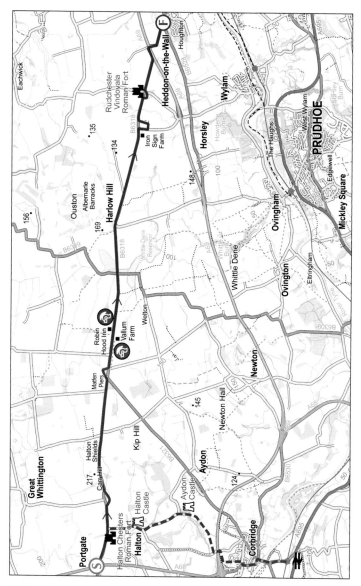

Eachwick

Great Whittington

Portgate

S

Halton Chesters Roman Fort
Halton
Halton Castle

Aydon Castle

Aydon

124

Corbridge

A68

A695

B6530

Newton

Newton Hall

145

Whittle Dene

Ovington

Etringham

River Tyne

B6309

Mickley Square

PRUDHOE

West Wylam

The Haughs

Eggewell

Ovingham

Horsley

100

A69

Wylam

Shelley Burn

Howden Burns

148

Welton

Whittle Dene Resevoir

100

Kip Hill

Halton Shields

Carr Hill

217

156

169

Ouston

Albemarle Barracks

Harlow Hill

134

135

B6318

B6309

Robin Hood Inn

Vallum Farm

Matfen Piers

Iron Sign Farm

Rudchester Vindovala Roman Fort

Heddon-on-the-Wall

Houghton

B6528

A69

50

A69

F

Down Hill vallum from Onnum Roman Fort

edition of the *Handbook to the Roman Wall* and be amazed. Now known as Halton Chesters, this cavalry fort, 4.3 acres in extent, lies seven miles west of Vindovala. That it was built by the VI Legion Augusta is verified by the stone plaque inserted above the west gate.

In 1936 a weathered building inscription was found face down in front of the west gate central pier, recording work by the Sixth Legion under Emperor Hadrian and his governor Aulus Platorius Nepos. A further inscription, referring to subsequent work by the II Legion during the reign of Antoninus Pius, now resides in the Museum of Antiquities in Newcastle.

The name Onnum is Celtic for 'water', and may simply refer to a sure supply of water, in contrast to Aesica (Great Chesters), with its seven-mile-long feeder aqueduct. One unusual feature was the bath-house, which lay within the vallum, close to the fort.

As you leave the Halton Chesters site, your attention will be drawn to the ditch-incised hill ahead. This is Down Hill, where the vallum has survived to a considerable extent and the Trail sets course to inspect it.

A GOOD 'CORIA' MOVE

Corbridge Roman Site Museum (English Heritage), with granary building floor

The importance of Corbridge is more than for accommodation and railway connections, it has major Roman significance, too. Walkers are encouraged to break from the National Trail at Onnum Roman Fort (Halton Chesters) to admire the town and specifically visit Coria Roman Fort at the Corbridge Roman Site. Walk down the open parkland drive, and go via a hand gate beside the cattle grid, passing a bungalow lodge. Keep with the road left of the tall hedge and after the pond access, passing below Halton parish church. You are encouraged to step up the church path and look inside; also at the west wall of the church find a quirky topiary yew pig from where there is a fine view of Halton Castle. Although not open to the public, this provides a fine perspective of this sturdy, high-chimneyed house set into a castellated peel tower – defensive medieval domesticity. Follow on with the road, keeping forward at the junction, guided by the brown English Heritage sign for Aydon Castle. This peaceful country road arrives at the car parking, where the road swings left. Keep forward to come to the outer bailey walls of the castle, beyond the cottages and farmyard.

Aydon Castle's situation is stunning, and it is often cited as the finest defended medieval manor house in England. In years gone by it has been a popular set for such films as *Ivanhoe*. The main body of the property is unadulterated 14th-century work, built by a Suffolk merchant who had cause to rue his adventure north. The Middle Ages in the Middle Marches were no place for peaceable people; Scottish raids and local reiving made farming life precarious and costly.

Aydon is perched upon a blunt bluff above a tight bend of Cor Burn. Go through the wooden gate to the right of the great entry doors, with its blue bridleway waymark arrow. The path swings down a gully into the wooded dell to cross the obvious footbridge, keeping straight on, rising in the woodland, coming by a field on the left before bending right to reach a hand gate exiting the woodland. Follow the popular pasture path straight on; this leads to a hand gate. Keep forward with fine views towards Hexham, identified by the smoke of Eggers timber factory. The path comes by a fence and switches sides at a hand gate and swings left to reach a hand gate beside a stock handling pen, entering a green lane. This leads down to a gate/stile into Milkwell Lane. Pass under the A69 flyover and go immediately right with the confined path, with the Hippingstones Field left. The path bends away from the road embankment; take the first fork left onto the tarmac path beside the new housing known as Stanegate Manor and Roman Field. This becomes a confined path again after the Middle School, ultimately coming down to St Helen's Lane. Go right to Stagshaw Road and stagger left and right with Trinity Terrace; this is Corchester Lane, which leads to the Roman Site within half a mile.

St Andrew's Church in Corbridge has a complete Roman arch, from the Roman town, incorporated into its original construction. On the west side of the church are the 14th-century King's Ovens – the townsfolk had to bake bread communally as dough was taxed. Dere Street is curiously and erroneously named Watling Street in the town.

Corbridge has a charm all its own and holds a pride of place in the Tyne valley, hence the pleasure one experiences in strolling in its environs, not the least its riverside paths. However, is has something unique to offer – the Roman town of Coria. Although apparently well removed from the town, the Roman fort and town of Coria extended to some 24 hectares, almost butting up to the modern settlement. It is worth noting that only some seven per cent of the Roman settlement has been revealed; you might judge archaeologists would just love to dig below the surface of the adjacent arable field. Close by, but unseen, a massive Roman bridge, built upon 10 piers, spanned the Tyne (many of the dredged stones are piled up on the south bank of the river); the river has drifted south from its Roman course.

In the north bank, footings of a triumphal gateway have been found: this originally stood over Dere Street, the road from York (Eboracum), and proclaimed southern entry into this evidently important military town. Pre-dating Hadrian's Wall, Coria is situated at the eastern end of the Stanegate, the Military Way from Carlisle.

In this area ridge and furrow abounds, the curved line betraying ox-ploughing, and there is considerable evidence of former quarrying ahead and to the right.

Pass the stone entrance to Halton Castle drive and proceed to a fence-stile, then go along the fenced passage via stiles to a wall stile into pasture. ◄ Bear half-right and cross the open track, ascending onto the brow of Down Hill and passing the stone Trail marker on the brow. The line of the Wall slices through the plantation over the field wall to the left.

This is the last really good exhibition of the **vallum** heading east. Notice its angular engineered turns ahead, a characteristic throughout its course. Just as the Romans liked straight or direct roads, so they preferred sharp turns rather than wavy lines; they tended to fight the contours as if to dominate the landscape. There are also 'crossings' in this section – gaps where the ditch was infilled during a later Roman period, when the tight rein of the military zone was relaxed; they served to funnel all movement through the Wall to the milecastle gates and, in this locality, the great Dere Street frontier control back at Portgate.

On a recent visit the author was reminded of a perennial issue caused by free access to such historic sites and the general availability of metal

Field-edge path leading to Vallum Farm

detectors, having met someone with such a device beavering away in the deep vallum ditch, seemingly oblivious to the illegality of what he was doing. He had unearthed horseshoes, nails and gun cartridges with a modest spade. Incidents of this nature should be reported to the English Heritage officer based at Bessie Surtees House in Newcastle.

The Path drifts leftward via successive wall stiles onto the verge. Cross the B6318 to a casual lay-by opposite the entrance to Carr Hill Farm. Follow the cinder path along the northern verge of the Military Road, passing the hamlet of **Halton Shields**. Note the phone box short of the old schoolhouse.

The **hamlet name** harbours more than you might suspect – Shields means 'a cluster of shepherds' summer dwellings', while Halton comes from the Saxon *haw-hyll*, meaning 'look-out hill'. Carr Hill is here a contraction of 'rocky hill', matching Carrawburgh Farm east of Brocolitia Roman Fort – which is curious as there is no hint of surface stone.

At the invisible site of Milecastle 20 the Trail crosses the Military Road. It is here that the route of St Oswald's Way joins the Hadrian's Wall Path, from where it continues westward (backwards, as far as you're concerned) to Heavenfield.

St Oswald's Way (stoswaldsway.com) came into being as a recreational route in 2007. The 96-mile (154km) route connects Heavenfield with the Holy Island of Lindisfarne through lovely Northumbrian countryside. The Way was originally devised by Embleton Church Council and then implemented by a partnership of public sector organisations led by Alnwick District Council. It is now managed by a small voluntary team, the St Oswald's Way Management Group, assisted by bodies, including Northumberland County Council, and by over

30 volunteer rangers, who help to look after the route. (A description of the Way is given in detail in *Walking St Oswald's Way and Northumberland Coast Path* by Rudolf Abraham, Cicerone Press.)

At a minor road junction, cross the wall stile opposite and continue alongside arable cropped fields on a fenced passage set below the roadside hedge bank, looking out for the odd surviving Wall stone at its base. A hand gate brings the Path to a road crossing at **Matfen Piers Gate**, with the Castle Morpeth District sign and entry into Hadrian's Wall Country indicating from whence we came.

The two Saxon village names on the road sign are intriguing: Matfen means 'Matta's peat marsh', while Ingoe means 'Inga's hill'.

The ball-topped stone pillars herald the approach road to Matfen Hall, now a country house hotel and spa complete with a 27-hole golf course. ◀ A wall stile gives entry to the confines of the Wall ditch, rampant with wildflower colour in summer since the trees were felled. The adjacent pasture is ribbed with curved ox-ploughing.

Another wall stile places you into a pasture; go left on an enlarged circumnavigation of the Wallhouses Farm to avoid the trauma of walking along the Military Road. Kissing gates and fenced passages largely shield the newly established path from encounters with farm stock.

Regaining the line of the Wall ditch at a kissing gate, stride on through the lightly wooded way, encountering a small fence stylepartway along, to emerge at a wall stile at Moorhouses road end. You might see a 'Hadrian Pet Hotel' panel here – quite appropriate, as the whole Wall thing was Hadrian's pet idea – although one might suspect he would have opted for Matfen Hall!

The bungalow 'Deneside' was once a petrol filling station.

Another wall stile and a quiet fenced passage beside the field leads to a footbridge over the dry Wall ditch; the Military Road verge is for a few paces unavoidable. ◀

Before going through the hand gate and down the steps into the depths of the Wall ditch, you should not miss the opportunity of visiting **Vallum Farm** only a short distance further along the main road on the right. More than a tearoom, more than a food hall, this is a real artisan business with a great connection with local producers – and still a working dairy farm. Vallum Farm creates its own cheese and scrumptious ice cream: a Trail treat! There is also an unofficial stamping station (see Appendix A). The impressive Wall-wide graphic in the main building was created by the now defunct Hadrian's Trust. The vallum can be detected passing through the field either side of the farm buildings.

Returning to the task in hand, the Trail leads on through the Wall ditch via a hand gate to pass in front of the **Robin Hood Inn** (which features an al fresco stamping station). After the Old Repeater House slip left, via the decking, and step down into the Wall ditch via hand gates and plank bridges along the field edge. Continue down by stone flags to cross the Stamfordham road into the road barrier passage over the linking channel bridge, in the midst of the **Whittle Dene Reservoir ponds**.

The **reservoirs**, set on various stepped levels, are popular with vagrant waterfowl. Watch out for young or female smew (a small sea duck with a red head) as well as grebes (great and little both nest here). Anglers, too, are given licence to enjoy these shining levels. Whittle means 'the hill with the large expanse of dry land' – but the dams have sorted that out good and proper! A gate gives access to the water compound nature reserve, heading up the fenced passage to the viewing hide: worth a pause to ponder on the movement of birds.

Through the next hand gate the fenced passage continues beside arable land, rising steadily to a wall-squeeze and along a rough patch to cross over a wall stile onto the road verge at **Harlow Hill**.

Inevitably, you will look intently at the **barns and cottages**, straining your eyes for evidence of Wall stone. (The inverted crescent motif on the cottage

Wall ditch east of Harlow Hill

wall comes from the Duke of Northumberland's crest.) The conversion of the Church of England chapel into a barn seems unfortunate – especially when contrasted with the adaptation of the main farm. 'No Boundaries' self-catering accommodation is on the site of Milecastle 16 (www.harlowhill-MXVI.co.uk).

The Trail wends down a fence-lined roadside verge (note the track to Northside Farm wigwam orchard over the road) to cross the access road to **Albemarle Barracks**.

Three instances of **military heritage** – Roman Wall, post-Jacobite road, and contemporary army camp – combine at what is now the home of the 39th Regiment Royal Artillery. Established in World War 2 to serve as an airfield for the Royal Air Force, it was decommissioned and became a motor racing circuit in the early 1960s. Jackie Stewart won his first race here in 1963, driving a Jaguar E-Type; the following year Jim Clarke presented the races

Ripe wheat beside the Path approaching Iron Sign

prizes, and the year after that racing moved to the Croft Circuit at Dalton-on-Tees.

The Trail continues via hand gates beside arable fields, crossing the Whitchester Farm road to retain its course in harmony with what passes for the Wall ditch, initially on stone flags, becoming quite bush-confined at one point. Clamber over a curious infill mound within the ditch that suggests an old access from the road.

Further hand gates lead on, as a fenced passage, until steps and decking bring the Trail to a careful crossing of the B6318. From the opposing steps continue beside the tall hedge, rising to the top of Eppies Hill. A roadside pathway leads to a minor crossroads; go right, passing the entrance to the former **Iron Sign Farm** (B&B).

The Path embarks on a curious square perambulation, as the chance to create a new section of public right of way in the paddock immediately east of Iron Sign Farm was denied. A sign to the left guides you along a narrow fence-side path, coming back up to the vicinity of the Military Road. Follow the field-edge path

The next pasture field contains ridge and furrow in two directions, the curved element indicative of ox-ploughing.

down to a footbridge over March Burn – which means 'boundary stream'. ◄

Coming up to a hand gate, enter the Rudchester Farm enclosure of **Vindovala Roman Fort**. Go right, skirting the shallow banks of the fort, by an interpretative panel and the farm buildings.

VINDOVALA ROMAN FORT AND MITHRAIC TEMPLE

As the first rural fort out of Newcastle, in an ideal world Vindovala (which means 'the fort with white walls') would make an ideal exhibition fort for visitors to the eastern country end of the Wall system. The fourth fort west of Segedunum, it covered an area of four-and-a-half acres and lies seven Roman miles west of Condercum (Benwell). The Military Road sliced through its middle.

The basic outline of the fort can be seen both to the north, defined by the wooden paddock fencing, and to the south, by the farm buildings. The sturdy sandstone barn would appear to contain a few Roman stones – particularly in its lower courses. The Wall's first serious commentator, J Collingwood Bruce, author of the *Handbook to the Roman Wall*, noted in 1860 that there were fragments of a Roman gravestone on an inside wall of the barn, inscribed with the letters: AVR, RIN, XIT, NIS.

A Mithraic temple has been excavated to the south-east of the fort. There were several temples to the god Mithras along the Wall – the focus of a religious cult. Derived from ancient Persia, the cult was preferred by officers, notably legionaries, although evidently auxiliaries drew inspiration from it too.

It was exclusively masculine in observance, associated with mysterious acts linked to the sacrificial slaying of bulls in a cave, and focused on the eternal battle between light (good) and dark (evil). In its heyday it rivalled Christianity in popularity. Ironically, the present farm name 'Rudchester' inverts the Roman chauvinism, for it translates as 'the former Roman fort now belonging to Rudda' – a feminine Scandinavian name.

Cross the minor road by facing kissing gates, angling half-left through the copse to continue beside the road-side hedge and through a hand gate: note the Roman Wall stone. At the foot go through the hand gate and follow the road verge of the realigned B6318 to the step over the barrier at the top. Go right, crossing the A69 flyover with the road and following the footway up to the Three Tuns crossroads in **Heddon-on-the-Wall**.

> For the last time on the Trail you are beside the **Military Road** constructed in 1747 after the Jacobite Rebellion. It ran from the heart of Newcastle to Sewingshields (en route to Carlisle). With robust symbolism the contracted engineers requisitioned the Wall as hardcore – and why not? It was simply a further example of recycling. The Wall ditch is evident to the left on the road wall. As you look back west, the road stretches out straight as a die with typical military directness.

WESTBOUND: HEDDON-ON-THE-WALL TO PORTGATE

After visiting the English Heritage Roman Wall enclosure (see 'Heddon-on-the-Wall', below), backtrack 60 metres to the National Trail signpost on Towne Gate. Go right, between houses with Chare Bank, coming behind the churchyard and down by the Memorial Garden and Village Hall. Cross the main road by The Three Tuns (public house), following the footway west beside the Military Road.

Cross the A69 road bridge and at the junction go left, stepping over the barrier and descending upon the verge. At the point the Military Road resumes, go through the kissing gate and advance within the pasture beside the road with hints of the remnant Wall. After a hand gate the Path comes into a copse; bear left to cross the minor road via facing hand gates.

Wall stones in roadside bank east of Rudchester

Advance, with the farm buildings of Rudchester close left, to an interpretative board (see 'Vindovala Roman Fort and

Mithraic Temple', above) and then bear right beside the fence to a kissing gate. Proceed beside the roadside hedge, dipping to cross a gated footbridge. The field-edge path rises to be guided left by a fence skirting round the paddocks of Iron Sign.

Encountering a minor road, turn right to come back to the Military Road. Follow the verge path left (the speed camera sign a caution to fleet-footed walkers, perhaps?); coming over the brow, the path switches into the field and follows the hedge downhill. A short flight of wooden steps brings the Trail to the Military Road: cross with care. From the decking stile, head on beside the roadside hedge. After a hand gate the Path runs up within the Wall ditch and is later stone-flagged to a gateway onto a farm lane. Cross over and continue along the field margin to a hand gate, then cross the access road to Albemarle Barracks. Continue via a hand gate in harmony with the Military Road, fenced from the field, to emerge onto the verge at **Harlow Hill**.

Follow the footway when, after the houses, a wall stile invites you off the verge. This leads to a fenced passage beside the hedge, which in turn leads to a hand gate with a reservoir-viewing bird hide close right. Continue to another hand gate and along the road verge, then negotiate the crossroads. The fenced field-side passage resumes, initially stone-flagged.

Continue via hand gates within the field beside the Wall ditch to reach steps onto the decking leading to the road at the Old Repeater House. Follow the verge, passing the Robin Hood Inn to regain the Wall ditch passage at a hand gate.

Climbing stone steps, follow the verge to be guided right over a footbridge spanning the Wall ditch and advance in a fenced passage. Crossing a minor road by facing wall stiles, continue close to the wooded Wall ditch with an intermediate stile leading to a kissing gate; turn right, thereby avoiding the road in front of Wallhouses Farm.

The Path leads by kissing gates and fenced passages, trending left via kissing gates. Keep left to step over a wall stile, re-entering the Wall ditch enclosure. Advance to a wall stile at the **Matfen Piers** road junction.

With great care, cross over the Military Road and slip through the hand gate to continue within the field, fence-confined beside the road. On reaching a road junction, cross the step over the wall and advance along the footway, switching sides at **Halton Shields**.

Beyond the lay-by stay with the verge until directed across the Military Road. Wall stiles lead by a fence passage; then from a fence styleveer part-left onto the brow of Down Hill with its pronounced vallum ditches. Skirt the

Ornate gateway at Onnum Roman Fort (Halton Chesters)

old quarry and cross over a track to reach the right-hand field corner, then cross another wall stile.

The Path continues, fence-confined with stiles, to enter the Halton Chesters Roman Fort site; cross the open estate road at the ornate gateway/ cattle grid (see 'A good 'Coria' move', above). Keep on to a ladder stile, dipping to a further ladder stile and footbridge. Continue via a fence stile to a ladder stile over the wall, which puts the Trail into the broad verge beside the Military Road. Go left to reach the **Portgate** roundabout at the Errington Arms (see 'Portgate' at the end of Stage 7).

STAGE 9
Heddon-on-the-Wall to Newcastle Quayside

Start	Heddon-on-the-Wall
Finish	Newcastle Quayside
Distance	10 miles (16km)
Walking time	6hr
Refreshments	Newburn: Tyne Riverside Country Park (café in visitor centre), The Keelman (ph), The Boathouse Branzino Restaurant; Lemington: community centre café; Newcastle upon Tyne: Quayside – variety of hotels, pubs and cafés
Accommodation	Wide variety of options including Newburn, Swallwell, Blaydon, Jesmond and Quayside
Railway link	Wylam, Newcastle Central

The marvellous eastbound frontier march forsakes the Wall's hypnotism as the Trail metaphorically tumbles into the Tyne valley to accompany Hadrian's Way. This largely trackbed cycleway is a popular social corridor leading to the iconic and vibrant waterfront of the great city of Newcastle upon Tyne. Suddenly, you enter the realm of frequent urban buses shuttling hither and thither, giving you mobility the like of which you will have dreamed of elsewhere on the Trail. Now you can 'head on' and complete the journey in a comfy seat, if you so desire. (Note the author's disapproving frown!)

For 1:25K route map see booklet pages 40–45.

Across the way the handy garage/shop is an alternative for refreshment supplies.

◄ Cross over the road at The Three Tuns public house – for many not so hastily done, as the bar may be of sufficient lure. ◄ Follow the village road ahead, to the right of the memorial gardens. A shortcut may be taken down Heddon Banks on the Trail – however, it is at the cost of a far greater prize: the fine stretch of Roman Wall that lies on the eastern edge of the village.

In front of the village hall go past the white barrier into the narrow pathway of Chare Bank; this emerges into Towne Gate. While the actual Trail is signed right,

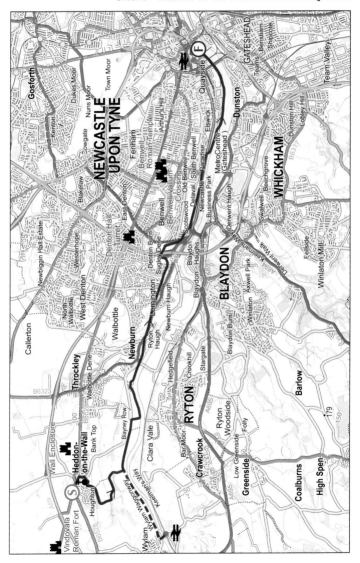

you should not lightly ignore the English Heritage enclosure, which is reached within 150ft (46m) to the left and accessed through a kissing gate and hedged passage.

HEDDON-ON-THE-WALL

After days of green fields, scattered farms and hamlets, Heddon heralds a real change in the character of the Trail. Before you make the transition down to the Tyne-focused final phase of the walk, put aside a little free time to enjoy the village.

The name translates as 'the heather-capped hill on Hadrian's Wall', and here it is seen in glorious isolation, as so often we have witnessed this great statement of the Classical Age. Spin your imagination back across the gulf of 19 centuries to when the Wall was a continuous high stone divide, the northern limit of Roman authority in Britannia. The cattle grazing in the adjoining ridge-and-furrow pasture symbolise the long continuity of civilian life in the intervening centuries.

This, the longest stretch of Broad Wall, mercifully survived quite simply because it veered from the convenient line off Great Hill for the Military Road to avoid the parish church on the hill crest ahead.

With the gorse bank of Great Hill as a backdrop and some evidence of the Wall ditch before us, you can gaze upon a credible length of Wall showing an original kink. It stretches for 330ft (100m) and rises to a maximum of six courses.

A rookery in the nearby beech trees gives a raucous country greeting.

Backtrack along Towne Gate, going by the bus shelter, the timber-built Women's Institute and the Methodist church to The Swan Hotel. Opposite, steps lead to St Andrew's Church, the prominent hilltop situation correctly suggesting a pious place of some antiquity. ◄

Evidence of a religious building on this **exalted site** exists back to AD650; little wonder, then, that the chancel is laden with fine courses of Roman masonry. The dedication hinting to old religious ties with Scotland, the saint is marked elsewhere on or near the Trail – Carlisle and Corbridge for instance, at either end of Stanegate.

*St Andrew's
Church, Heddon*

Before turning left down Heddon Banks by the interpretative board you might wish to inspect the handsome Victrix: a Roman soldier carved from a chestnut tree in Taberna shopping arcade, accessed by a passage behind the Leighs Nursery.

As you descend through the estate, with names such as Trajan Walk and Centurion Way you can have no doubt of the Roman influence. Continue down by Heddon Banks, where several scenically well-favoured houses enjoy a fine Tyne valley view towards Newburn and, to the left, the suburban skyline of Benwell Hill. (Benwell is the location of the lost site of Condercum Roman Fort, although there are two interesting relics to hunt for among the modern housing: a temple and, uniquely, a vallum crossing – both are worth discovering.) The bungalow South Lodge shows exaggerated Mediterranean touches.

The road becomes a track by West Acre. Slipping beneath power lines, the lane bears left from the woodland of Heddon Common, down by a cottage and via a gate into a wooded, partially cobbled lane lined with holly to the rear of Close House.

Built in 1779 in the classical style for the Berwicke family, successful Merchant Adventurers in Newcastle, more recently **Close House** has been connected with the University of Newcastle. It is now in private hands as a stylish hotel overlooking its integral golf course.

Close House overlooks an impressive golf course, which has been developed with the fairways and sand traps designed by course tour professional Lee Westwood

Bear left, passing the old walled garden, with glasshouses, now neatly lawned. Bear right, down through the adjacent woodland strip. Emerge left to rejoin the country club access road and follow it down to the entrance of the golf course car park. Turn left along the track to cross a wooden bridge. Bearing right, skirt the edge of the driving range, and rugby field, and bear right again with a fairway to reach a kissing gate onto the **Wylam Waggonway**.

Here find the last National Trail signpost and a potentially revealing interpretative panel, but being cast-iron it

is sadly difficult to read in the tree shade. Henceforward, you are strictly on Hadrian's Way.

Wylam Waggonway

William Hedley's famous *Puffing Billy* ran this way; this and the *Wylam Dilly* are the oldest surviving **locomotives** in the world, and they are both on display at York Railway Museum. Robert Stephenson lived for a time in Newburn, although there is no truth in the claim that he first experimented with his innovative *Rocket* locomotive on the Waggonway.

The Waggonway was built in 1748 to a 5' gauge, the standard 4'8½" gauge Scotswood, Newburn & Wylam track being laid much later in 1876. In 1814 the famous *Wylam Dilly* and *Puffing Billy* locomotives began hauling coal waggons. The Waggonway was essential, as the river at the time was too shallow for keeled boats. An interesting fact is that the standard gauge of these railways precisely matches the width of a Roman cart – 4'8½". Surely this is a coincidence... or maybe not...

At this point the walking link from Wylam railway station (see Appendix C) joins from the right, having passed George Stephenson's birthplace (born 9 June 1781). This humble cottage, in the care of the National Trust, has a welcome tearoom.

Turn left and get up your own head of steam, always aware of the occasional tingling bells warning of cyclists scooting up from behind! You may also be tempted to copy the habit of locals and follow the scenic path along the eroding bank of the Tyne. ◀ After about a kilometre the tree-shaded level Trail reaches the gate onto the open road before **Blayney Row** (at a Sustrans totem). Turn right and follow the lane in front of the cottage terrace, situated on what is still called Ryton Island – from the time before the river was dredged into the great waterway we see today and ran in strands, placing this spot firmly in County Durham. From the kissing gate at the end pass to the left of the Hadrian's Way stone to join the path hugging the banks of the Tyne.

This is part of the Tyne Riverside Country Park, a recreational tendril that runs the six miles from Low Prudhoe to Newburn.

Upstream from the stone a wooden post in the **riverbank** indicates where a ferry once operated, to the boatman's house; it still exists on the far bank by the railway. Some 900ft (274m) further the Tide Stone, indicating the normal limit of the highest tides, once stood – riverbank erosion sealing its fate and that of the National Trail, which followed the bank until 2010.

Pass round by the slipway, often animated with waterskiers, canoeists and oarsmen, backed by the visitor centre (and tearoom). The Keelman restaurant, accommodation lodges and Big Lamp microbrewery are located further back; these will have their own appeal to Trail walkers. (The restaurant – famous for excellent bar food and such fine house ales as Big Lamb Bitter, Prince Bishop and Sunnydaze, which can be purchased in two-pint jugs for the price of 1½ pints – may be bad news for thirsty walkers trying to cultivate a good walking pace!)

It can get crowded here, so walk on by the Tyne Amateur Rowing Clubhouse, resplendent with the head of Old Father Tyne sporting a twisted beard and capped with a basket of coal. Next up is The Boathouse in Water Row, which has been the Branzino Italian Restaurant since 2021. From 1798 to 1801 George Stephenson was in charge of Robert Hawthorn's new pumping engine at Water Row Coal Pit, where his father, Robert, was a fireman.

> The **flood marks** cut on the quoins indicate the 1771 flood, which swept away a string of bridges downstream from Bywell, including the central section of Newcastle's Tyne Bridge (on the site of the Swing Bridge).
> Although the Tyne was dredged to improve river traffic for the industrial growth of Tyneside, and in spite of the tidal nature of the river beyond this point to Wylam, this was historically the lowest fording point on the river. In recent times dredgings were used to level the sites of the old coal-powered power stations of North and South Stella on the far bank. Numerous canonballs were sieved during this process – remnants from the Battle of Newburn, when a Scottish army, led by General Lesley, overwhelmed Charles I's English army positioned on the Ryton bank on 28 August 1640.

It would seem the community name **Newburn-on-Tyne** records a traumatic centuries-old flood event whereby New Burn, flowing down through the line of the Wall between Throckley and Walbottle, radically changed its course, but we are talking at least 900 years ago, as in 1121 the stream was known as Neuburna! Once a signal box stood next to a level crossing at the former toll-road over Newburn Bridge.

Watch the traffic flow as you cross the single-carriage road bridge. ▶ Keep to the hard tarmac cycle path, passing the timber-boarded building (now a scrap car depot) – originally the site of a pumping house for the Isabella Colliery.

This is the course of the first Carlisle to Newcastle Railway, which was later used as a mineral line when the new main line forged a route on the south bank of the Tyne.

177

The **coal** was transformed into coke, the sulphur being removed in ovens (horrid for workers), thus enabling it to be used at Spenser's Steelworks, which was located from 1822 on what is now the Newburn Industrial Estate. The steelworks were of such proportions that Newburn became known as 'New Sheffield'. Mind you, the village-name is far from new, as it was known as Neuburna in 1121.

Crossing the Newburn road bridge, pass the Warburton bakery and then the landscaped site of Percy Pit Colliery – named after the Duke of Northumberland, who owned the manorial rights. An incline from Walbottle Colliery once delivered coal down to wagon sidings here. Leading on, the old railway track-bed trail comes close to Tyne View (with its useful rows of shops), affording views of the 18th-century beehive-shaped glass furnace cone to the right, while to the left there is welcome refreshment at the **Lemington** Community Centre café. ◄

Whisper it: you might even hop on a bus here that could skip you forward to Wallsend if urban walking is not to your inclination.

Lemington, largely composed of red-brick terraces of colliery dwellings, has very rural roots. The place name translates as 'the farm where brooklime grew'; this plant is otherwise known as water pimpernel (a member of the speedwell family).

The track-bed Trail comes by the wooded dell of **Sugley Dene** (Nature Reserve), which enchantingly means 'the valley clearing attracting hedge sparrows'.

Arriving at an estate road in Bell's Close, cross by the traffic-calming island and head up the tarmac path in a landscaped open space frequented by dog walkers. Cross the footbridge spanning the **A1** – an incessantly noisy traffic artery (how one may yearn for the Trail's more peaceful rural idylls in our wake). From here there is an opportunity for a nostalgic visit to our old friend Hadrian's Wall, and specifically the Denton Hall turret. This is achieved by bearing right on the footway and bearing left with the signposted footpath up Denton Dene's semi-wooded parkland to reach West Road and into the city centre. Return to

Hadrian's Way on the east side of the A1 footbridge and continue on the Trail.

On the east side of the A1 footbridge, the green space now entered is Denton Dene. Bear half-right, following the tarmac footway through the parkland, passing the Newcastle Blue Star football ground, an amateur club in the Northern Alliance Premier Division, to reach Denton Road. ▸ Follow the footway to a pedestrian crossing by the Amma Restaurant (Sri Lankan dishes a speciality). Pause to admire the steel sculpture of a collier with his lamp, pit pony and children, a shining example of positive poignant reflection.

Follow on with the open road, where once ran brick terracing; the hillside is honeycombed with drift coalmines, all thoroughly sealed and forgotten. At Kelly's Yard turn right by the fencing to step back onto the old Carlisle & Newcastle Railway track-bed cycle trail. (In this vicinity was the site of Scotswood Junction.) After you gain a glimpse of the green, traffic-thronged **Scotswood Road Bridge** over the Tyne, the tarmac Trail leads on, becoming progressively more open.

The area from Scotswood Bridge to Paradise has modern industrial buildings, successors to the great Vicker's Armaments Works – hence the stationary chieftain tank perched at the main entrance. ▸ In due course, however reluctantly you may wish it, gently descend to join a footway beside the noisy Scotswood Road (you can tell the author is a countryman!).

The music hall song **'Blaydon Races'**, first sung by George Ridley in 1862, refers to this busy thoroughfare, recalling the lively scenes associated with the annual foot race (earlier horse race), which sped along the road and over Scotswood Bridge into the town of Blaydon. The chorus will be familiar to many:

Oh! lads ye shud a'seen us gannin,
Passin' the folks upon the road just as they
were stannin,

If you fancy a reviving cuppa or light snack, St Margaret's Church – located up to the left along Armstrong Road – runs a community café on Tuesdays and Thursdays, 10.30am–2.30pm.

A drift coal mine entrance is visible from the main road; the mine ran into the bank and therefore lies beneath the Trail.

Tidal mud from Elswick walkway

*Thor wis lots a lads and lasses there all wi smilin faces
Gannin alang the Scotswood Road to see the Blaydon Races.*

The song includes the line 'Noo when we gat to Paradise thor wes bonny gam begun': paradise latterly existed as cement works set upon the site of the exotic riverside Paradise Garden, laid out by the Hodgkins family from Benwell House. A tiny replacement garden exists below the Path and above the main road, but it has not been properly tended.

Cross Scotswood Road at the traffic light/pedestrian crossing, follow the footway left and bear right into **Newcastle Business Park** via William Armstrong Drive, with its surround of prestigious car dealerships. Take a moment to look across the Tyne to the horizon in a south-easterly direction above the Team Valley, to spot Anthony Gormley's 'Angel of the North' – icon of the 1990s. Just above this, Elswick has been transformed by a regeneration programme providing modern housing to replace the Victorian terraces.

Take the first opportunity to bear right on a cycle/pedestrian incline leading easily down to the Riverside Walkway. The interpretative panels are well worth reading to grasp a sense of what this pleasant area was like in the Industrial Age – quite, quite different! Imagine the clamour of Armstrong's Elswick Engineering Works. The office blocks are backed at mid-point by a flight of stairs focused on the Armstrong coat of arms; across the water the Dunston Staithes dominate the scene.

En route to The Close, follow the paved Walkway, passing beneath the sequence of high-stilted bridges, occasional decking tempting you 'onto the water'. First comes the sleek-lined concrete New Redheugh road bridge, built by Nuttalls, then the King Edward Mainline Railway Bridge, then the Queen Elizabeth I Metro Bridge, and finally the double-decker High Level Bridge carrying a road topped by a railway. ▶

The oldest of these bridges was built in 1849.

Fish Market and High Level Bridge

Just short of the Swing Bridge see the old Fish Market and Lloyds Bar (Wetherspoons) with its adapted warehousing.

From medieval times onwards this area was a place of **merchants**. With the coming of the 'Coaly Tyne', the movement of coal along the river was handled by a rare breed of men known as keelmen. They are remembered in the lilting traditional song 'The Keel Row' (paraphrased): 'As I came through Sandgate I heard a lassie sing "Weel may the keel row The boat that my love's in".'

They were hard-living men, often paid in beer. John Wesley, a founder of Methodism, observed their uncouthness and bad language. They became extinct with the building of the coal staithes; a large one at Wallsend is long gone, although the massive timber-framed Dunston Staithes lingers still.

WESTBOUND: NEWCASTLE QUAYSIDE TO HEDDON-ON-THE-WALL

Hadrian's Way goes on under the Swing Bridge, passing Wetherspoons. Keep to the Riverside Walkway; ultimately, the low path ends and you climb a flight of steps onto William Armstrong Drive in Newcastle Business Park.

Reaching the traffic lights, turn left on the footway beside busy Scotswood Road, crossing at the pedestrian lights. Follow the path inclining upwards and rightwards from the busy traffic thoroughfare. This wends along the course of the old Newcastle & Carlisle Railway to the old Scotswood Junction. Watch out for the fork with the Keelman's Way. The cycle path comes out at Kelly's yard on an open area below Whitfield Road.

Passing the shiny 'Men of Steel' pitman pony sculpture, cross Denton Road at the pedestrian lights and follow the footway to where a footpath is signed left; it passes the sports centre and weaves on to cross the footbridge over the **A1**. The tarmac footway trends left, being visually (if not audibly) screened from the terrific traffic artery. A traffic-calming island enables the suburban approach to Ottringham Close to be crossed with ease.

Rising with the footway, rejoin the line of the rail trail, last experienced when close to the Scotswood interchange. A small chicane and the

Pitman sculpture in Scotswood

cycle path pass the foot of **Sugley Dene** Nature Reserve, then **Lemington** Community Centre (with café) in Tyne View. After passing under a road bridge, the way forks; keep left, duly crossing the Newburn road bridge above the Warburton's Bakery. The Path comes to a fork: go left to the traffic lights beside the single-carriageway Newburn Bridge. Ignore the bridge, cross over, and go down Water Row by The Boathouse pub. Pass the Tyne Rowing Club, arriving at the **Tyne Riverside Country Park**, with its visitor centre and café, and The Keelman pub behind. Continue upstream beside the river.

As the Path splits, take the right-hand fork from the riverbank, passing the 'Hadrian's Way' stone, guided right by the fingerpost to a kissing gate and on along the lane beside the cottage terrace. Join the Wylam Waggonway, turning left within the metalled, tree-shrouded cycleway. Continue to and beyond barriers at Heddon Haughs to reach a Wylam Waggonway interpretative panel.

Here turn right, via the kissing gate, and follow the new path adjacent to the rugby field. Between the golf fairway and driving range the Path bears right and then crosses a wooden bridge to follow a connecting track to the country club car park. Turn right along the access roadway and then promptly bear left into the adjacent woodland, rising within, to step back onto the access road.

Turn left, passing the walled garden to come behind Close House. Switch acutely right, up the holly-lined lane signed for Heddon. The partially cobbled track runs through woodland to a gate by a cottage. The track encounters another woodland, beneath a pylon line; at this point bear right, passing West Acre and then rising by Heddon Banks into the village of **Heddon-on-the-Wall**. The Trail turns right into Towne Gate, passing a bus shelter and timber-built Women's Institute. Only another 60 metres ahead find an enclosure featuring a fine curved length of **Roman Wall** (see 'Heddon-on-the-Wall', above).

A stretch of Wall in Heddon, with medieval pottery kiln base in the foreground

STAGE 10

Newcastle Quayside to Segedunum

Start	Newcastle Quayside
Finish	Segedunum, Wallsend
Distance	5 miles (8km)
Walking time	2½hr
Refreshments	Newcastle upon Tyne: Quayside (variety of hotels, pubs and cafés); Ouseburn: It's All About The Bike (café); St Peter's Marina: The Merchants Tavern (formerly known as the Bascule Bistro & Bar); Wallsend: Segedunum Roman Fort museum and café, other cafés near the railway station
Accommodation	Newcastle City Centre, Wallsend
Railway link	Newcastle Central
Metro link	Wallsend

Now begins the easternmost and most thoroughly urban part of the trek, with a choice of two end points. The National Trail finishes, you might think conclusively, at Wallsend – specifically at the Segedunum Museum and Roman Fort. This stage describes the route to that earlier end-point. But the truth of the matter is that while you might be 'walking' the Wall, the Romans 'ran' a frontier. They relied on access to the North Sea, so a supply harbour and fort was needed at the mouth of the Tyne. Stage 11 describes walking on to that further-flung finish.

The red, hydraulically operated **Swing Bridge** was installed by William Armstrong in 1876 to develop his shipping and armaments factory along the Elswick riverside. It's thought that it rests where the Romans spanned the river with their Pons Aelius, dedicated to and possibly designed by Emperor Hadrian himself. It's known that Hadrian came to these shores after inspecting the Rhine frontier; logic therefore suggests that he would have landed at this upstream Roman port in the vicinity of Lort Burn.

That a bridge was built with the Wall lends weight to the suggestion that there was a fort on the Gateshead side. Hadrian's influence in the design explains why his family name was ascribed to it; during his reign he was renowned for touring his empire and encouraging the restoration and reconstruction of both civic and religious buildings – there were even several Hadrianopolis 'towns' named in his honour. He was an emperor defined as much by his love of architecture as his affection for and by his army.

For 1:25K route map see booklet pages 45–48.

◀ Slipping under the arch of the bridge onto Quayside proper, you may merrily stroll on with all the distractions of a vibrant city waterfront to excite you. However, the walking link from Central Station (see Appendix C) comes

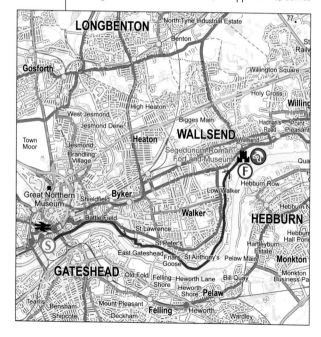

Tyne Bridge and the Sage Gateshead

in by Watergate, close to the Customs House – follow it to visit some of the majestic buildings in the heart of this architecturally impressive city.

NEWCASTLE – CULTURAL CAPITAL OF THE NORTH-EAST

Renowned for its majestic Victorian architecture, Newcastle has arguably the finest streetscapes in Britain. This guide can do scant justice to the experience, but to get you underway, slip through Watergate into Sandhill, keeping left of Bessie Surtees House (a handsome 16th-century merchant's house now the north-east regional offices of English Heritage), and climb the Castle Stairs, a long flight of stone steps; these lead through the city walls at the Postern Gate, installed at the behest of Dominican monks, to the cobbled Castle Garth, with the Greek Revival-style Moot Hall to the right.

Ahead stands the massive Castle Keep, symbolising the strength of a proud city. Visitors may enter the keep via the staircase upon the fore building, which is rather after the stamp of Dover Castle – indeed, the two castles are thought to have been designed by a common architect.

The keep stands amid the site of Pons Aelius, and parts of it are laid out in the cobbles close to the base of the keep on the west side. Excavations,

187

Newcastle's great Castle Keep

begun in 1978, were inevitably greatly hampered by the restricted nature of available sites; to date, these have not revealed the Wall's entrance to, or exit from, the fort. Features revealed within the fort include the headquarters building, with underground strongroom to stash the cash (the Romans knew the power of money in securing allegiances); the commanding officer's buildings, with various granaries; and the Via Principalis, the main thoroughfare through the centre of the fort.

The granaries are marked by three parallel lines of paving beneath the embankment arch, with a further square feature of real masonry under the arch closest to the keep. The fort was first 'slighted' during the eighth century by its conversion into a Saxon Christian cemetery in the vicinity of the keep. This was possibly associated with the monastery that gave Newcastle its pre-Conquest name of 'Monkchester'.

The importance of the Tyne as the north country equivalent of the Thames is shown by the creation of the 'new castle' in 1080 by Robert Curthose, eldest son of William the Conqueror. The medieval stone castle came in the 12th century, the surviving elements being the keep from 1168, the south curtain wall, postern and north gates.

Medieval defences were completed during the mid-13th century by the addition of an outer north gate or barbican, now known as the Black Gate. The castle never repelled a siege, and when the town wall was completed in the mid-14th century, it stood forlorn. By the end of the 16th century only the basement of the keep and the Great Hall were still in use – as a prison and court of assize, respectively.

During the 17th century, houses appeared within its walls. The Civil War brought new defences – excavations in 1992 revealed a wall beneath the railway viaduct arch north of the keep. By the mid-17th century shops thronged the environs of the keep, surviving until the upheavals of the 19th century, when, with ruthless efficiency, the railway embankment swept through in 1846.

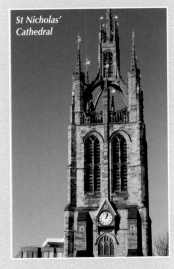

St Nicholas' Cathedral

Pass on by Black Gate, proceeding up St Nicholas Street, one's attention transfixed by St Nicholas' Cathedral. The lantern tower held high is unique in England, a 14th-century embellishment of stunning beauty. Only becoming a cathedral in 1882, the building retains the intrinsic quality of a parish church. Note the memorial bust of Thomas Bewick in Amen Corner. In 1776 Thomas moved from Eltringham near Prudhoe to a workshop located here; his wood engravings remain a vital archive, recording rural life just before the Industrial Revolution drove people from the land to labour in congested towns and cities. (It is well worth visiting the museum of rural life at Bewick's birthplace in Cherryburn, near Prudhoe.)

Now walk along Collingwood Street, then onto the paved isthmus to cross the traffic island with the impressive monument to George Stephenson, erected in 1882. George, of Stockton & Darlington Railway fame, and his son Robert, of *Rocket* fame, lived and developed their fascination in the emergent railway revolution in works situated behind Central Station in South Street.

Begin up Westgate Road, on the line of the Roman Wall. Turn into Grainger Street, which connects Central Station with Grey's Monument. The Tyne and coal brought commerce and wealth to the city, but it was Richard Grainger's speculative building enterprise in the 1830s that brought its classical style and dignity. Booming commerce coupled with the seemingly limitless expansion of trading links with the empire (shades of Rome) brought tremendous growth – the city witnessed a doubling of its population during the first half of the 19th century. Grainger took advantage of the municipal wealth to put forward ideas of a coherent new Newcastle. He harnessed the architectural talent of John

189

Dobson, and together they produced such impressive boulevards as Grainger, Grey and Clayton Streets. John Clayton of Chesters House (and, of course, of Hadrian's Wall fame), the quietly spoken town clerk and lawyer who worked in an eminent city law firm, was an influential ally.

Thus, through the major building works of the Victorian Age, they created the only truly planned city centre in Britain – an ebulliently classical composition. Indeed, a few years ago Grey Street was voted the most beautiful street in England by a national poll.

Dobson's final and grandest statement was Central Station; yet for all its merits, and for all the good it has brought the city over 150 years, there will still be those visitors with a love of history who rue the loss of the castle bailey and so much else associated with pre-Industrial Newcastle – all swept aside as the railway was brought puffing and steaming into the heart of the city.

A very special place to visit is at the foot of Westgate Road, off Neville Street: the Literary and Philosophical Society Library (commonly known as the Lit & Phil), a cultural focus of Newcastle since 1793 and still going strong.

City Guides – volunteers working in association with Newcastle Gateshead Visitor Information Centre – provide entertaining historical guided walks. Contact: Newcastle Visitor Information Centre, 8–9 Central Arcade, 28 Market Street, Newcastle upon Tyne NE1 5BQ, tel 01912 778 000, visitorinfo@ngi.org.uk (www.NewcastleGateshead.com).

Wall walkers with a keen interest in the Roman legacy should visit the £26 million state-of-the art Great North Museum, which opened in 2009 and is a marriage of the two university museums and the Hancock natural history collection. It contains a remarkable collection, including a large model of the entire Wall in the Roman Gallery. It also contains the best Wall-related material found east of the North Tyne valley, most of which has hitherto not been on public view through lack of space. There are scale models of a Mithreum (Mithraic temple); bridge altars from Pons Aelius; and a fine inscription, circa AD158, recording the arrival of troops from the Rhine to reinforce the British legions. The altars, dredged from the Tyne in the 19th century, would have originally been set prominently on the Roman bridge. As Pons Aelius fort was constructed in the late second century, there is speculation regarding the possible existence of a yet unidentified camp on the Gateshead side, coinciding with the building of the Wall. So much remains unknown about the course and nature of the Wall in this area.

When you've finished basking in the history and architecture, retrace your steps to Quayside and the Swing Bridge.

Geordies, defined as those born beside the tidal Tyne, have an emotional allegiance with **Tyne Bridge**, a sturdy icon of their city. The massive green structure uniquely forms the only urban nesting place of kittiwake, more normally associated with the Farne Islands or more generally sea cliffs. Since the first two pairs arrived in 1997, the colony has risen to 150 nesting pairs, their presence causing a flap among businesses not overjoyed by the debris that inevitably collects on The Quayside paving.

The walkway leads naturally on by Wesley Square to pass the enticingly graceful 'winking' Gateshead Millennium Bridge, the most inspiring of the seven Tyneside spans. It is an access point for the shining armadillo, alias the Sage Gateshead, home of the Royal Northern Sinfonia and the Baltic Flour Mill – hence the Baltic Centre for Contemporary Art, the biggest of its kind in the world.

The Quayside is well endowed with architectural splendour and sculptural embellishment – not to mention

Gateshead Millennium Bridge

Cycle Hub at Ouseburn

a tempting array of places of refreshment; on a sun-drenched day it is a scene to match any cosmopolitan city waterfront. Stride on, as you must, on the generous curve of the river, by major office suites and Mariners Wharf apartments to the mouth of the Ouseburn.

Crossing Ouseburn Bridge, look above The Tyne Bar and the overbearing Glasshouse Bridge, then gaze in amazement at the twin-pagoda-towered brick building – all the more amazing as it was built as a primary school!

The Roman Wall crossed the **Ouseburn** a little upstream in the vicinity of Byker Bridge. It is a very deep cleft and must have posed quite some engineering problems – no wonder the section of Wall from Pons Aelius to Segedunum was not part of the original grand design.

Further upstream still is Jesmond Dene, 'a ribbon of green' bequeathed to the city by Lord Armstrong, who died in 1900 and left one of the biggest industrial legacies in British history. You may notice the statue to William Coulson above the viaduct; he was a significant benefactor to the vulnerable people and animals of Newcastle.

Go past the Saddle Skedaddle Cycle Hub café and then the Spillers car park, now along St Lawrence Road by railings that shield the cleared site of the former Spillers Flour Mill, a massive siloed building. (Its demise has opened up the scene wonderfully – one wonders what will take its place.) Pass between the engineering works of BEL Valves, turning right into Glasshouse Street then left along Bottlehouse Street to arrive at St Peter's Marina – a colourful scene with yachts in a marina pool surrounded by a modern red-brick apartment 'village', opened in 1991 by Princess Diana. ▶

The one possible recourse for refreshment here is the Bascule Bar & Bistro.

By Chandlers Quay cross the bascule bridge at the entrance to the marina; the riverside cycle path continues via the bijou Trinity Courtyard and The Ropery.

In leaving these cosy abodes behind, allow the **tidal river** to take centre stage. Invariably, coarse fishermen can be seen along this quiet riverside walk, patiently trying to entice codling and whiting onto their hooks. Suddenly, the tangle of bladderwrack seaweed and the flight of gulls gives a sense that the sea is nigh.

Approaching **St Anthony's Point**, the Trail leaves the waterfront within the Walker Riverside Park – either switch steeply up steps (no sign) or take the longer, more leisurely cycle route – to gain the higher level of the old railway track. From here the walk to Segedunum couldn't be more straightforward: keep to the cycle path, with just two road crossings after passing under the Benton Way road bridge beside the National Centre for Subsea & Offshore Engineering (Newcastle University). The Segedunum Bathhouse reconstruction hoves into view ahead, a red sign guiding you acutely right, down a brief path to where you can view the excavated site of the actual Roman bath-house, with its hypercaust pillars. Formerly, a pub stood on the site, one of several in the vicinity slaking the thirst of shipyard workers after a hard

The old Swan Hunter company, with its distinctive red swordfish logo, was synonymous with the Tyne.

Foundations of the original Roman bath-house at Segedunum. In the background see the orange pantiles of the bathhouse reconstruction and the museum tower.

day's labour. The open space below has been stripped of all traces of the shipyard, all bar one inlet dock.

So we arrive at the real Wall's end – a tiny section of Roman Wall can be seen emerging from the fort railings, slipping down into the oblivion in the fenced-off and cleared site of the former Swan Hunter shipyard ◀ . Across the broad river see a tall, slender rocket-like church spire in Hebburn, formerly a United Reform Church, now, like many religious buildings, repurposed as the Dhammakaya Meditation Centre of Newcastle, a Buddhist Temple, no less.

There was a time when a quarter of the world's **shipping** was built or fitted on the Tyne. A native of Sunderland is known as a 'Makum' because many ships were built (make them: 'makum') on the Wear and then towed to be fitted on the Tyne. Until 2010 there were at least 20 cranes here, like giant

angle-poise lamps in cheery tones of yellow, red and blue. The site is now geared to more modest wind turbine construction.

You can access Segedunum Museum by steps and a gate, with the welcoming 'I walked Hadrian's Wall' board ahead. Or pass on to go left with the old Swan Hunter access road (see the Swans building right) and behind the museum (location of the Passport stamping station), coming to the ornate shipyard clock to reach Buddle Street. Wallsend Metro station is seen invitingly ahead, with the Asda supermarket to the right.

Wallsend Metro station lies across Buddle Street from the rear of the museum, along Station Road opposite. But don't be in a hurry to leave; certainly, walkers with a coast-to-coast mindset have six more merry miles to march to reach the sea proper, including the fabulous Shields Ferry and a brilliant exhibition Roman fort to boot.

SEGEDUNUM
(WHERE ROME'S GREAT FRONTIER BEGINS… OR, MORE LIKELY, ENDS!)

The North Tyneside Council and Tyne & Wear Museum Service created the hugely impressive interpretative focus surrounding the fort, with Wall and bathhouse reconstructions (modelled on Cilurnum), a fitting tribute to the importance of this easternmost end of the Roman Wall. Annually, it attracts 50,000 visitors, a considerable proportion being school parties from all around the country.

Standing proud among the forest of gigantic cranes in the nearby shipyard, the panoramic viewing tower evokes the engineering heritage of the Tyne shipyards and echoes of nautical architecture. In certain respects it can be said to serve a similar function to that of the London Eye.

Trail walkers, whether weary eastbounders or those about to embark for the west, should consider investigating all parts of the museum as an essential part of their coast-to-coast expedition. The rather odd approach to the reception lobby is the result of archaeology associated with the Roman trackway, which led from the eastern gate into the Barbarian territory on which the museum stands. Enter the lift to reach the high viewing gallery: a screen gives a rolling story of the site below – a most imaginative and

Segedunum Museum gallery tower

stirring scene-setter. The Segedunum Project, including the laying out of the fort you see before you, began in 1997; after the colliery brick terraces had been demolished in the 1970s, homeowners transferred to newly built properties in the Battle Hill Estate.

Looking west, you can discern the line of the Roman Wall to the right of a pair of tower blocks as the Fossway – the road name a reference to the Wall's north ditch. To the right of this is the turquoise Parsons Engineering Works, and in the distance catch a glimpse of the architecturally renowned Byker Wall community housing, short of the Ouseburn.

The museum's galleries are fascinating – they really do get you into Roman frontier 'time trekker' mood. If the decision to 'do' the Wall got you here, you will need no further encouragement! If you are at the end or latter stages of your walk to Arbeia, then this holds your focus beautifully.

With all that has happened to the fort site in recent centuries – most notably the advent of coal mining – there can be no surprise that few items of genuine fort masonry remain. However, a good look inside the red pantile-roofed bathhouse reconstruction is a priority; its domed and painted interior is quite magical, conveying the sophistication of Roman culture.

The area just before the bathhouse reconstruction was where the Roman civilian settlement (vicus) lay; here native British traders lived and worked in harmony with the life of the fort. They would have serviced the ancillary needs of the garrison. In light of the auxiliaries' unmarried status, services might have been of the flesh too!

In AD122 Wall construction commenced from Hadrian's first 'grand design', yet only a few years elapsed before numerous adaptations were deemed essential to make the frontier more effective; and there can be little doubt that Hadrian was consulted. One such change was to extend the Wall from the bridging point of Pons Aelius to a new fort here at Segedunum, as the Celts were capable of crossing the Tyne downstream of the Ouseburn.

Perhaps the unrecorded fort at Gateshead was brought forward to the site of the present Newcastle keep, in the same way that Vindolanda was replaced by Vercovicium – the impressive Housesteads. Segedunum appears to mean 'strong' or 'victory' fort, clearly named to enthuse the garrison that built the Wall extension. The fort was originally garrisoned by bargemen from present-day Iraq – the skills of these early keelmen were essential in bringing garrison provisions from Arbeia.

A branch Wall originally led from the south-eastern corner of the fort down to the banks of the Tyne, which was closer to the fort than it is today. In 1903 the few remaining Wall stones, now set beside the cycle path, were removed from a site within the shipyard when it was expanded to build the transatlantic liner *Mauretania*, the biggest ship ever made here.

Walkers really must visit the first true length of Roman Wall leading westwards, located within a secure enclosure outside the main fort railings, across Buddle Street. Next to the Wall stands a reconstruction showing a variety of possible finishes. The whole Wall was probably rendered and/or pointed, with the aim of leaving the 'humbly cultured' barbarian tribes in a constant state of awe. The set of spikes or cippi on view are thought to have been placed in front of the Wall as an impenetrable entanglement (for reasons of public safety they are reconstructed in blunt form).

Also visible is the sealed site of 'B' colliery shaft; the earlier 'A' pit was sunk in 1778 and lay near the west gate of the fort. Although both pits produced fine household coal, they had a terrible reputation for gas explosions: in 1835 104 men and boys lost their lives in a single pit disaster.

WESTBOUND: SEGEDUNUM TO NEWCASTLE QUAYSIDE

You are now on the National Trail. Exit the museum's 'back door' and cross the former Swan Hunter approach road, joining a path connection to Hadrian's Way cycle route. Turn right and pass the repositioned remnant Roman Wall and Roman bathhouse reconstruction, following the tarmaced Waggonway, which duly crosses a road and continues in a semi-wild environment – although the urban and industrial surroundings are never far from sight. After the second road crossing, pass modern houses, then as the great gasworks frame looms, fork left as directed within Walker Riverside Park, coming gradually down towards the river with one hairpin bend. Now the cycleway progresses at the tidal river level along **St Anthony's** shore, passing along The Ropery to St Peter's Marina.

Cross the lift bridge, passing by the boat-bedecked harbour to bear right then left opposite the Bascule Bistro & Bar, following Bottlehouse Street. At the end go right by BEL Valves and left by British Engines, gaining the wide roadway where the huge Tyne Mill building stood until recently. Hug the fencing, as indicated by the cycleway lines, to reach the large Spiller's car park and 'It's all about the Bike' café.

After crossing the Ouseburn veer half-left to regain the Tyne shore railings, overlooked by grand, modern galleried flats. The subsequent vibrant city waterfront provides plenty of distraction for an earnestly striding walker; head along the Quayside by the pedestrian Millennium Bridge and under the iconic Tyne Bridge to reach the Swing Bridge. (See 'Newcastle – Cultural Capital of the North-East', above.)

Downstream to St Anthony's Point

STAGE 11

Segedunum to South Shields
(Hadrian's Cycleway)

Start	Segedunum, Wallsend
Finish	Arbeia Roman Fort, South Shields
Distance	6 miles (10km)
Walking time	3½hr
Refreshments	Segedunum Roman Fort museum and café, other cafés near the railway station; North Shields: variety of hotels, pubs and cafés; South Shields: South Shields Museum and Art Gallery – café
Accommodation	Wide range of options, including Wallsend, Whitley Bay, Tynemouth, North Shields and South Shields
Metro link	South Shields

This section follows the concluding stretch of Hadrian's Cycleway route 72 – in its entirety a 174-mile route on the National Cycle Network coast to coast from Ravenglass to South Shields.

▸ Segedunum Museum lies roughly equidistant between Newcastle Quayside and North Shields on Hadrian's Cycleway (route 72), which you now join from the back door exit of the Museum, crossing the former access road to the Swan Hunter Shipyard. Go left (east), signed 'Royal Quays/North Shields'. A pleasant windy trail leads to and through an orange-painted arch onto the footway beside Hadrian Road.

For 1:25K route map see booklet pages 48–51.

Take the pedestrian crossing near the **Hadrian Road** Metro station, just before the Hadrian's Lodge Hotel. Now advancing on the north side of the road, come down below the high Metro bridge and join a path/cycleway through woodland closer to the bridge, then cross Willington Gut in Wallsend Burn – a haven for ducks. Joining the road, go right with Ropery Lane, which becomes Western Road. Bear left before the Albion Inn.

A cycle path leads through to the brick terrace of Armstrong Road; note brief evidence of the underlying cobble paving. At the end swing left with Auburn Close into the rising Howdon Lane. Go over the pedestrian crossing, from where the cycleway runs through open ground (a reclaimed refuse tip), coming by the Tyne Tunnel toll, seen through the hedge. The tarmac path crosses the pedestrian Brewers Lane bridge and bears right, coming down to a pedestrian crossing at **East Howdon** (ignore path right to the pedestrian Tyne Tunnel).

Follow on left with the Howdon Road footway. At the second roundabout bear right by Royal Quays

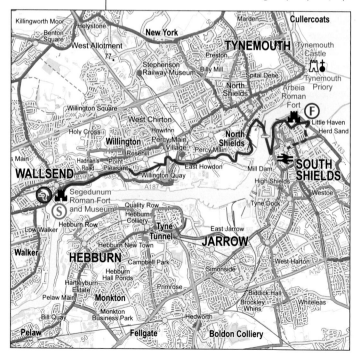

retail outlet, and at the next pedestrian crossing go over and keep right, signed 'Shields Ferry' – now following the modern landscaped Earl Grey Way by decorative groynes, passing the Wet'n'Wild Water Park leisure facility to reach the Albert Edward Dock Marina.

Keep left by the waterfront apartments, skirting round the marina via a footbridge on a footway that rises with Ballast Hill Road and Dock Road. Bear right with Lawson Street and at the end go right to join a footway leading down to the New Quay landing stage. ▶

The half-hourly **Shields Ferry** carries pedestrians over the Tyne to the South Shields terminal pier for £2.30. Feel the thrill of being at the mouth of a great river. The ferry's frequency is dependent on 'giving way' to great ocean-going cargo and passenger ships being piloted into the North Sea.

From South Shields floating ferry terminal pier, walk up the incline and turn left along the broad footway; you might keep to the left at the tall flats of Market Dock

Shields Ferry waiting room facing across the wide waters of the Tyne towards South Shields

Before stepping aboard, take a look at the Collingwood Mansions, built in 1816; the central portion was originally the Northumberland Arms Inn.

along the boardwalk, thereby visiting the bronze Spirit of South Shields.

> Icon of regeneration, this **prow figurehead** cradles a golden collier brig, carriers of the famed coals from Newcastle. She guards the passage of ships through the maritime thoroughfare to and from the North Sea. In the Captain's Wharf dry dock pool, set back from here, find seven stainless steel model collier brigs, known as *The Fleet* – both are part of Tyne & Wear's Art on the Riverside project.

Continue with Long Row, noting the interpretative panel as the roadway leads into Wapping Street ('Wapping' meaning marsh) – a row of slipway boat repair businesses – and spot the tiny Boomerang Boat Museum, then pass the Marine Safety & Fire Training Centre. Ignore the cycleway switchback, instead crossing River Drive to climb the flight of steps opposite. Go left through the traffic-hampering posts with Greens Place to turn right onto Baring Street and arrive at what is most definitely the eastern culminating point of the frontier Trail.

To complete your personal coast-to-coast odyssey, follow Fort Street to cross Lawe Road, striding on through North Marine Park. Descend a flight of steps and cross Harbour Drive to reach the promenade, where you might inspect *The Eye* sculpture with its song lyrics 'Blow the wind southerly', made famous by Kathleen Ferrier. ◄

This symbolises a lovely link across the frontier, as the contralto singer – otherwise known as Kathleen Wilson – was a bank manager's wife in Silloth, on the western seaboard of Hadrian's Wall (where today you can find Mrs Wilson's Coffee House and Eatery, named in her memory).

Ahead the sandy beach of **Little Haven** is a sure invitation for you to anoint your boots in the North Sea.

> The **shifting sands** at the mouth of the Tyne historically caused shipping all sorts of problems, ultimately only resolved when the North and South Piers were completed in 1885. Now you can regularly see ocean-going ships being piloted to and fro through this extended mouth of the Tyne.

Tynemouth Castle in the middle of the 'Eye' on Little Haven Promenade

but my eye could not see it, wherever might be it; the barque that is bearing my lover to me

ARBEIA ROMAN FORT

Tyne & Wear Archives & Museums has done a fabulous job of bringing the fort to life; and entry is free, so assuming it's open, and you have the time, you have no excuse not to give it your avid attention. Non-walking visitors will be at a distinct disadvantage, for only the walker will truly know the significance of the setting – especially when you wander on seaward after your visit here to complete the coast-to-coast trek.

Captivating attention immediately is the massive West Gate reconstruction – you'll pinch yourself to see if it's real! Set on a prominent hilltop, Arbeia commanded a great maritime perspective over the mouth of the Tyne: from here Roman ships had an open-water, umbilical-like connection with their continental seaboard and Mediterranean-surrounding empire. While today the Tyne is dredged deep, in Roman times is was considerably shallower – hence, to supply their frontier upstream they brought in Tigeris bargemen from Mesopotamia (now Iraq) to mastermind the movement of commodities and equipment. This explains the fort name 'place of the Arabs'. Interestingly, there is an altar in the museum that strongly suggests the formal name of the fort had been Lugudunum and that Arbeia was a Roman colloquialism that stuck.

Reconstruction of the commanding officer's quarters and barracks in the SE corner of Arbeia

Anyone who believes small is beautiful will love the museum, which is rich with intimate treasures but not overbearing. The actual fort site itself is special, having been thoroughly excavated; but what really deserves your time are the various reconstructions beyond the magnificent gatehouse with its crenellated wall. Inspect the barrack blocks, latrines and headquarters building – so authentic one might expect a Roman officer or auxiliary to stroll in behind you at any moment! There is even a 'wet weather trail' – although it's quite possible you'll have experience of that already!

Link to South Shields Metro station (for Newcastle Central Station)

Recross Harbour Drive and ascend the steps, thus following the footway through North Marine Park, past the bandstand, to reach Lawe Road at its junction with Sea Road. Now go right, heading into town with Ocean Road and advancing to the traffic roundabout.

No visit to South Shields is quite complete unless you've admired the beautiful **Town Hall**, reached from the roundabout along Anderson Street to the right. Empress Queen Victoria stands heroically before the majestic building, surmounted by a symbolic galleon weathervane, with every carefully crafted stone reflecting the sense of pride of the time in Empire and Rule Britannia.

Backtrack to follow Ocean Road from Morrison's, soon a pedestrian street, passing the South Shields Museum & Art Gallery to reach **South Shields Metro station**, from where you can make the all-important link to Newcastle Central Station.

WESTBOUND: SOUTH SHIELDS TO NEWCASTLE QUAYSIDE

From **South Shields Metro station** descend the steps to enter King Street, heading east past the marvellous South Shields Museum & Art Gallery – first on a pedestrian way then after a roundabout on the busy town thoroughfare Ocean Road.

At the end of Ocean Road bear half-left within North Marine Park, following the footway and passing the bandstand to step down over Harbour Drive and via the car park to inspect *The Eye* sculpture on the promenade. Steps lead onto the sandy Little Haven beach for the ceremonial anointing of the boots in the North Sea!

Switch directly back over Harbour Drive, ascending the flight of steps, and stroll on to cross Lawe Road and join Fort Street. Arrive at **Arbeia Roman Fort and Museum**. Follow Baring Street to the right, and at its northern end bear left with Greens Place. Once through the bollards go right, down the flight of steps and cross straight over River Drive, immediately switching left with Wapping Street. This lowest road leads through to Long Row and the modern estate of Market Dock to reach the South Shields Ferry landing stage via the inclined walkway. (Ferries are half-hourly and tickets cost £2.10.)

Upon reaching the North Shields landing stage, walk onto New Quay road, going right then left up Borough Road. Watch for the Hadrian's Way cycleway signage guiding left through suburban Addison Street and on by the business premises of Lawson Street; at the end go left with Dock Road and Ballast Hill Road to reach the Albert Edward Dock Marina.

At the south-west corner switch right, passing up over a road and through the landscaped path, Earl Grey Way, to come by the Royal Quays retail park to Howdon Road. Keep left at the third roundabout, find the pedestrian crossing and walk through the open ground on a tarmac walkway to cross a footbridge over the A191 Tyne Tunnel Approach.

Continue left, then go right to reach a pedestrian crossing of Howdon Lane. Turn left then right with Auburn Close, entering Armstrong Road. The cycleway leads on, entering Western Road behind The Albion and soon afterwards becoming Ropery Lane. Bear left with a path that crosses a tubular footbridge over Wallsend Burn, rising beyond into Hadrian Road. Cross by the Hadrian Lodge Hotel and follow the cycleway on to, and by, **Segedunum Museum** (see 'Segedunum Roman Fort and Museum', above).

STAGE 12

Heddon-on-the-Wall to Segedunum
(Hadrian's Toon Trail)

Start	Towne Gate, Heddon on the Wall
Finish	Segedunum, Wallsend
Distance	12.5 miles (20km)
Walking time	Allow 6½hr
Refreshments	Inevitably as an urban walk there is a abundance of choice. The very first Greggs shop is passed in Shields Road, Byker, a business founded in 1939.

Having devoted your largely rural walk to Hadrian's Wall all the way from the Solway Firth, there is an extremely good case for sticking the course and following the frontier all the way to Wallsend. This unwaymarked route, an immersive urban ramble, is richly endowed with the heritage of Newcastle. Geordies always refer to Newcastle as 'the Toon' – from the area of Town Moor. While Newcastle Utd fans are known as the Toon Army. Indeed, Toon is a genuine Borderers' term for 'town'.

From The Three Tuns pub cross the road into the confined path left of the Knott Memorial Hall, in harmony with

Hadrian's Wall at Heddon, with medieval pottery kiln in the foreground

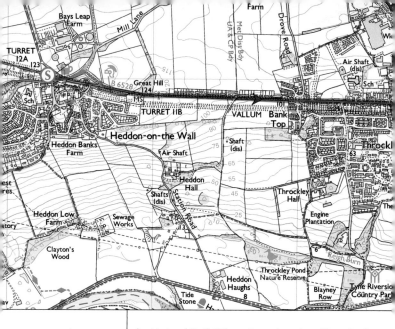

Map scale is 1:25,000.
Map continues
on page 210

the National Trail. Where the path ends at Chare Bank, veer left to come into the rock-cut section of the Military Road; now fenced off to the left this is close to the site of Milecastle 12.

Go right (obviously) and cross the road into the hedge lined path accessing the English Heritage enclosure to inspect the 100m-long stretch of low Roman Wall, with a medieval pottery kiln at the near end. A slight dip in the adjacent pasture gives a clue to the line of the **vallum**. Exit by steps onto the road and cross to join the Military Road footway on **Great Hill**.

Crossing the boundary line out of Northumberland into the city of Newcastle, come by Frenchmen's Row, a terrace built in 1796 for workers at the former Heddon Colliery. Frenchmen's Row was usurped to provide homes for French loyalist clergy refugees, hence the name. However, the houses there now are replacements, built in 1960, although a sundial from the original buildings has been incorporated into the new row. The private house standing adjacent was formerly the Royal French Arms.

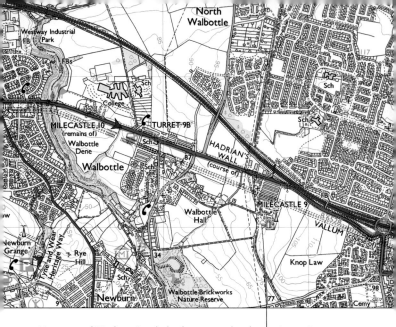

Now termed Hexham Road, the footway makes for speedy progress, with open country to the right with faint hints of the vallum in the cropped fields. ▶ Entering the former coal mining village of **Throckley**, the road descends, passing a brick-walled reservoir. Arriving at a roundabout, you switch to the south side and, crossing Newburn Road, come by the parish church of St Mary's, possibly set upon the Wall.

The footway next dips through the wooded dingle of Throckley Dene (interpretative panel), where the builders of Hadrian's Wall must have had a mighty constructional challenge, as it is a noticeably deep ravine. The road, by contrast, dips gently, being set on an embankment.

Next up is **Walbottle**, which simply meant 'house on the Wall'. Passing the entrance to Walbottle Academy, with its novel topiary hedge, be aware that **Milecastle 10** lay in the open farmland to the right, a useful measure of your progress. As you look down the field towards the wire fence, the dip in the field marks the line of the vallum, the southern defensive ditch that kept the nasty

The Aged Miners' Homes remind us of the short lives colliers led, with early onset respiratory conditions common.

Map continues
on page 213

The Engine Inn at
Hawthorn Terrace is
the first proper pub
to lure you from your
pavement plodding
since The Three
Tuns. All along the
Hexham Road there
has been a sequence
of bus stops, perhaps
the most useful bus
you'll see is the 685,
which travels all the
way to Carlisle.

Brittunculi (what the Romans called the native Brits) out
of the Roman military area. It can also be discerned if you
venture down Grove Road beside St Cuthbert's School
and look west up the field. ◄

Passing the top of the North Walbottle Waggonway,
which carried coal down to Lemington, where it in effect
merges with the Hadrian's Way part of Hadrian's Wall
Path. As a further reminder of the age of coal mining, see
right the seven brick terraces of the old Blucher Colliery,
comprising some 140 tightly packed houses. It is fascinating walking up the narrow passages between them to get a
sense of the tight community, in both its senses.

Immediately after the terraces, in the arable field
on the right of the fence, is the site of Milecastle 9. This
is significant as it was here that Eric Birley, as a young
archaeology graduate, overheard fellow excavators talking about the sale of Vindolanda. This prompted him to
ask his father for the cash to attend the estate's auction,
where he duly purchased the site along with Chesterholm
House. The rest is history!

The footway comes to a considerable roundabout at the **A69** junction, where you bear right with Union Hall Road then left with West Denton Road. At the Alan Shearer Centre (St Cuthbert's Care) in West Denton Close, a narrow path leads on to come by the busy dual carriageway. Keep right, passing the footbridge, to come upon the next evidence of Hadrian's Wall, first as a grassy bank then, after the next footbridge spanning the A69, as exposed stones (identified as West Denton on the interpretative panel).

The A1 interjects but walkers are not hampered as a path leads right through the slip road underpass and over a footbridge spanning the major road itself, then a further underpass leads to the eastern side and a Welcome to the City of Newcastle upon Tyne sign. Across the main road peering above trees is Denton Hall, built in 1622 by the Erringtons, who also owned Beaufront Castle above Corbridge.

Soon, another fine stretch of Hadrian's Wall is encountered, this time with the sole surviving Broad Wall turret in situ. The internal platform was the base for a wooden ladder to the first of two floors. The pavement

Length of Wall foundation beside the A69 approaching the A1

*Wonderwall:
Denton Dene's
celebration of the
1900th anniversary
of Hadrian's
visit in AD122*

plod continues past shops, and after a tyre depot you will find a further brief length of wall. In 2022, to celebrate the 1900th anniversary of Hadrian's visit, Denton Dene set 'Wonderwall' on the backing fence. Across the road see the parkland of the Dene and the Denton Turret Medical Centre. Within a few paces behind Solomon's Punjabi Cuisine, at the edge of the Esso garage forecourt, find a tiny fragment of rearranged stones, not precisely on the line of the wall, but it does show that the garage owner had an appreciation of the passage of the Roman wall.

Beyond the junction, keep to the right-hand footway beside West Road, ascending Benwell Hill, passing the cricket club and the entrance to West Road Crematorium over to the left. The brow duly arrives and after the unlikely named Fox and Hounds pub, with a lane of that name to the right, watch out for the Wallquest information panel on the adjacent wrought-iron fencing. This heralds Benwell Hill's contribution to the Roman Wall story, namely Condercum Roman fort, which translates as 'the fort with the wide-open prospect' – hard to imagine today. The artist's impression lacks a vicus settlement, which must have been considerable.

A unique find in 1751, when the Military Road was being built, was an **altar** inscribed 'lamiis tribus', which translates as 'the three witches'. Classical lamia is a single female demon associated with devouring children, and never travels in threes. The dedicator of this altar is most probably trying to venerate the triple mother goddesses that were very common on the Wall (and often depicted wearing hooded capes, as can be seen in Chesters Museum, Chollerford). The altar features in the seal of the Society of Antiquaries of Newcastle upon Tyne. Pass the dormant Pendower Hall, formerly the city council's education development centre.

As a mast becomes evident to the left, see the top of the reservoir, which, in turn, sits unreverentially upon the Roman fort. Fortunately, however, two Roman

Map continues
on page 215

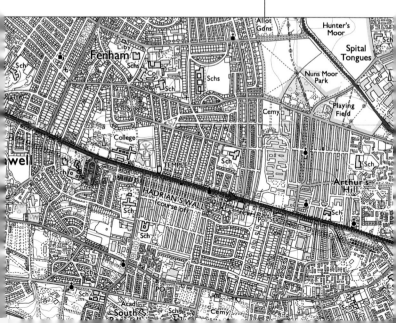

elements associated with the fort remain. First, turn right into Denhill Park (from the interpretative panel) and, following the looping estate road at the bottom of the cul-de-sac, find another unique frontier feature: the vallum crossing gate – with its road layers evident – a guarded access road up to Condercum fort.

Coming back to West Road, continue east then bear next right with Weidner Road, right again with Westholme Gardens and then left a short way down Broomridge Avenue to find a small enclosure containing the Temple of Antenocitius (pronounced Ann-tenno-city-cus), a native male god uniquely associated with this spot.

As the Sage building first peeks into eyeshot ahead, spy the beautiful golden dome of Newcastle's Muslim Temple over to the left.

Pace back to West Road and march merrily east by a large shopping centre and then the multicultural mingle of pavement shops that distinguish Benwell Hill, further emphasised by the Hindu Temple, after which the name changes to Westgate Road. The road now begins a steady descent, passing the handsome Hotel Balmoral, which will have been in quite a rural setting when built, then three tower blocks. ◄

No 1 has a black plaque to the remarkable Labour MP Mo Mowlam, who lived in this house. In 1996 Mo's persistence and persuasive manner helped seal the Good Friday Agreement in Northern Ireland.

At this point a pleasing variation to sticking with the main road is to bear right at Elswick Road into Summerhill Street, passing the parish church. Then go left with Summerhill Grove to cross the little park in the midst of the Summerhill community and so with Summerhill Terrace. ◄ As you return to Westgate Road, admire Swinburne Place to the left, a handsome brick terrace, the nearest dwelling having decorative reverse 'S' wall tiles.

Coming down to the major intersection with St James Boulevard, see an ultra-modern skyscraping glass tower to the left and the old Robert Sinclair tobacco buildings on the right. Carefully negotiate the pedestrian crossings, getting a brief glimpse left of St James Park, the home ground of Newcastle Utd FC. Continue to take a brief veer left to inspect the striking medieval city wall at West Walls, with its D-shaped towers: it mimics the probable original height of Hadrian's Wall. After Clayton Street West pass Pink Lane in Grainger Town and look out for the Black Swan pub by the arts centre, set upon a

milecastle. If you peek into the yard, you will see a metal man installation.

Map continues on page 216

> Curiously, the **milecastle** does not fit in with the acknowledged sequence of such features – part of the mystery of the route the Wall followed to Pons Aelius Roman bridge over the Tyne. So much shrouds the course of Hadrian's Wall in urban Newcastle, the industrial revolution banishing more than 99.9% of it to 'king coal'. The phrase 'coals to Newcastle' was coined in 1530, when a Royal Act gave the city a monopoly in exports.

Coming past Cross House and the grand Assembly Rooms, a long glimpse left up Grainger Street reveals the Earl Grey monument, designed by the same man who fashioned Nelson's Column in Trafalgar Square in London. Angle over the partly pedestrianised space, with its imposing monument to George Stephenson, at

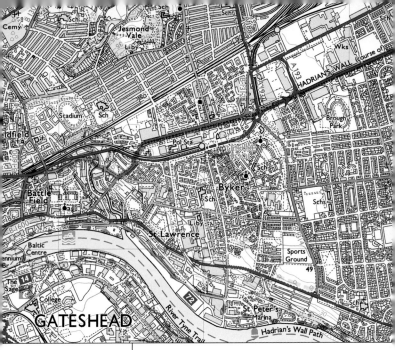

Map continues
on page 219

the junction with Neville Street (with the **Central Station**
right). Come to the North of England Institute of Mining
and Mechanical Engineers, in front of which is marked
the line of Hadrian's Wall. Next door is the much adored
Lit & Phil, where enlightenment has been nurtured since
the society's founding in 1793.

Come to St Nicholas' Street with Black Gate ahead.
Bear right under the road arch and visit the castle keep.

Outlined in the paving and under the arches are elements of the Roman fort, **Pons Aelius**, constructed
in stone by Septimus Severus some 60 years after
the Wall had first been constructed on this spot. At
that time the Tyne was shallow; indeed, it flowed
in several tidal channels, the Roman bridge sited
where the Swing Bridge now stands. Pons was Latin
for 'bridge' and Aelius was Hadrian's family name.
The extension to Segedunum (Wallsend) began in

AD127, built to the narrow 8ft gauge. The imperious Castle Keep, built in 1080, deserves a dedicated visit. Climb the steep stairs to reach the high-set great hall of the castle, which replicates Dover Castle and is thought to have been designed by the same architect. It was purchased by the Newcastle Corporation in 1810 as a ruin, and from the late 1840s onwards the Society of Antiquaries held the lease (as well as paying to restore it). More recently, the management of the Keep and the Black Gate was transferred to the Heritage Lottery Fund-funded Heart of the City Project, with which the society remains partners.

Thread back through the arches and come round the back of Black Gate on the walkway to see the interpretative panels. Passing out, bear right below steps into the Side roadway to turn right at Amen Corner. A path leads around St Nicholas' **Cathedral**, passing the welcoming entrance. In the next right-hand corner see a bust of Thomas Bewick, on the site of his workshop. ▶

Coming by the seated statue of Queen Victoria, go right with Mosley Street and across the junction, with the very grand architecture of Grey Street on the left. The road rises towards an island office block, seemingly on stilts, known as '55 Degrees North' (formerly Swan House). Use the light-controlled pedestrian crossing on Pilgrim Street and go round to the right, descending stairs to pass under the circulating road. Come beside the 17th-century Holy Jesus Hospital, with its dutch gable end, which was built on the site of a 13th-century Augustinian Friary.

Passing under the Metro Bridge, cross into City Road and view to the right an isolated corner portion of the city walls. Keep to the left-hand portion of City Road to cut acutely back up Tower Street to inspect the Sallyport Tower. Then bear right with Garth Heads, walking between the handsome brick Industrial Dwellings block and Keelman's Hospital. Bear left with Jubilee Street into Melbourne Street. Turning right, this becomes Buxton Street and after passing the student accommodation, turn next left up Gibson Street.

The famous wooden engraver's art recorded the life of the area before the Industrial Revolution had a serious impact on rural life – and Tyneside was largely rural, for all the burgeoning colliery activity.

At the top, bear right by the old baths and then St Dominic's Priory alongside New Bridge Street, in the area known as **Battle Field**. This was not the scene of a skirmish; like Walbottle it's a corruption of 'botel' meaning 'dwellings along the Wall'. With such a paucity of Hadrian's Wall on show it comes as a blessed relief to glance right by St Vincent's catholic centre with Crawhall Road to view a modest brick dwelling at Red Barns. Picked out in darker brick and mortar is the cross-section of Hadrian's Wall, including the notional parapet up to the eaves and paving in front. This further confirms the alignment of the Roman Wall, proof that the frontier did once ghost through this latterday suburbia.

Across the road, where Stepney Bank begins, prior to the construction of student accommodation, archaeologists recently found the actual Wall and the north wall of Turret 3a, the only one identified east of Pons Aelius. The site of the turret was strategic, overlooking the Ouseburn Valley. Regular Roman measurements would suggest it might have been located in Melbourne Street.

Descend Stepney Bank by the ever-popular Ship Inn pub, and Ouseburn Road, in the shadow of Byker railway viaduct, to cross the Ouseburn footbridge. Head on up the roadway, rising with Leighton Street upon irregular-shaped whinstone cobbles by Fearon's. At the top turn left with Byker Bank – the name Byker refers to a Viking farm that lay beside an alder carr (marsh).

Spot the 39 metal studs set into the paving, which represent the wooden spike obstacles (cippi) on the berm in front of the Wall that were found here during excavations.

A further small ascent brings you beside a portion of the distinctive Byker Wall housing community. Use the pedestrian crossing and advance beneath the Metro viaduct, keeping forward by Morrison's to turn right into Shields Road, a shop-lined street of mixed businesses. Towards the top end find Hadrian Square in front of the **Byker Leisure Centre** set back to the right. On the paved area fronting this is the footing course of Hadrian's Wall. The first genuine curtain wall seen since the foot of Benwell Hill. ◄

Coming to the top, fork right with the truncated Union Road. At the end, and by Edinburgh Cycles, find the apparent foundation course of Hadrian's Wall,

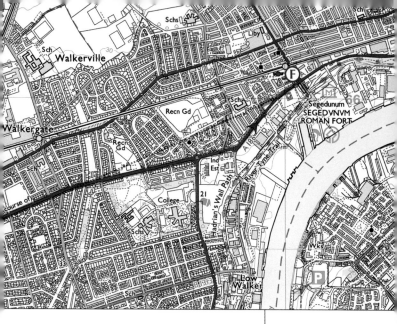

although this is fake. Fewer than 2 miles to go – orbit the great traffic roundabout clockwise, and after negotiating the Huddeston Road junction, with its retail park follow Fossway, which means 'the ditch-lined road', it was formerly called Double Dykes.

Pass Seimens Energy, formerly Parson's marine engineering works. Further intimated with the small pub Turbinia, which refers to the world's first turbine-propelled vessel, the creation of Charles Parsons. A few paces before the pub on the left-hand pavement, the slightly askew line identifies where Hadrian's Wall once ran. Fossway segways into Maurice Road, cornering left as Neptune Road, morphing again as Buddle Street, duly reaching the site of **Segedunum Roman Fort**.

Just before the fort, on the left, wend by Plantation Street to inspect a modern simulation of the Wall, with cippi. This is the only full-height construction along the entire length of Hadrian's Wall and is a valuable educational aid for school parties.

WESTBOUND: SEGEDUNUM TO HEDDON-ON-THE-WALL

Begin at the entrance to Segedunum Museum car park, following Buddle Street to Carville Road. Join the footpath adjacent to Plantation Road to view the Wall reconstruction. Rejoining Buddle Street, hold to the pavement by Neptune Road, continuing as Fossway, and passing the massive Seimens Energy building.

After negotiating the Huddleston Road junction, skirt anti-clockwise round the great roundabout into Union Road and thus down Shields Road in Byker. Bear left by Morrison's, walking beneath the Metro viaduct (although you can stick with New Bridge Road over Byker Bridge to Crawhall Road, thereby avoiding the descent into the Ouseburn).

It's more fun, however, to go down Byker Bank and right by Leighton Street to cross the Ouseburn footbridge, ascending Stepney Bank to reach Crawhall Road. Pass St Vincent's catholic centre, bearing right with Gibson Street and left with Buxton Street into Melbourne Street. Turn left with Jubilee Street, and right along Garth Heads into Tower Street, passing the Sallyport Tower. Go right with City Road, going under the Metro bridge by the 17th-century Holy Cross Hospital, ascending a short flight of steps and under the traffic, circulating the 55 Degrees North building. Using a pedestrian crossing, go down Mosley Street. Turn left by the seated statue of Queen Victoria, walking round the east side of Newcastle Cathedral and go left by Side to

Replica Roman Wall at Segedunum

come by the Black Gate and the railway viaduct, beyond which you will find the Castle Keep.

Bear right with Westgate Road, angle over the partly pedestrianised space with its imposing monument to George Stephenson, and set course with the footway on the long, uncomplicated ascent west, which rises inexorably towards Benwell Hill. This becomes West Road as the road begins to plateau short of Benwell Grove, now lined by shops. The high point on the hill is crowned by a reservoir directly on top of Condercum Roman Fort, identified by the mast. To visit the temple of Antenociticus, watch for Weidner Road on the left by Westholme Gardens and Broomridge Avenue, and further descend Denhill Park to view the vallum crossing.

The pavement now descends by the cricket ground. Immediately after the Denton Road roundabout, find, beyond the garage, a length of Roman Wall. Just short of the A1 interchange you will find a fine section with a turret. Use the nifty pedestrian underpasses and footbridge to cross the noisy A1, advancing with a further tiny section of the Wall beside the dual carriageway.

After the second A69 footbridge, bear left with the path and road by the Alan Shearer Centre and West Denton Road. At the end turn right with Union Hall Road. Cross to the west side and keep left, approaching the great roundabout. The footway is now sustained along Hawthorn Terrace by the old colliery hamlet of Blucher and through the wooded dip of Walbottle Dene. Now called Hexham Road (most commonly referred to as the Military Road), keep to the unremitting pavement through Throckley. After passing the Welcome to Northumberland sign at Frenchman's Row, come onto Great Hill and go down the steps left to inspect the fine stretch of Roman Wall and so, delightfully, enter Heddon-on-the-Wall.

APPENDIX A

Stamping stations

BOWNESS-ON-SOLWAY

- The Banks promenade, available 24hr

- The Kings Arms pub, available during normal opening hours. (The pub usually stocks passports, certificates and purple badges.)

- Indoor stamping point in the Lindow Hall (Bowness Village Hall) next door to the pub, open daily during normal working hours. (The Hall has a WC and a visitor book for walkers to sign.)

CARLISLE

- Sands Centre café (no passports or certificates or badges). The Sands Centre opens early and closes late.

- Back-up stamping point introduced a few years ago at the Sheepmount Athletics Stadium because some walkers mistook it for the Sands Sports Centre. (No passports or certificates or badges.)

- Tullie House has its own 'Tullie House' stamp at the museum entrance, available during normal opening hours (no passports or certificates or badges). The stamp goes in the same Sands Centre space on the card.

BIRDOSWALD ROMAN FORT

- Indoor stamping point at museum entrance, available during normal opening hours (no passports or certificates or badges).

- Outdoor box on the obvious facing wall approaching the museum entrance, available when the museum is closed.

HOUSESTEADS ROMAN FORT

- The stamping point is outside the museum entrance, available 24hr (no passports or certificates or badges). Heading east: from the hand gate at the east end of Housesteads Wood, go through and head for the museum, then continue around the south perimeter and around to Knag Burn gateway. Heading west: from Knag Burn gateway, walk around the south perimeter of the fort and head for the museum (now with refreshments), then continue in the same clockwise direction back up to the Trail and Wall, heading for Housesteads Wood.

- This stamping point was introduced some years after the Trail opened, as a conservation measure. It helps to take some of the pressure off the steep Knag Burn slope.

CHESTERS ROMAN FORT (CHOLLERFORD)

- Indoor stamping point at the museum entrance, available during normal working hours (no passports or certificates or badges).

- Outside stamping box on the field wall at the car park entrance leaving the Military Road. Sometimes it is locked during the museum's opening hours.

EAST WALLHOUSES

- The Robin Hood Inn has an outside stamping box, available all hours (no passports or certificates or badges).

- The Vallum Farm café is an unofficial back-up stamping point (open daily; no passports or certificates or badges).

WALLSEND

- Stamping point at the Segedunum museum reception, available during normal opening hours only. Segedunum stocks passports, as well as the souvenir purple enamel badges and certificates for people finishing their walk at Wallsend.

- There is a 24-hour stamping box at the rear entrance of the museum – go through the iron gate and the box is on the right-hand wall.

- ASDA supermarket, across the road from the museum, is a back-up stamping point. It also stocks passports, certificates and badges. ASDA keeps long hours and walkers tend to get a warm welcome from the staff.

- The TOTAL petrol station, about 450ft (137m) west of Segedunum, is another back-up stamping point (no passports, certificates or badges). It keeps long hours.

Should you finish your walk with a stamp missing, you only have to send your National Trail passport and a stamped addressed envelope (with the correct postage from the UK to your return address!) to the Hadrian's Wall Trail Manager, (Northumberland National Park Authority, Eastburn, South Park, Hexham NE46 1BS) and they will add the missing stamp. Trail walkers can buy their passports, badges and certificates online from www.trailgiftshop. co.uk. Additionally, on-the-spot purchases can be obtained at either end of the trail, at Segedunum Museum and the Kings Arms in Bowness-on-Solway.

APPENDIX B
Accommodation

Stage 1
Wallsend Guest House & Glamping Pods
CA7 5AF
tel 01697 351 055
info@thewallsend.co.uk
www.thewallsend.co.uk

Rose Cottage B&B
CA7 5AF
tel 01228 576 138
info@katescumbriancottages.co.uk

Kings Arms B&B
CA7 5AF
tel 01697 351 426
info@kingsarmsbowness.co.uk
www.kingsarmsbowness.co.uk

The Old Chapel B&B/campsite
CA7 5BL
tel 01697 351 126
oldchapelbowness@hotmail.com

Bowness House B&B
& Garrison Shepherd's Huts
CA7 5AF
tel 016973 52418
bownesshousearmholidaycomplex.co.uk

Shore Gate House B&B
CA7 5BH
tel 0169 7351 308
bookings@shoregatehouse.co.uk
www.shoregatehouse.co.uk

The Hope and Anchor Inn B&B
CA7 5BU
tel 01697 351 460
www.hopeandanchorinn.com

Hesket House B&B
CA7 5BU
tel 01697 351 876
stay@heskethouse.com

Highland Laddie Inn
CA7 5DT
tel 016973 51839

The Grange Cottages B&B
CA7 5DW
tel 01228 576 551
messrs.hodgson@tesco.net

Highfield Farm B&B campsite
CA5 6AA
tel 01228 576 060 or 07976170538
info@highfield-holidays.co.uk
www.highfield-holidays.co.uk

Hillside Farm B&B
CA5 6AA
tel 01228 576 398
sandrahillsidefarm@gmail.com
www.hadrianswalkbnb.co.uk

Rosemount Cottage B&B
CA5 6AN
tel 01228 576 440
tweentown@aol.com

Stage 2
Roman Wall Lodges
tel 07784 736423
enquiries@romanwall-lodges.co.uk
hadrians-wall-accommodation.co.uk

Knockupworth Hall B&B
CA2 7RF
tel 01228 523 531
knockupworthdi@aol.com

Vallum House Hotel
CA2 7NB
tel 01228 521 860
denmar39@tiscali.co.uk

Etterby Country House Hotel
CA3 9QS
tel 01228 510472
info@etterbycountryhouse.co.uk

Cumbria Park Hotel (Best Western)
CA3 9DG
tel 01228 522 887
enquiries@cumbriaparkhotel.co.uk
cumbriaparkhotel.com

Avar House B&B
CA3 9DG
tel 01228 540 636
vacancies@avarhouse.co.uk

Angus Hotel & Almonds Restaurant
CA3 9DG
tel 01228 523 546
hotel@angus-hotel.co.uk
www.angus-hotel.co.uk

Marlborough House B&B
CA3 9NW
tel 01228 512 174
Ian_mc_brown@hotmail.com

Warwick Lodge Guest House
CA1 1LP
tel 01228 523 796
www.warwicklodgecarlisle.co.uk

Holly Trees Hotel
CA1 1LP
tel 01228 547 243
www.hotel-carlisle.co.uk

Courtfield Guest House
CA1 1LP
tel 01228 522 767
www.courtfieldguesthouse.co.uk

Cambro House
CA1 1LP
tel 01228 543 094
www.cambrohouse.co.uk

Howard Lodge
CA1 1LP
tel 01228 529 842
www.howard-lodge.co.uk

Cherry Grove Guest House
CA1 2AW
tel 01228 598 782
www.cherrygroveguesthouse.co.uk

Townhouse B&B
CA1 1LP
tel 01228 598 782
www.townhousebandb.com

Stage 3
Madgwick B&B
CA6 4QN
tel 01228 573 283
madgwickonwall@yahoo.co.uk

High Crosby Farm Glamping Pods
CA6 4QZ
tel 01228 573000

Newtown Farm B&B
CA6 4N
tel 0169 772 768
s.grice@btconnect.com

Howard Arms Hotel
CA8 1NG
tel 016977 42758
www.howardarms.co.uk

Sycamore Gap B&B
CA8 1SB
tel 07817 750777

Scotch Arms Mews
CA8 1SB
tel 07786 115621
www.thescotcharmsmews.co.uk

Lanercost Country B&B
CA8 2HL
tel 01697 543009

Belted Will Hotel
CA8 2NJ
tel 016977 46236

Stage 4
Townhead Farm B&B
CA8 2DJ
tel 016977 2730
armstrong_townhead@hotmail.com

Sandysike Bunkhouse
CA8 2DU
tel 07725 645929
sandysike@gmx.com

Florrie's Bunkhouse
CA8 2DH
tel 07909 965851
hello@florriesonthewall.co.uk

Greenacres B&B
CA8 2DJ

Old Vicarage Brewery B&B
CA8 2DP
tel 01697 543002

Low Rigg Farm B&B
CA8 2DX
tel 016977 3233

Quarryside camp site
CA8 2JH
tel 01697 72538
campingatbanks@gmail.com
www.quarryside.co.uk

Stage 5
Bush Nook Group Accommodation
CA8 7AF
tel 01697 747 194
info@bushnook.co.uk
www.bushnook.co.uk

Brookside Villa B&B
CA8 7DA
tel 01697 747 300
info@brooksidevilla.com
www.brooksidevilla.com

Hill on the Wall B&B
CA8 7DA
tel 01697 747 214
info@hillonthewall.co.uk
www.hillonthewall.co.uk

Howard House B&B
CA8 7AJ
tel 01697 747 285
elizabeth@howardhousefarm.fstnct.co.uk

Willowford Farm B&B
CA8 7AA
tel 01697 747 962
stay@willowford.co.uk
www.willowford.co.uk

Samson Inn
CA8 7DR
tel 01697 747 880
samson@gmail.com

Four Wynds Guest House
CA8 7HN
tel 01697 747 972
info@four-wynds-guest-house.co.uk
www.four-wynds-guest-house.co.uk

Holmhead Guest House & Camping Barn
CA8 7HY
tel 01697 747 402
holmhead@forestbarn.com
bandbhadrianswall.com

Greenhead Hotel & Hostel
CA8 7HB
tel 01697 747 411
enquiries@greenheadhotelandhostel.co.uk
www.greenheadhotelandhostel.co.uk

Fell End Farm B&B
CA8 7HZ
tel 01434 320 316
enquiries@fellendfarm.co.uk

Walltown Lodge B&B
CA8 7JD
tel 01697 747 514 or 7415 058350
diane@walltownlodge.com

Burnhead B&B
NE49 9PJ
tel 01434 320 841
enquiries@burnheadbedandbreakfast.co.uk
www.burnheadbedandbreakfast.co.uk

The Old School House B&B
NE49 9EE
tel 01434 312013
office@oldschoolhousehaltwhistle.com

Wydon Farm
NE49 0LG
tel 01434 331702
www.wydonfarm.co.uk

Grey Bull B&B
NE49 0DL
tel 01434 321991

Hillis Close Farm
NE49 0PA
tel 07746 876308

Bridge House B&B
NE49 9NW
tel 01434 320 744
info@bridgehousecawfields.co.uk
www.bridgehousecawfields.co.uk

Vallum Lodge B&B
NE47 7AN
tel 01434 344 248
stay@vallum-lodge.co.uk
www.vallum-lodge.co.uk

Twice Brewed Inn
NE47 7AN
tel 01434 344 534
info@twicebrewedinn.co.uk
www.twicebrewedinn.co.uk

Saughy Rigg B&B
NE49 9PT
tel 01434 344 120
info@saughyrigg.co.uk
www.saughyrigg.co.uk

YHA The Sill
NE47 7AN
tel 0345 2602702

Stage 6
Old Repeater Station B&B
NE47 6NQ
tel 01434 688 668
les.gibson@tiscali.co.uk
www.hadrians-wall-bedandbreakfast.co.uk

Beggar Bog Farmhouse B&B
NE47 6NN
tel 01434 344 652
stay@beggarbog.com

Carraw Farm B&B
NE46 4DB
tel 01434 689 857
relax@carraw.co.uk
www.carraw.co.uk

Stage 7
Green Carts Farm campsite & bunkhouse
NE46 4BW
tel 01434 681 320
sandra@greencarts.co.uk
www.greencarts.co.uk

Hadrian Lodge Hotel
NE47 6NF
tel 01434 684 867
www.hadrianlodge.co.uk

The Reading Rooms B&B
NE47 6JQ
tel 01434 688 802
thereadingrooms@aol.com
www.thereadingroomshaydonbridge.co.uk

Anchor Hotel
NE47 6AB
tel 01434 684 227
anchorhotel@stay.uk.fsnet.co.uk

Langley Castle Hotel
NE47 5LU
tel 01434 688 888
manager@langleycastle.com

Red Lion Inn
NE47 5AR
tel 01434 674 226
redlionnewbrough@hotmail.co.uk

Carr Edge Farm
NE47 5EA
tel 01434 674 788
stay@carredge.co.uk
www.carredge.co.uk

Simonburn Guest House & Tearoom
NE48 3AW
tel 01434 681 321
simonburn.guesthouse@btopenworld.com

Hallbarns B&B
NE48 3AQ
tel 01434 681 419
enquiries@hallbarns-simonburn.co.uk

Battlesteads Hotel
NE48 3LS
tel 01434 230 209
info@battlesteads.com
www.battlesteads.com

Barrasford Arms Hotel
NE48 4AA
tel 01434 681 237
barrasfordarms@outlook.com
www.barrasfordarms.co.uk

The George Hotel
NE46 4EW
tel 01434 681611

Hadrian Hotel & Restaurant
NE46 4EE
tel 01434 681 232

Crag House B&B
NE46 4HA
tel 01434 681 276

The Sun Inn
NE46 4PW
tel 01434 602 934
suninn.acomb@gmail.com

The Queens Arms
NE46 4PT
tel 01434 607 857

Oakwood Cottage B&B
NE46 4LE
tel 01434 602 013
steveturner@treecorner.freeserve.co.uk

Fallowfield Dene B&B/campsite
NE46 4RD
tel 01434 603 553
info@fallowfielddene.co.uk

Loughbrow House B&B
NE46 1RS
tel 01434 603 351
enquiry@loughbrowhouse.co.uk

High Reins B&B
NE46 3AT
tel 01434 603 590
walton45@hotmail.com

Beaumont Hotel (Best Western)
NE46 3LT
tel 01434 602 331
beaumont.hotel@btinternet.com

Stage 8

DeVere Slaley Hall Hotel
NE47 0BX
tel 01434 673 350
victoria.williams@devere-hotels.com

Priorfield B&B
NE45 5JP
tel 01434 633 179

Peartree House B&B
NE45 5JN
tel 01434 632 223
contactus@peartreebedandbreakfast.com

Norgate B&B
NE45 5HS
tel 01434 633 736
norgatecorbridge@btinternet.com

Golden Lion B&B
NE45 5AA
tel 01434 634507
thegoldenlion77@gmail.com

Dilston Mill B&B
NE45 5QZ
tel 01434 633 493
susan@dilstonmill.com
www.dilstonmill.com

Broxdale B&B
NE45 5AY
tel 01434 632 492
broxdale@btinternet.com

Fellcroft B&B
NE45 5AY
tel 01434 632 384
ove@fellcroft.co.uk
www.fellcroftbandb.com

Duke of Wellington Inn
NE43 7UL
tel 01661 844 446
info@thedukeofwellingtoninn.co.uk
www.thedukeofwellingtoninn.co.uk

The Robin Hood Inn
NE18 0LL
tel 01434 672 2549
robinhood_northumberland@outlook.com

Matfen Hall Hotel
NE20 0RH
tel 01661 855 715
www.matfenhall.com

Matfen High House B&B
NE20 0R
tel 01661 886 592
struan@struan.enterprise-plc.com
www.matfenhighhouse.co.uk

Church House B&B
NE18 0PB
tel 01661 886 736
bedandbreakfast@stamfordham.fsbusiness.
co.uk

Dukes Cottages
NE42 6AD
tel 0191 268 8749
info@dukescottages.co.uk

Stage 9
Wormald House
NE41 8DN
tel 01661 852 529/07815 903167
jr.craven@tiscali.co.uk

Iron Sign Country House
NE15 0JB
tel 01661 853 802
lowen532@aol.com

Tyne Valley Views B&B
NE15 0DD
tel 07963 655972
john.riddell62@gmail.com

Ramblers' Repose
NE15 0DD
tel 01661 852 419
pmillward155@btinternet.com

Heddon Lodge B&B
NE15 0BU
tel 01661 854 042
info@heddonlodge.co.uk

Close House Country Club
NE15 0HT
tel 01661 852 255
www.closehouse.com

The Keelman Lodging (Newburn)
NE15 8NL
tel 01911 2670772
admin@biglampbrewers.co.uk

Stages 10/12
Holiday Inn Express Newcastle-Metro Centre
NE16 3BE
tel 0371 902 1548
newcastle@morethanhotels.com

Hedgefield House
NE21 4LR
tel 0191 413 7373/07958 304942
david@hedgefieldhouse.co.uk
www.hedgefieldhouse.co.uk

Westland Hotel
NE2 1JR
tel 0191 281 0412

The Dorset Arms Hotel
NE28 8DX
tel 0191 209 9754
info@dorsetarmshotel.co.uk
www.dorsetarmshotel.co.uk

Holiday Inn Express (Newcastle City
Centre)
tel 08704 009030
gm.newcastle@expressholidayinn.co.uk

Clifton House Hotel
NE4 6XH
tel 0191 272 7345
cliftonhousehotel@hotmail.com

Avenue Hotel
NE2 2LU
tel 0191 281 1396
avenue.hotel@amserve.com

Oaktree Lodge
NE26 2AH
tel 0191 252 8587
oaktreelodge@aol.com

Verne Hotel
NE28 6TZ
tel 0191 295 0003

Premier Inn (North Shields)
NE29 6DL
tel 033332 11356
www.premierinn.com

Annie's Guest House
NE33 2NE
tel 0191 456 6088
www.anniesguesthouse.co.uk

Premier Inn (Port Of Tyne)
NE34 9PU
tel 033332 19003
www.premierinn.com

The Sir William Fox Hotel
NE33 3PS
tel 0191 456 4554
www.sirwilliamfoxhotel.com

The Sea Hotel (Best Western)
NE33 2LD
tel 0191 427 0999
www.bestwestern.co.uk

Little Haven Hotel
NE33 1LH
tel 0191 45 54455
www.littlehavenhotel.com

APPENDIX C

Walking links to the Path from nearby railway stations

Apart from the 12-mile section west of Carlisle, it is possible for walkers to join the National Trail from year-round railway services on the Carlisle–Newcastle Railway and from the Metro on Tyneside. Should you add the maritime frontier of Hadrian's Coast by alighting at Maryport railway station on the Cumbrian Coast Line, you can walk 127 miles (204km) to South Shields Metro Station – with intermediate stations should you wish to modify your walk plans or gather the journey up piecemeal.

CARLISLE STATION LINK
1 MILE (1.6KM) (SEE STAGE 3)

From the Citadel Station advance to the traffic lights, cross the road and pass the bus stops beside the Citadel building in English Street. Keep straight ahead, crossing at the next traffic lights to enter the pedestrian shopping area leading into the Market Place, focused on the Market Cross and backed by the Old Town Hall TIC (up steps).

Keep to the left of the bandstand to enter Castle Street. Bear left to pass Carlisle Cathedral, go through The Close and via Abbey Gatehouse arch into Abbey Street. After 150ft (46m) bear right to pass through the gardens of Tullie House Museum, exiting into Castle Street. Turn left and take the underpass in front of Tullie House beneath Castle Way, a busy dual carriageway. Emerging with Carlisle Castle ahead, go up the steps left onto the footway and go left again after the castle walls. Bear left by a car park into Bitts Park, advancing to join the National Trail approaching Eden Bridge.

BRAMPTON STATION LINK
4 MILES (6.5KM) (SEE STAGE 4)

Leave the remote station platform joining the Dandy Line, signed 'public footpath Brampton ½ mile'. The eastbound platform backs onto the old horse-drawn carriage platform, which until 1923 gave the town of Brampton a link with the rail network. (Railway enthusiasts may like to know that when the station was opening in 1836, the station master Thomas Edmondson instituted the world's first cardboard tickets for passengers, later also developing the first date-stamping machine.)

The path leads largely through woodland and, floodlit, under the A69 to step down into Station Road. Turn left, keeping right at the green, via two short connecting roads over the old Newcastle Road to enter Lanercost Road. (Bus travellers alighting from the 685 (Carlisle–Newcastle) Arriva service in Brampton's Market Square can reach this spot via High Cross Street, turning right into The Sands under the wooded hill The Moat.)

Follow the footway leading out of town along charmingly named The Swartle. Where a side road joins from the left, go right through the metal kissing gate and follow a footpath that leads down the wooded Quarry Beck valley to emerge onto the road. Cross the elegant pedestrian high-arched Abbey Bridge, following the road by Lanercost Tearoom and Priory Garth. At the T-junction, go within the beech-hedge lined bridle-lane between the houses from the handsome signpost. After this swings left, fork right and climb within the private road to connect with the National Trail at Haytongate, with its picnic tables and refreshment cabin.

HALTWHISTLE STATION LINK
2½ MILES (4KM) (SEE STAGE 5)

Exit Haltwhistle station platform to follow Station Road via Westgate into Main Street, thereby leading through the Market Place. Pass by the Centre of Britain Hotel, bearing left along Town Hall Crescent and veering right with a path onto Fair Hill. Directly after the entry to Fairfield Park find a path signed left that leads down by a fence, turning left to walk along the edge of a playing field and join Willa Road. Follow this road upstream, initially beside Haltwhistle Burn, and stay on the road as it climbs to Lees Hall Farm.

Pass on through the farm buildings via gates onto the succeeding track, which meets the Military Road at a gate. Carefully cross the B6318 by Leeshall Cottage, bearing in mind that the traffic can be fast. Follow the side road by Markham Cottage. After the gate the road runs on enclosed – and can be followed to Walltown – but to quickly

link up with the National Trail cross the cattle grid and follow the farm track up towards Great Chesters Farm, entering the Aesica Roman Fort enclosure.

BARDON MILL STATION LINK
3 MILES (5KM) (SEE STAGE 6)

From the platform, walk along the approach lane to the street close to the Village Store. Cross the road, entering the yard of Errington Reay Pottery. The path is indicated straight up ahead, at the top of the yard; bear left with an incline path leading to an open crossing of the A69. Cross this road with the utmost care (traffic can be very fast but fortunately there is a long clear view in both directions). A further short incline path leads up to a kissing gate entering a pasture.

Accompany the field wall to a kissing gate then join an open track, go left via a cattle grid and then through a gate to reach a minor road. Turn right, and at the junction bear left (actually more straight on), a road sign showing the blue cycleway 68/72 and Vindolanda/Once Brewed. Passing cottages, the road dips then rises to where a fenced drive enters from the right, footpath sign 'Vindolanda'.

Follow this roadway, passing Cragside Riding Stables, and continue with the gravel trackway leading by a footbridge/ford and on past Low Fogrigg cottage. At a field gate the track enters a pasture; advance with the lovely wooded dingle of Chainley Burn to the right. Go through a hand gate and continue, passing the bare foundations of a ruin, to dip into the valley.

Abbey Bridge, looking to Lanercost Priory

Go through a 'v' stile and along a boardwalk via two further 'v' stiles to come close to the burn. Obviously ignore the skeletal footbridge, crossing instead by the subsequent sturdy footbridge; you can gain a partial view of the Chesterholm gardens. The path completes its confined journey at the access roadway to Vindolanda Museum. (The opportunity to pay, enter and explore the greater site, including the Stanegate fort of Vindolanda as well as café and toilets, is hugely rewarding.)

Follow on by the Hedley Centre to meet the minor road – a surviving portion of Stanegate, the pre-Hadrianic frontier road from Carlisle to Corbridge. Turn left, entering the field right at the ladder stile. To the left note the fine, in-situ, Codley Roman milestone; interestingly, the severed base of a further milestone, exactly one Roman mile distant, stands beside the Vindolanda approach road (Stanegate) – you may thereby stride a Roman mile as the Romans knew it.

However, our link route to the National Trail heads up the field. As height is gained the view back onto Vindolanda improves, and you can also judge the grooved course of Stanegate in the adjacent pasture to the east. Higher still, follow on with a fence to a stile, the ensuing field drawing into a narrow strip. At the top, cross the wall via a ladder stile by High Shield, with its solar-panelled roof. Exit the bushy fringe of the garden by a fence styleand traverse the next field, latterly beside the vallum, to a wall stile stepping into burdock.

Now there is no choice: you must follow the verge along the Military Road right, crossing to the gate (National Trust sign attached), and follow the farm-track (access to Hot Bank Farm). Notice, before the track enters the confines of Milking Gap and unites with the National Trail, an irregular ring of large stones on the left – this was an Iron Age farmstead of five round houses and a farmyard, the farmers ousted when the vallum-to-Wall zone was militarized.

HEXHAM STATION LINK
4 MILES (6.4KM) (SEE STAGE 7)

Leave the station car park, turning right with Station Road by the Wentworth Leisure Centre to reach the roundabout. Cross and follow the footway over the railway, then cross the River Tyne at the entrance to Tyne Green after the next roundabout. (The weir under the bridge gives the impression of a great river upstream; it is used by rowers and canoeists.)

Advance by the busy dual-carriageway and take pleasure in branching left on the bridleway signed 'St John Lee Bridge', the traffic-free country lane leading to a bridge over the A69 dual carriageway. Bear right up to the minor road, then go left by the tree stump and continue on to the five-ways at Peaslaw Gate. Follow the 'no through road', keeping forward, with brick cottages on the left at The Riding, to enter a narrow, hedged bridle path signed 'Acomb'. This leads down to cross Birkey Burn and continues in a walled passage rising to The Green in Acomb. (Note the odd sculpted stone on the right as the path opens, found at the South and North Tyne confluence.)

Turn left down the village Main Street by the Miners Arms and The Sun. At the crossroads by the Queens Arms turn right to follow the minor road leading out of the village and up the hill to Fallowfield Farm. Keep with the road through the farm community; after a cattle grid it continues unenclosed, rising easily to a galvanised road gate (note the bare bedrock through the field gate on the right). Keep with the road via a further road gate to reach St Oswalds Cottage at Heavenfield and the Military Road, opposite the access to the historic field island site of St Oswald's Church, thus joining the National Trail.

Vindolanda from Barcombe Hill

CORBRIDGE STATION LINK
4 MILES (6.4KM) (SEE STAGE 8)

Leave the platform (the station premises is now The Valley – an Indian restaurant and a novel evening train ride destination in its own right) and follow the approach road by The Dyvels pub, joining the main road to cross the Tyne Bridge into Corbridge. Turn left along Middle Street into the Market Place. Pass St Andrew's Church, following on with the main road and cornering at The Wheatsheaf Hotel.

Directly after Corchester Lane on the left (leading to Corbridge Roman site), turn right into St Helen's Lane, then left into Hippingstones Lane. Before the school, slip into the hedge lined pathway which leads to a kissing gate into Hippingstones Field (the blue panel explaining the significance of the field will soon become history itself as sadly houses are planned to be built in the field). The path runs across the field, entering the Cow Lane path at a hand gate. Cow Lane was severed with the construction of the A69; hence, as a fenced path it veers right to meet a minor road.

Turn left, going under the A69, then turn first right with a bridleway sign 'Aydon Castle'. Go through the double gate and along the green lane to a hand gate beside a cattle holding pen. Enter then traverse a pasture on a tangible path to a hand gate, bearing left above the fence to meet up with a bridle path at a hand gate. Traverse the next field to enter the woodland at a hand gate.

Aydon Castle

The potentially muddy holloway leads to a footbridge over Cor Burn, the path then rising to a hand gate with the high walls of Aydon Castle looming. Pass the entrance to this amazing fortified 13th-century manor house, now in the care of English Heritage. Follow the approach road, keeping ahead (signed 'Halton') to reach Halton Castle – an impressively embellished peel tower with a parish church resting beside; spot the Roman altar and topiary pig!

Continue via the cattle grid to follow the unenclosed road through the park, connecting with the National Trail at the entrance gateway. Located on both sides of the Military Road, the earthworks of Halton Chesters Roman Fort are not easily discernable.

WYLAM STATION LINK
1½ MILES (2.3KM) (SEE STAGE 9)

(For anyone walking west and wishing to avoid all the suburban tangle of Tyneside, this is also a great solution.) Cross the Tyne Bridge and head on to enter the Tyne Riverside Country Park car park, joining the Wylam Waggonway. Going right, pass/visit Stephenson's Cottage (National Trust), the birthplace of the railway pioneer George Stephenson, with a welcome tearoom at the back. Continue via golf course fairways to a Waggonway interpretative panel and National Trail signpost directing left.

NEWCASTLE-UPON-TYNE
STATION LINK
½ MILE (0.6KM) (SEE STAGE 10)

The simple and efficient link leaves Central Station, turning right with Neville Street to join the staggered Westgate Road by the famous Lit & Phil Library. Passing the railway arches, join St Nicholas' Street with the cathedral left and Black Gate opposite. Go under the railway arch near the Castle Keep, crossing the cobbled Castle Garth. Descend Castle Stairs and turn left by Bessie Surtees House (English Heritage), then turn right through Watergate onto The Quayside, joining Hadrian's Way.

Segedunum Museum viewing tower from Wallsend Metro Station

APPENDIX D
Bus and taxi services

Buses

While it's possible to have confidence in the regular passage of trains, there is far less certainty in rural bus services. Urban Tyneside, and to a lesser extent rural Northumberland, with bigger populations to underpin their services, are better served with buses.

The seasonal AD122 Hadrian's Wall Country Bus has become something of a ghost bus in Cumbria due to budget cuts in that county. Some semblance of a service may exist; you should seek local public transport advice before you commit yourself and avoid a futile wait at a 'lost cause' bus stop. Too often old timetables are posted up at bus stops, so be warned!

Indeed, the seasonal plans at the time of writing (2023) are only to provide a service, in terms of the Trail, from Walltown via Haltwhistle, Milecastle Inn, Once Brewed, Vindolanda, Housesteads, Chesters and Hexham.

Arriva, meanwhile, reliably plies the A69 with its 685 service, stopping at Carlisle, Brampton, Greenhead, Haltwhistle, Bardon Mill, Hexham, Corbridge, Heddon, Lemington and Newcastle (Eldon Square).

Taxis

Carlisle
Radio Taxis – tel 01228 527 575
AAA Taxis – tel 01228 808 777
Carlisle Drivers – tel 01228 515 818
Carlisle Taxi – tel 01228 424 242
City Taxis – tel 01228 520 000
Executive Cabs – tel 01228 529 957
Marks Taxi Service – tel 01228 891 244
C&P Taxis – tel 01228 535 425

Brampton
Airbus 2000 – tel 01697 73 735
Brampton Cars – tel 01697 73 386
Atkinson of Brampton – tel 01697 73 929

Haltwhistle
Diamond Private Hire – tel 07597 641 222
Turnbull Taxis – tel 01434 320 105
Melvin's Taxis – tel 07903 760 230
Sproul Taxis – tel 01434 321 064

Alston
Alston Taxis – tel 07990 593 855

Hexham
New Haydon Taxis – tel 01434 684 658
AAA Taxis – tel 01434 688 799
Langley Taxis – tel 01434 684 658
Baynes Travel – tel 01434 683 269
Advanced Taxis – tel 01434 606 565
Batey's Taxis – tel 01434 602 500
Ecocabs – tel 01434 600 600
Colin Taxi – tel 07771 860 688

Barrasford
A2B Taxis – tel 07796 397 006

Corbridge
Corbridge Village Taxi – tel 01434 634 006

Prudhoe

Gilmore Taxis – tel 01661 833 797
Arran Cabs – tel 01661 830 999
Prudhoe Taxis – tel 01661 833 833
A1 Castle Cabs – tel 01661 834 800

Ponteland

Broadway Cabs – tel 01661 822 200
Darras & Pont Taxis – tel 01661 871 736
Tony's Taxis – tel 01661 823 937

Newcastle

Airport Taxis – tel 0191 214 6969
Dean Taxis – tel 0191 444 4444
Phoenix Taxis – tel 01670 540 222
Denton Taxis – tel 0191 274 1010
Rowland Gill Taxis – tel 07860 620 973
Lemington Labour Club – tel 0191 267 4898
Dixons Taxis – tel 0191 273 3339
Fenham Taxis – tel 0191 272 2722
Geordie Cabs – tel 0191 275 0002
ABC Taxis – tel 0191 233 1000
Five Star Taxis – tel 0191 222 0555
LA Taxis – tel 0191 287 7777
Walker Taxis – tel 0191 265 2237

Wallsend

Battle Hill Taxis – tel 0191 263 8883
Westholme Taxis – tel 0191 234 5533
Blueline Taxis – tel 0191 209 8013

North Shields

Silverline – tel 0191 262 2020
Central Taxis – tel 0191 258 1000
Fleetline Taxis – tel 0191 296 1919
Priory Taxis – tel 0191 257 6061
Express Taxis – tel 0191 483 7777

South Shields

Richmond Taxis – tel 0191 455 3131
Westoe Taxis – tel 0191 454 4941
Dial a Cab – tel 0191 455 8888
Central Taxis – tel 0191 427 1111

APPENDIX E
Useful contacts

Considerable changes have taken place in the delivery of tourist information throughout the Wall corridor, brought about by the demise of Hadrian's Wall Trust in 2014.
www.nationaltrail.co.uk/ hadrians-wall-path
www.hadrianswallcountry.co.uk

www.visitnorthumberland.com managed by Northumberland Tourism for Northumberland County Council

www.englandsnortheast.co.uk England's North East

www.northumberlandnationalpark.org.uk Covering the scenically famous Whin Sill section of the Wall

www.heartofhadrianswall.com Heart of Hadrian's Wall Tourist Association

www.discovercarlisle.co.uk for Cumbria sector of the Trail.

www.haltwhistle.org for Haltwhistle

www.visithexham.net for Hexham

www.visitsouthtyneside.co.uk for South Shields

www.solwaycoastaonb.org.uk for Solway Firth lowlands

www.nationaltrust.org.uk

Consult North-East England for their Hadrian's Wall Estate

Museums and Roman sites

Tullie House (Carlisle)
tel 01228 534781
www.tulliehouse.co.uk

Carvoran Roman Army Museum (Greenhead)
tel 016977 47485

Vindolanda Fort and Museum
tel 01434 34427
www.vindolanda.com

English Heritage sites

www.english-heritage.org.uk

Housesteads Roman Fort
tel 01434 344363

Chesters Roman Fort
tel 01434 681379

Corbridge Roman Site
tel 01434 632349,

Birdoswald Roman Fort (Gilsland)
tel 016977 47602,

Carlisle Castle
tel 01228 591922

Lanercost Priory
tel 016977 3030

Aydon Castle
tel 01434 632450

Great North Museum: Hancock
tel 0191 208 6765,

Segedunum Roman Fort and Museum (Wallsend)
tel 0191 236 9347

Arbeia Roman Fort and Museum (South Shields)
tel 0191 456 1369

www.twmuseums.org.uk

Tourist information centres

Carlisle
CA3 8JH
tel 01228 625600

Haltwhistle
NE49 0AX
tel 01434 322002

The Sill:
National Landscape Discovery Centre
NE47 7AN
tel 01434 341200

Hexham
NE46 1XE
tel 01434 652220

Newcastle
NE1 5AF
tel 0191 277 8000

Youth hostels and camping barns

(campingbarns@yha.org.uk)

Carlisle
tel 08707 705752

Bankshead Camping Barn
tel 08707 706113

Greenhead
tel 01697 747411

Once Brewed
tel 08707 75980

Newcastle-upon-Tyne
tel 08707 705972

Public transport

Journey Planner
www.traveline.info

Rail Travel
www.northernrailway.co.uk

Tyne Valley Community Rail Partnership
www.tvcrp.org.uk

Northumberland and Tyne & Wear
bus services
www.gonortheast.co.uk

For parking information see
www.northumberlandnationalpark.org.uk/
visitor-info/car-parks/

Walking tour companies

Shepherds Walks Holidays
www.shepherdswalksholidays.co.uk

Contours Walking Holidays
www.contours.co.uk

Macs Adventure
www.macsadventure.com

Mickledore
www.mickledore.co.uk

The Walking Holiday Company
www.thewalkingholidaycompany.co.uk

Celtic Trails Walking Holidays
www.celtic-trails.com

Easyways Bespoke Walking Tours
www.easyways.com

Ramblers Walking Holidays
www.ramblersholidays.co.uk

Baggage transfer

Hadrian's Wall Baggage Transfer Service
www.hadriansbags.co.uk
tel 07976 356459

Walkers' Baggage Transfer
tel 08714 238803
bookings@walkersbags.co.uk

Lake District Baggage Transfer
tel 07485 657548
hello@lakedistrictbaggagetransfer.com

Brigantes Walking Holidays and Baggage
Transfer
tel 01756 770402
support@brigantesenglishwalks.com

Sherpa Van
tel 017488 26917
info@sherpavan.com

Hadrian's Haul Ltd Wall-wide baggage
transfer service
tel 07799 828282

Blue Badge Guides

www.cumbriatouristguides.org
www.northeastenglandtouristguides.co.uk

APPENDIX F
Further reading

Breeze, David J, *Handbook to the Roman Wall* Fourteenth Edition, Society of Antiquities of Newcastle-upon-Tyne 2006 (affectionately known as The Purple Brick, this is the primary reference for exploring the frontier for studious Wall walkers)

Breeze, David J, *The Frontiers of Imperial Rome,* Pen & Sword Military, 2011

Breeze, David J, *Hadrian's Wall: A History of Archaeological Thought* Cumberland & Westmorland A&A Society, 2014

Breeze, David J, Savin, Peter and Richards, Mark, *Hadrian's Wall: A Journey Through Time* Bookcase, 2019

Leach, Stephen & Whitworth, David, *Saving the Wall: The Conservation of Hadrian's Wall* Amberley, 2011

Whitworth, David, *Hadrian's Wall Through Time* Amberley, 2012

Bedoyere, Guy de la, *Hadrian's Wall: History and Guide*, Tempus, 1998

Bidwell, Paul, *Hadrian's Wall 1989–99*, South Shields, 1999

Breeze, David J. and Dobson, Brian, *Hadrian's Wall*, 5th ed, Penguin, 2004

Crow, James, *Books of Housesteads*, English Heritage/Batsford, 1995

Crow, James and Woodside, Robert, *Hadrian's Wall, An Historical Landscape*, National Trust, 1999

Davies, Hunter, *A Walk along the Wall*, Weidenfeld and Nicolson, 1984

Hutton, William, *The First Man to Walk Hadrian's Wall*, 1802, Frank Graham, 1990

Johnson, Stephen, *Hadrian's Wall*, Batsford/English Heritage, 1989

McCarthy, Mike, *Roman Carlisle and the Lands of the Solway*, Tempus, 2002

Wilmott, Tony, *Birdoswald Roman Fort: 1800 years on Hadrian's Wall*, Tempus, 2001

Moffat, Alistair, *The Wall: Rome's Greatest Frontier,* Birlinn, 2008

Mothersole, Jessie, *Hadrian's Wal,l* John Lane, 1922, (out-of-print gem)

Kipling, Rudyard *Puck of Pook's Hill* 1906 (a children's classic, short fanciful stories from history written while Kipling was staying as a guest at Stagshaw House, near Portgate. Donald Mackenzie, who wrote the introduction for the Oxford World's Classics edition of the book in1987, has described this book as an example of archaeological imagination that, in fragments, delivers a look at the history of England, climaxing with the signing of Magna Carta.)

Roger Clegg and Mark Richards, *The Spirit of Hadrian's Wall – an atmospheric photographic essay about the Wall in all its seasons*

The Trail has spawned an excellent range of pocket guides published by Aurum Press, Trailblazer, Rucksack Readers and Knife Edge. However, you might like to track down, via second-hand sources, the author's two original hand-scribed Cicerone guides from before the advent of the National Trail, The Wall Walk and Wall Country Walks, published in 1993 and 1996, respectively.

Maps

Harvey Maps, HADRIAN'S WALL PATH
    National Trail Map, detailed waterproof map – perfect for far-moving walkers

Ordnance Survey, HADRIAN'S WALL, Historical Map & Guide
    Suitable for casual visitors and keen monument-hunters alike

Ordnance Survey, MAP OF HADRIAN'S WALL, 1972 edition.
    Only found (all too rarely, as they are treasured) in second-hand bookshops; this is the best map for studious walkers with a eye landscape history.

Current Ordnance Survey maps covering HADRIAN'S WALL PATH
    Landranger (1:50,000): 85, 86, 87, 88
    Explorer (1:25,000): OL43, 314, 315, 316

NOTES

NOTES

LISTING OF CICERONE GUIDES

BRITISH ISLES CHALLENGES, COLLECTIONS AND ACTIVITIES

Cycling Land's End to John o' Groats
Great Walks on the England Coast Path
The Big Rounds
The Book of the Bivvy
The Book of the Bothy
The Mountains of England & Wales:
    Vol 1 Wales
    Vol 2 England
The National Trails
Walking the End to End Trail

SHORT WALKS SERIES

Short Walks Hadrian's Wall
Short Walks in Arnside and Silverdale
Short Walks in Dumfries and Galloway
Short Walks in Nidderdale
Short Walks in the Lake District:
    Windermere Ambleside and Grasmere
Short Walks on the Malvern Hills
Short Walks in the Surrey Hills
Short Walks Winchester

SCOTLAND

Ben Nevis and Glen Coe
Cycle Touring in Northern Scotland
Cycling in the Hebrides
Great Mountain Days in Scotland
Mountain Biking in Southern and Central Scotland
Mountain Biking in West and North West Scotland
Not the West Highland Way Scotland
Scotland's Best Small Mountains
Scotland's Mountain Ridges
Scottish Wild Country Backpacking
Skye's Cuillin Ridge Traverse
The Borders Abbeys Way
The Great Glen Way
The Great Glen Way Map Booklet
The Hebridean Way
The Hebrides
The Isle of Mull
The Isle of Skye
The Skye Trail
The Southern Upland Way
The West Highland Way
The West Highland Way Map Booklet
Walking Ben Lawers, Rannoch and Atholl
Walking in the Cairngorms
Walking in the Pentland Hills
Walking in the Scottish Borders
Walking in the Southern Uplands

Walking in Torridon, Fisherfield, Fannichs and An Teallach
Walking Loch Lomond and the Trossachs
Walking on Arran
Walking on Harris and Lewis
Walking on Jura, Islay and Colonsay
Walking on Rum and the Small Isles
Walking on the Orkney and Shetland Isles
Walking on Uist and Barra
Walking the Cape Wrath Trail
Walking the Corbetts
    Vol 1 South of the Great Glen
    Vol 2 North of the Great Glen
Walking the Galloway Hills
Walking the John o' Groats Trail
Walking the Munros
    Vol 1 – Southern, Central and Western Highlands
    Vol 2 – Northern Highlands and the Cairngorms
Winter Climbs: Ben Nevis and Glen Coe

NORTHERN ENGLAND ROUTES

Cycling the Reivers Route
Cycling the Way of the Roses
Hadrian's Cycleway
Hadrian's Wall Path
Hadrian's Wall Path Map Booklet
The Coast to Coast Cycle Route
The Coast to Coast Walk
The Coast to Coast Walk Map Booklet
The Pennine Way
The Pennine Way Map Booklet
Walking the Dales Way
Walking the Dales Way Map Booklet

NORTH-EAST ENGLAND, YORKSHIRE DALES AND PENNINES

Cycling in the Yorkshire Dales
Great Mountain Days in the Pennines
Mountain Biking in the Yorkshire Dales
The Cleveland Way and the Yorkshire Wolds Way
The Cleveland Way Map Booklet
The North York Moors
The Reivers Way
Trail and Fell Running in the Yorkshire Dales
Walking in County Durham
Walking in Northumberland
Walking in the North Pennines
Walking in the Yorkshire Dales: North and East
Walking in the Yorkshire Dales: South and West

Walking St Cuthbert's Way
Walking St Oswald's Way and Northumberland Coast Path

NORTH-WEST ENGLAND AND THE ISLE OF MAN

Cycling the Pennine Bridleway
Isle of Man Coastal Path
The Lancashire Cycleway
The Lune Valley and Howgills
Walking in Cumbria's Eden Valley
Walking in Lancashire
Walking in the Forest of Bowland and Pendle
Walking on the Isle of Man
Walking on the West Pennine Moors
Walking the Ribble Way
Walks in Silverdale and Arnside

LAKE DISTRICT

Bikepacking in the Lake District
Cycling in the Lake District
Great Mountain Days in the Lake District
Joss Naylor's Lakes, Meres and Waters of the Lake District
Lake District Winter Climbs
Lake District:
    High Level and Fell Walks
Lake District:
    Low Level and Lake Walks
Mountain Biking in the Lake District
Outdoor Adventures with Children – Lake District
Scrambles in the Lake District – North
Scrambles in the Lake District – South
Trail and Fell Running in the Lake District
Walking The Cumbria Way
Walking the Lake District Fells –
    Borrowdale
    Buttermere
    Coniston
    Keswick
    Langdale
    Mardale and the Far East
    Patterdale
    Wasdale
Walking the Tour of the Lake District

DERBYSHIRE, PEAK DISTRICT AND MIDLANDS

Cycling in the Peak District
Dark Peak Walks
Scrambles in the Dark Peak
Walking in Derbyshire
Walking in the Peak District – White Peak East
Walking in the Peak District – White Peak West

SOUTHERN ENGLAND

20 Classic Sportive Rides in South East England
20 Classic Sportive Rides in South West England
Cycling in the Cotswolds
Mountain Biking on the North Downs
Mountain Biking on the South Downs
Suffolk Coast and Heath Walks
The Cotswold Way
The Cotswold Way Map Booklet
The Kennet and Avon Canal
The Lea Valley Walk
The North Downs Way
The North Downs Way Map Booklet
The Peddars Way and Norfolk Coast Path
The Pilgrims' Way
The Ridgeway National Trail
The Ridgeway National Trail Map Booklet
The South Downs Way
The South Downs Way Map Booklet
The Thames Path
The Thames Path Map Booklet
The Two Moors Way
The Two Moors Way Map Booklet
Walking Hampshire's Test Way
Walking in Cornwall
Walking in Essex
Walking in Kent
Walking in London
Walking in Norfolk
Walking in the Chilterns
Walking in the Cotswolds
Walking in the Isles of Scilly
Walking in the New Forest
Walking in the North Wessex Downs
Walking on Dartmoor
Walking on Guernsey
Walking on Jersey
Walking on the Isle of Wight
Walking the Dartmoor Way
Walking the Jurassic Coast
Walking the South West Coast Path
Walking the South West Coast Path Map Booklets
 – Vol 1: Minehead to St Ives
 – Vol 2: St Ives to Plymouth
 – Vol 3: Plymouth to Poole
Walks in the South Downs National Park

WALES AND WELSH BORDERS

Cycle Touring in Wales
Cycling Lon Las Cymru
Glyndwr's Way
Great Mountain Days in Snowdonia
Hillwalking in Shropshire
Mountain Walking in Snowdonia
Offa's Dyke Path
Offa's Dyke Path Map Booklet
Ridges of Snowdonia
Scrambles in Snowdonia
Snowdonia: 30 Low-level and Easy Walks – North
Snowdonia: 30 Low-level and Easy Walks – South
The Cambrian Way
The Pembrokeshire Coast Path
The Pembrokeshire Coast Path Map Booklet
The Snowdonia Way
The Wye Valley Walk
Walking in Carmarthenshire
Walking in Pembrokeshire
Walking in the Brecon Beacons
Walking in the Forest of Dean
Walking in the Wye Valley
Walking in Gower
Walking the Severn Way
Walking the Shropshire Way
Walking the Wales Coast Path

INTERNATIONAL CHALLENGES, COLLECTIONS AND ACTIVITIES

Europe's High Points
Walking the Via Francigena Pilgrim Route – Part 1

AFRICA

Kilimanjaro
Walking in the Drakensberg
Walks and Scrambles in the Moroccan Anti-Atlas

ALPS CROSS-BORDER ROUTES

100 Hut Walks in the Alps
Alpine Ski Mountaineering Vol 1 – Western Alps
The Karnischer Hohenweg
The Tour of the Bernina
Trail Running – Chamonix and the Mont Blanc region
Trekking Chamonix to Zermatt
Trekking in the Alps
Trekking in the Silvretta and Ratikon Alps
Trekking Munich to Venice
Trekking the Tour of Mont Blanc
Walking in the Alps

PYRENEES AND FRANCE/SPAIN CROSS-BORDER ROUTES

Shorter Treks in the Pyrenees
The GR11 Trail
The Pyrenean Haute Route
The Pyrenees
Walks and Climbs in the Pyrenees

AUSTRIA

Innsbruck Mountain Adventures
Trekking Austria's Adlerweg
Trekking in Austria's Hohe Tauern
Trekking in Austria's Zillertal Alps
Trekking in the Stubai Alps
Walking in Austria
Walking in the Salzkammergut: the Austrian Lake District

EASTERN EUROPE

The Danube Cycleway Vol 2
The Elbe Cycle Route
The High Tatras
The Mountains of Romania
Walking in Hungary

FRANCE, BELGIUM AND LUXEMBOURG

Camino de Santiago – Via Podiensis
Chamonix Mountain Adventures
Cycle Touring in France
Cycling London to Paris
Cycling the Canal de la Garonne
Cycling the Canal du Midi
Cycling the Route des Grandes Alpes
Mont Blanc Walks
Mountain Adventures in the Maurienne
Short Treks on Corsica
The GR5 Trail
The GR5 Trail – Benelux and Lorraine
The GR5 Trail – Vosges and Jura
The Grand Traverse of the Massif Central
The Moselle Cycle Route
The River Loire Cycle Route
The River Rhone Cycle Route
Trekking in the Vanoise
Trekking the Cathar Way
Trekking the GR10
Trekking the GR20 Corsica
Trekking the Robert Louis Stevenson Trail
Via Ferratas of the French Alps
Walking in Provence – East
Walking in Provence – West
Walking in the Ardennes
Walking in the Auvergne
Walking in the Brianconnais
Walking in the Dordogne
Walking in the Haute Savoie: North
Walking in the Haute Savoie: South
Walking on Corsica
Walking the Brittany Coast Path

GERMANY

Hiking and Cycling in the Black Forest
The Danube Cycleway Vol 1
The Rhine Cycle Route
The Westweg
Walking in the Bavarian Alps

For full information on all our
guides, books and eBooks,
visit our website:
www.cicerone.co.uk

CICERONE

Trust Cicerone to guide your next adventure,
wherever it may be around the world...

Discover guides for hiking, mountain walking, backpacking,
trekking, trail running, cycling and mountain biking, ski touring,
climbing and scrambling in Britain, Europe and worldwide.

Connect with Cicerone online and find inspiration.

- buy books and ebooks
- articles, advice and trip reports
- podcasts and live events
- GPX files and updates
- regular newsletter

cicerone.co.uk